W9-BHF-068

**5**

# Ready® Mathematics
## Practice and Problem Solving

## Teacher Guide

$2 \div \frac{1}{3} = 6$

$0.25 \times 10$

Curriculum Associates

## Teacher Advisors

Rachel Adelstein, Assistant Principal, Briggs Avenue Academy, Bronx, NY

Crystal Bailey, Math Impact Teacher, Eastern Guilford Middle School, Guilford County Schools, Gibsonville, NC

Max Brand, Reading Specialist, Indian Run Elementary, Dublin City School District, Dublin, OH

Dinah Chancellor, Professional Development Mathematics Consultant, Southlake, TX

Helen Comba, Supervisor of Basic Skills & Language Arts, School District of the Chathams, Chatham, NJ

Cindy Dean, Classroom Teacher, Mt. Diablo Unified School District, Concord, CA

Leah Flynn, Classroom Teacher, Brockton Public Schools, Brockton, MA

Randall E. Groth, Ph.D, Associate Professor of Mathematics Education, Salisbury University, Salisbury, MD

Bill Laraway, Classroom Teacher, Silver Oak Elementary, Evergreen School District, San Jose, CA

Jennifer Lerner, Classroom Teacher, PS 57, New York City Public Schools, New York, NY

Susie Legg, Elementary Curriculum Coordinator, Kansas City Public Schools, Kansas City, KS

Sarah Levine, Classroom Teacher, Springhurst Elementary School, Dobbs Ferry School District, Dobbs Ferry, NY

Nicole Peirce, Classroom Teacher, Eleanor Roosevelt Elementary, Pennsbury School District, Morrisville, PA

Donna Phillips, Classroom Teacher, Farmington R-7 School District, Farmington, MO

Maria Rosati, Classroom Teacher, Harwood Elementary School, Warren Consolidated Schools, Warren, MI

Kari Ross, Reading Specialist, MN

Sunita Sangari, Math Coach, PS/MS 29, New York City Public Schools, New York, NY

Eileen Seybuck, Classroom Teacher, PS 57, New York City Public Schools, New York, NY

Mark Hoover Thames, Research Scientist, University of Michigan, Ann Arbor, MI

Shannon Tsuruda, Classroom Teacher, Mt. Diablo Unified School District, Concord, CA

## Acknowledgments

Editorial Director: Cynthia Tripp
Cover Designers, Illustrators: Julia Bourque, Matt Pollock
Book Designer: Scott Hoffman

Executive Editor: Kathy Kellman
Supervising Editors: Pamela Halloran, Grace Izzi
Director–Product Development: Daniel J. Smith
Vice President–Product Development: Adam Berkin

Common Core State Standards © 2010. National Governors Association Center for Best Practices and Council of Chief State School Officers. All rights reserved.

ISBN 978-0-7609-9595-2
©2015—Curriculum Associates, LLC
North Billerica, MA 01862
No part of this book may be reproduced
by any means without written permission
from the publisher.
All Rights Reserved. Printed in USA.
15 14 13 12 11 10 9 8 7 6 5 4 3 2

# Table of Contents

Student Book includes a Family Letter for every lesson and Unit Vocabulary pages.

## Unit 2: Number and Operations—Fractions

Student Book includes a Family Letter for every lesson and Unit Vocabulary pages.

## Unit 3: Operations and Algebraic Thinking

## Unit 4: Measurement and Data

Student Book includes a Family Letter for every lesson and Unit Vocabulary pages.

## Unit 5: Geometry

## Teacher Resource Blacklines

Teacher Resource blackline masters are provided for use with the collaborative practice games in *Ready Practice and Problem Solving*. Full instructions for use of these teacher resources can be found in the Step by Step for each unit game.

Student Book includes a Family Letter for every lesson and Unit Vocabulary pages.

# *Ready*® Program Overview

*Ready* is an integrated program of assessment and data-driven instruction designed to teach your students rigorous national and state standards for college and career readiness, including mathematical practice standards. You can use the program as a supplement to address specific standards where your students need instruction and practice, or more comprehensively to engage students in all standards.

**Built for the new standards. Not just aligned.**

## For Students

***Ready Instruction*** provides differentiated instruction and independent practice of key concepts and skills that build student confidence. Interim assessments give frequent opportunities to monitor progress.

***Ready Practice and Problem Solving*** complements ***Ready Instruction***, through rich practice, games, and performance tasks that develop understanding and fluency with key skills and concepts.

***Ready Assessments*** provides three full-length assessments designed to show student mastery of standards.

## For Teachers

The ***Ready Teacher Resource Book*** and ***Ready Practice and Problem Solving Teacher Guide*** support teachers with strong professional development, step-by-step lesson plans, and best practices for implementing rigorous standards.

***Ready Teacher Toolbox*** provides online lessons, prerequisite lessons from previous grades, center activities, and targeted best-practice teaching strategies.

## *Ready* Program Features

 Built with **all-new content** written specifically for rigorous national and state standards for college and career readiness

 Uses a research-based, **gradual-release** instructional model

 Requires **higher-order thinking** and complex reasoning to solve problems

 Integrates **Standards for Mathematical Practice** throughout every lesson

 Embeds thoughtful **professional development**

Encourages students to develop **deeper understanding** of concepts and to understand and use a variety of mathematical strategies and models

 Promotes **fluency** and connects hands-on learning with clearly articulated models throughout

**A7**

©Curriculum Associates, LLC   Copying is not permitted.

# What's in *Ready® Practice and Problem Solving*

Building on ***Ready Instruction, Ready Practice and Problem Solving*** encourages students to reason, use strategies, solve extended problems, and engage in collaborative learning to extend classroom learning. Designed for flexibility, ***Ready Practice and Problem Solving*** can be used for homework, independent classroom practice, and in after-school settings.

## Lesson Practice Pages

Practice specific to each part of every ***Ready Instruction*** lesson gives students multiple opportunities to reinforce procedural fluency and synthesize concepts and skills learned in the classroom.

- Lesson practice pages can be used at the end of a lesson or after completing each part of a lesson.

- For ease of use, each part of a ***Ready Practice and Problem Solving*** lesson includes a ***Ready Instruction*** page reference indicating when they could be assigned.

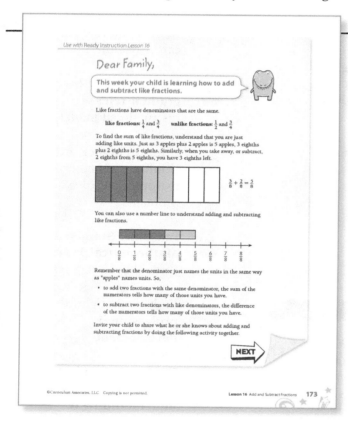

## Family Letters

- Family Letters can be sent home separately before each lesson, or as part of a family communication package. They include a summary statement, vocabulary definitions, and models that help adult family members support their child's mathematical learning.

- Each letter concludes with a simple activity that encourages students to share their math knowledge with family members while practicing skills or concepts in a fun, engaging way.

- A Spanish version of each letter is available on the Teacher Toolbox.

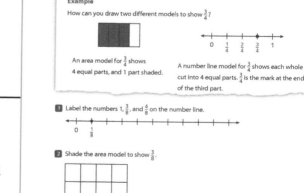

## Prerequisite Skill Practice

- Students apply lesson **prerequisite concepts or skills** as they work with models that support those in the ***Ready Instruction*** lesson Introduction.

- This serves as a review of previous understandings and prepares students for the next section of the ***Ready Instruction*** lesson.

©Curriculum Associates, LLC   Copying is not permitted.

Name: _____

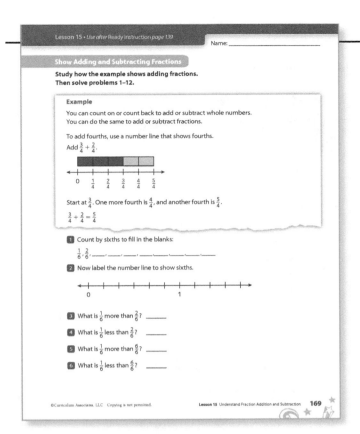

## Skills and Concepts Practice

- **Worked-out examples** support and reinforce students' classroom learning, and can also serve as an explanation of the math content for adult family members if the practice pages are used as homework.

- Problems are **differentiated** to provide maximum flexibility when assigning practice as independent classwork or homework. The differentiation is marked in the Teacher Guide as basic **B**, medium **M**, or challenging **C**.

- **Vocabulary** is defined at the point where terms are used in the practice problems.

- Students are encouraged to show their work and use models and strategies they learned in the ***Ready Instruction*** lesson.

- Lessons conclude with **mixed practice** problems that vary in type, including multiple choice, yes-no formats, and open-ended questions.

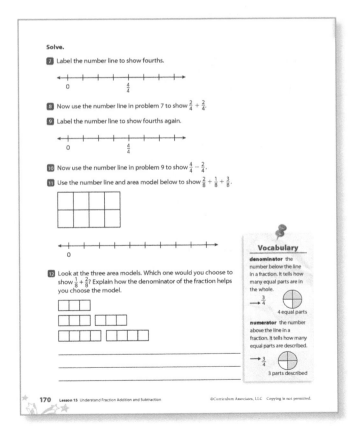

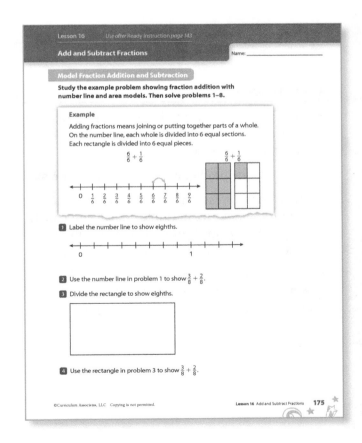

©Curriculum Associates, LLC   Copying is not permitted.

# Unit Practice Pages

Unit materials cover multiple skills and concepts, helping students make connections across standards.

## Unit Game

- Unit Games are engaging collaborative experiences, designed to encourage students to use **strategic thinking** as they play the game with a partner.

- Students record the mathematics of each game to **promote fluency** and reinforce learning. The recording sheet also serves as an opportunity for informal assessment by providing a written record for teachers to monitor students' work.

- These partner games can be used at classroom centers and/or sent home for play with an adult family member.

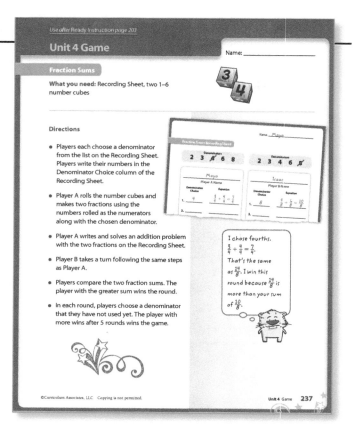

## Unit Practice

- The Unit Practice provides **mixed practice** of lesson skills and concepts, and includes visual or stepped-out support for students.

- Unit Practice problems **integrate multiple skills**.

- These pages present problems with a **variety of formats**, including multiple choice and constructed response, to help students become familiar with items they will encounter on their state tests.

- The unit practice pages can be assigned as homework, used as independent or small group practice, or for whole class discussion.

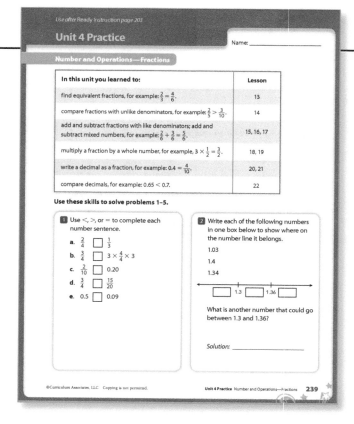

©Curriculum Associates, LLC   Copying is not permitted.

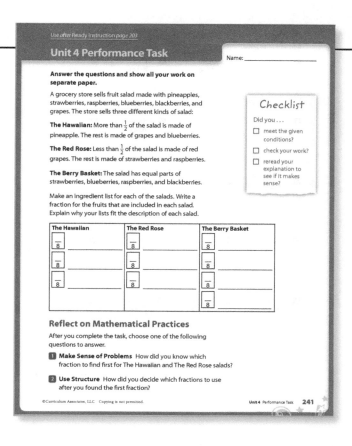

## Unit 4 Performance Task

Name: _____

**Answer the questions and show all your work on separate paper.**

A grocery store sells fruit salad made with pineapples, strawberries, raspberries, blueberries, blackberries, and grapes. The store sells three different kinds of salad:

**The Hawaiian:** More than $\frac{1}{2}$ of the salad is made of pineapple. The rest is made of grapes and blueberries.

**The Red Rose:** Less than $\frac{1}{2}$ of the salad is made of red grapes. The rest is made of strawberries and raspberries.

**The Berry Basket:** The salad has equal parts of strawberries, blueberries, raspberries, and blackberries.

Make an ingredient list for each of the salads. Write a fraction for the fruits that are included in each salad. Explain why your lists fit the description of each salad.

*Checklist*

Did you . . .
- ☐ meet the given conditions?
- ☐ check your work?
- ☐ reread your explanation to see if it makes sense?

| The Hawaiian | The Red Rose | The Berry Basket |
|---|---|---|
| $\frac{\phantom{x}}{8}$ _____ | $\frac{\phantom{x}}{8}$ _____ | $\frac{\phantom{x}}{8}$ _____ |
| $\frac{\phantom{x}}{8}$ _____ | $\frac{\phantom{x}}{8}$ _____ | $\frac{\phantom{x}}{8}$ _____ |
| $\frac{\phantom{x}}{8}$ _____ | $\frac{\phantom{x}}{8}$ _____ | $\frac{\phantom{x}}{8}$ _____ |
| | | $\frac{\phantom{x}}{8}$ _____ |

### Reflect on Mathematical Practices

After you complete the task, choose one of the following questions to answer.

**1 Make Sense of Problems** How did you know which fraction to find first for The Hawaiian and The Red Rose salads?

**2 Use Structure** How did you decide which fractions to use after you found the first fraction?

©Curriculum Associates, LLC   Copying is not permitted.                    **Unit 4** Performance Task   **241**

## Unit Performance Task

- Real-world Unit Performance Tasks require students to **integrate skills and concepts**, apply higher-order thinking, and explain their reasoning.

- Engaging real-world tasks encourage students to become active participants in their learning by requiring them to organize and manage mathematical content and processes.

- **Performance Task Tips** help students organize their thinking.

- Students are asked to reflect on **Mathematical Practices** after they have concluded their work.

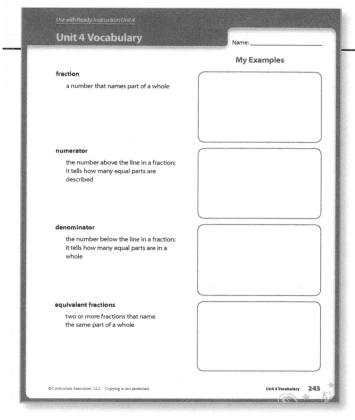

## Unit 4 Vocabulary

Name: _____

**My Examples**

**fraction**
a number that names part of a whole

**numerator**
the number above the line in a fraction; it tells how many equal parts are described

**denominator**
the number below the line in a fraction; it tells how many equal parts are in a whole

**equivalent fractions**
two or more fractions that name the same part of a whole

©Curriculum Associates, LLC   Copying is not permitted.                    **Unit 4** Vocabulary   **243**

## Unit Vocabulary

- The Unit Vocabulary is a way for students to integrate vocabulary into their learning. Vocabulary pages provide a **student-friendly definition** for each new and review vocabulary term in the unit.

- Students are given space to write **examples** for each term to help them connect the term to their own understanding.

- After students have completed these pages, they can use them as a reference.

- Throughout the units, students are given opportunities to further personalize their acquisition of mathematics vocabulary by selecting terms they want to define.

©Curriculum Associates, LLC   Copying is not permitted.

# Fluency Practice Pages

## Skills Practice

- Fluency facts practice and multi-digit computation worksheets in multiple formats provide flexibility and promote the use of grade-appropriate strategies and algorithms.

- These worksheets for grade-level facts and operations can be used any time after the skill has been taught.

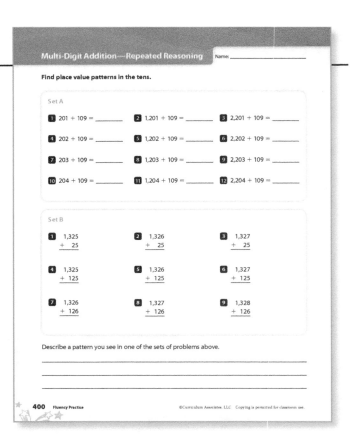

## Repeated Reasoning Practice

- Repeated Reasoning practice worksheets encourage students to make use of **structure** and look for **regularity** as part of their development of grade-level fluency.

- In this type of fluency practice, students identify and describe patterns in the relationship between the answers and the problems. This develops their abstract reasoning skills, mental math skills, and a deeper understanding of fractions and base ten numbers.

©Curriculum Associates, LLC   Copying is not permitted.

# Correlation Chart

## Common Core State Standards Practice in *Ready® Practice and Problem Solving*

The table below shows the standards addressed in lesson practices, unit practices, games, and performance tasks all of which correspond to **Ready Instruction** lessons and units. Use this information to plan and focus meaningful practice.

| Common Core State Standards for Grade 5 — Mathematics Standards | | Content Emphasis | *Ready® Practice and Problem Solving* |
|---|---|---|---|
| **Operations and Algebraic Thinking** | | | |
| **Write and interpret numerical expressions.** | | | |
| **5.OA.A.1** | Use parentheses, brackets, or braces in numerical expressions, and evaluate expressions with these symbols. | Supporting/ Additional | Lesson 19 Practice<br>Unit 3 Practice<br>Unit 3 Game: Most Valuable Expressions |
| **5.OA.A.2** | Write simple expressions that record calculations with numbers, and interpret numerical expressions without evaluating them. *For example, express the calculation "add 8 and 7, then multiply by 2" as $2 \times (8 + 7)$. Recognize that $3 \times (18932 + 921)$ is three times as large as $18932 + 921$, without having to calculate the indicated sum or product.* | Supporting/ Additional | Lesson 19 Practice<br>Unit 3 Practice |
| **Analyze patterns and relationships.** | | | |
| **5.OA.B.3** | Generate two numerical patterns using two given rules. Identify apparent relationships between corresponding terms. Form ordered pairs consisting of corresponding terms from the two patterns, and graph the ordered pairs on a coordinate plane. *For example, given the rule "Add 3" and the starting number 0, and given the rule "Add 6" and the starting number 0, generate terms in the resulting sequences, and observe that the terms in one sequence are twice the corresponding terms in the other sequence. Explain informally why this is so.* | Supporting/ Additional | Lesson 20 Practice<br>Unit 3 Practice<br>Unit 3 Performance Task |
| **Number and Operations in Base Ten** | | | |
| **Understand the place value system.** | | | |
| **5.NBT.A.1** | Recognize that in a multi-digit number, a digit in one place represents 10 times as much as it represents in the place to its right and $\frac{1}{10}$ of what it represents in the place to its left. | Major | Lesson 1 Practice |
| **5.NBT.A.2** | Explain patterns in the number of zeros of the product when multiplying a number by powers of 10, and explain patterns in the placement of the decimal point when a decimal is multiplied or divided by a power of 10. Use whole-number exponents to denote powers of 10. | Major | Lesson 2 Practice |
| **5.NBT.A.3** | Read, write, and compare decimals to thousandths. | Major | Lesson 3 Practice |
| | **5.NBT.A.3a** Read and write decimals to thousandths using base-ten numerals, number names, and expanded form, e.g., $347.392 = 3 \times 100 + 4 \times 10 + 7 \times 1 + 3 \times \left(\frac{1}{10}\right) + 9 \times \left(\frac{1}{100}\right) + 2 \times \left(\frac{1}{1000}\right)$. | Major | Lesson 4 Practice<br>Unit 1 Practice<br>Unit 1 Game: Decimal Race to 100 |
| | **5.NBT.A.3b** Compare two decimals to thousandths based on meanings of the digits in each place, using >, =, and < symbols to record the results of comparisons. | Major | |
| **5.NBT.A.4** | Use place value understanding to round decimals to any place. | Major | Lesson 4 Practice<br>Unit 1 Practice<br>Unit 1 Performance Task |

**The Standards for Mathematical Practice are integrated throughout the lesson practices, unit practices, and unit games.**

Common Core State Standards © 2010. National Governors Association Center for Best Practices and Council of Chief State School Officers. All rights reserved.

**A13**

©Curriculum Associates, LLC    Copying is not permitted.

| Common Core State Standards for Grade 5 — Mathematics Standards | Content Emphasis | Ready® Practice and Problem Solving |
|---|---|---|

## Number and Operations in Base Ten (continued)

### Perform operations with multi-digit whole numbers and with decimals to hundredths. (continued)

| | | |
|---|---|---|
| **5.NBT.B.5** Fluently multiply multi-digit whole numbers using the standard algorithm. | Major | Lesson 5 Practice<br>Unit 1 Practice |
| **5.NBT.B.6** Find whole-number quotients of whole numbers with up to four-digit dividends and two-digit divisors, using strategies based on place value, the properties of operations, and/or the relationship between multiplication and division. Illustrate and explain the calculation by using equations, rectangular arrays, and/or area models. | Major | Lesson 6 Practice<br>Unit 1 Practice |
| **5.NBT.B.7** Add, subtract, multiply, and divide decimals to hundredths, using concrete models or drawings and strategies based on place value, properties of operations, and/or the relationship between addition and subtraction; relate the strategy to a written method and explain the reasoning used. | Major | Lesson 7 Practice<br>Lesson 8 Practice<br>Lesson 9 Practice<br>Unit 1 Practice<br>Unit 1 Game: Decimal Race to 100<br>Unit 1 Performance Task<br>Unit 4 Game: Measurement Match |

## Number and Operations—Fractions

### Use equivalent fractions as a strategy to add and subtract fractions.

| | | |
|---|---|---|
| **5.NF.A.1** Add and subtract fractions with unlike denominators (including mixed numbers) by replacing given fractions with equivalent fractions in such a way as to produce an equivalent sum or difference of fractions with like denominators. *For example, $\frac{2}{3} + \frac{5}{4} = \frac{8}{12} + \frac{15}{12} = \frac{23}{12}$. (In general, $\frac{a}{b} + \frac{c}{d} = \frac{(ad + bc)}{bd}$.)* | Major | Lesson 10 Practice<br>Unit 2 Practice<br>Unit 2 Game: Fraction Sums and Differences<br>Unit 2 Performance Task |
| **5.NF.A.2** Solve word problems involving addition and subtraction of fractions referring to the same whole, including cases of unlike denominators, e.g., by using visual fraction models or equations to represent the problem. Use benchmark fractions and number sense of fractions to estimate mentally and assess the reasonableness of answers. *For example, recognize an incorrect result $\frac{2}{5} + \frac{1}{2} = \frac{3}{7}$, by observing that $\frac{3}{7} < \frac{1}{2}$.* | Major | Lesson 11 Practice<br>Unit 2 Practice |

### Apply and extend previous understandings of multiplication and division.

| | | |
|---|---|---|
| **5.NF.B.3** Interpret a fraction as division of the numerator by the denominator $\left(\frac{a}{b} = a \div b\right)$. Solve word problems involving division of whole numbers leading to answers in the form of fractions or mixed numbers, e.g., by using visual fraction models or equations to represent the problem. *For example, interpret $\frac{3}{4}$ as the result of dividing 3 by 4, noting that $\frac{3}{4}$ multiplied by 4 equals 3, and that when 3 wholes are shared equally among 4 people each person has a share of size $\frac{3}{4}$. If 9 people want to share a 50-pound sack of rice equally by weight, how many pounds of rice should each person get? Between what two whole numbers does your answer lie?* | Major | Lesson 12 Practice<br>Unit 2 Practice |
| **5.NF.B.4** Apply and extend previous understandings of multiplication to multiply a fraction or whole number by a fraction. | Major | Lesson 13 Practice<br>Lesson 14 Practice<br>Unit 2 Practice<br>Unit 2 Performance Task |
|     **5.NF.B.4a** Interpret the product $\left(\frac{a}{b}\right) \times q$ as a parts of a partition of $q$ into $b$ equal parts; equivalently, as the result of a sequence of operations $a \times q \div b$. *For example, use a visual fraction model to show $\left(\frac{2}{3}\right) \times 4 = \frac{8}{3}$, and create a story context for this equation. Do the same with $\left(\frac{2}{3}\right) \times \left(\frac{4}{5}\right) = \frac{8}{15}$. (In general, $\left(\frac{a}{b}\right) \times \left(\frac{c}{d}\right) = \frac{ac}{bd}$.)* | Major | |
|     **5.NF.B.4b** Find the area of a rectangle with fractional side lengths by tiling it with unit squares of the appropriate unit fraction side lengths, and show that the area is the same as would be found by multiplying the side lengths. Multiply fractional side lengths to find areas of rectangles, and represent fraction products as rectangular areas. | Major | |

©Curriculum Associates, LLC   Copying is not permitted.

| Common Core State Standards for Grade 5 — Mathematics Standards | | Content Emphasis | Ready® Practice and Problem Solving |
|---|---|---|---|
| **Number and Operations—Fractions (continued)** | | | |
| **5.NF.B.5** | Interpret multiplication as scaling (resizing), by: | Major | Lesson 15 Practice |
| | **5.NF.B.5a**   Comparing the size of a product to the size of one factor on the basis of the size of the other factor, without performing the indicated multiplication. | Major | Unit 2 Practice |
| | **5.NF.B.5b**   Explaining why multiplying a given number by a fraction greater than 1 results in a product greater than the given number (recognizing multiplication by whole numbers greater than 1 as a familiar case); explaining why multiplying a given number by a fraction less than 1 results in a product smaller than the given number; and relating the principle of fraction equivalence $\frac{a}{b} = \frac{(n \times a)}{(n \times b)}$ to the effect of multiplying $\frac{a}{b}$ by 1. | Major | |
| **5.NF.B.6** | Solve real world problems involving multiplication of fractions and mixed numbers, e.g., by using visual fraction models or equations to represent the problem. | Major | Lesson 16 Practice<br>Unit 2 Performance Task |
| **5.NF.B.7** | Apply and extend previous understandings of division to divide unit fractions by whole numbers and whole numbers by unit fractions. | Major | Lesson 17 Practice<br>Lesson 18 Practice |
| | **5.NF.B.7a**   Interpret division of a unit fraction by a non-zero whole number, and compute such quotients. *For example, create a story context for* $\left(\frac{1}{3}\right) \div 4$*, and use a visual fraction model to show the quotient. Use the relationship between multiplication and division to explain that* $\left(\frac{1}{3}\right) \div 4 = \frac{1}{12}$ *because* $\left(\frac{1}{12}\right) \times 4 = \frac{1}{3}$. | Major | Unit 2 Practice<br>Unit 2 Performance Task |
| | **5.NF.B.7b**   Interpret division of a whole number by a unit fraction, and compute such quotients. *For example, create a story context for* $4 \div \left(\frac{1}{5}\right)$*, and use a visual fraction model to show the quotient. Use the relationship between multiplication and division to explain that* $4 \div \left(\frac{1}{5}\right) = 20$ *because* $20 \times \left(\frac{1}{5}\right) = 4$. | Major | |
| | **5.NF.B.7c**   Solve real world problems involving division of unit fractions by non-zero whole numbers and division of whole numbers by unit fractions, e.g., by using visual fraction models and equations to represent the problem. *For example, how much chocolate will each person get if 3 people share* $\frac{1}{2}$ *lb of chocolate equally? How many* $\frac{1}{3}$*-cup servings are in 2 cups of raisins?* | Major | |
| **Measurement and Data** | | | |
| **Convert like measurement units within a given measurement system.** | | | |
| **5.MD.A.1** | Convert among different-sized standard measurement units within a given measurement system (e.g., convert 5 cm to 0.05 m), and use these conversions in solving multi-step, real world problems. | Supporting/ Additional | Lesson 21 Practice<br>Lesson 22 Practice<br>Unit 4 Practice<br>Unit 4 Game: Measurement Match |
| **Represent and interpret data.** | | | |
| **5.MD.B.2** | Make a line plot to display a data set of measurements in fractions of a unit $\left(\frac{1}{2}, \frac{1}{4}, \frac{1}{8}\right)$. Use operations on fractions for this grade to solve problems involving information presented in line plots. *For example, given different measurements of liquid in identical beakers, find the amount of liquid each beaker would contain if the total amount in all the beakers were redistributed equally.* | Supporting/ Additional | Lesson 23 Practice |

**A15**

©Curriculum Associates, LLC   Copying is not permitted.

| Common Core State Standards for Grade 5 — Mathematics Standards | Content Emphasis | Ready® Practice and Problem Solving |
|---|---|---|
| **Measurement and Data (continued)** | | |
| **Geometric measurement: understand concepts of angle and measure angles. (continued)** | | |
| **5.MD.C.3** Recognize volume as an attribute of solid figures and understand concepts of volume measurement. | Major | Lesson 24 Practice<br>Unit 4 Practice |
|     **5.MD.C.3a** A cube with side length 1 unit, called a "unit cube," is said to have "one cubic unit" of volume, and can be used to measure volume. | Major | |
|     **5.MD.C.3b** A solid figure which can be packed without gaps or overlaps using $n$ unit cubes is said to have a volume of $n$ cubic units. | Major | |
| **5.MD.C.4** Measure volumes by counting unit cubes, using cubic cm, cubic in, cubic ft, and improvised units. | Major | Lesson 25 Practice<br>Unit 4 Practice |
| **5.MD.C.5** Relate volume to the operations of multiplication and addition and solve real world and mathematical problems involving volume. | Major | Lesson 26 Practice<br>Lesson 27 Practice |
|     **5.MD.C.5a** Find the volume of a right rectangular prism with whole-number side lengths by packing it with unit cubes, and show that the volume is the same as would be found by multiplying the edge lengths, equivalently by multiplying the height by the area of the base. Represent threefold whole-number products as volumes, e.g., to represent the associative property of multiplication. | Major | Unit 4 Practice<br>Unit 4 Performance Task |
|     **5.MD.C.5b** Apply the formulas $V = l \times w \times h$ and $V = b \times h$ for rectangular prisms to find volumes of right rectangular prisms with whole-number edge lengths in the context of solving real world and mathematical problems. | Major | |
|     **5.MD.C.5c** Recognize volume as additive. Find volumes of solid figures composed of two non-overlapping right rectangular prisms by adding the volumes of the non-overlapping parts, applying this technique to solve real world problems. | Major | |
| **Geometry** | | |
| **Graph points on the coordinate plane to solve real-world and mathematical problems.** | | |
| **5.G.A.1** Use a pair of perpendicular number lines, called axes, to define a coordinate system, with the intersection of the lines (the origin) arranged to coincide with the 0 on each line and a given point in the plane located by using an ordered pair of numbers, called its coordinates. Understand that the first number indicates how far to travel from the origin in the direction of one axis, and the second number indicates how far to travel in the direction of the second axis, with the convention that the names of the two axes and the coordinates correspond (e.g., $x$-axis and $x$-coordinate, $y$-axis and $y$-coordinate). | Supporting/ Additional | Lesson 28 Practice<br>Unit 5 Practice<br>Unit 5 Performance Task |
| **5.G.A.2** Represent real world and mathematical problems by graphing points in the first quadrant of the coordinate plane, and interpret coordinate values of points in the context of the situation. | Supporting/ Additional | Lesson 29 Practice<br>Unit 5 Practice<br>Unit 5 Performance Task |
| **Classify two-dimensional figures into categories based on their properties.** | | |
| **5.G.B.3** Understand that attributes belonging to a category of two-dimensional figures also belong to all subcategories of that category. For example, all rectangles have four right angles and squares are rectangles, so all squares have four right angles. | Supporting/ Additional | Lesson 31 Practice<br>Unit 5 Practice<br>Unit 5 Game: Triangle Bingo |
| **5.G.B.4** Classify two-dimensional figures in a hierarchy based on properties. | Supporting/ Additional | Lesson 31 Practice<br>Unit 5 Practice<br>Unit 5 Game: Triangle Bingo |

©Curriculum Associates, LLC Copying is not permitted.

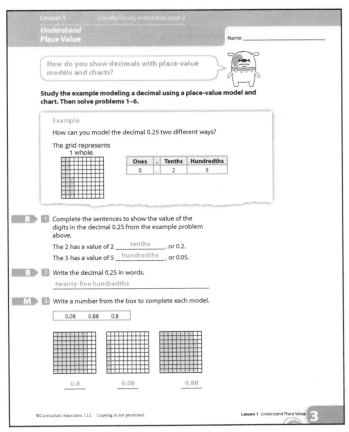

Lesson 1          *Use after Ready Instruction page 3.*

**Understand**
**Place Value**

Name: _____

How do you show decimals with place-value models and charts?

**Study the example modeling a decimal using a place-value model and chart. Then solve problems 1–6.**

**Example**

How can you model the decimal 0.25 two different ways?

The grid represents
1 whole.

| Ones | . | Tenths | Hundredths |
|------|---|--------|------------|
| 0 | . | 2 | 5 |

**B** ▸ **1** Complete the sentences to show the value of the digits in the decimal 0.25 from the example problem above.

The 2 has a value of 2 ____tenths____ , or 0.2.

The 5 has a value of 5 ____hundredths____ , or 0.05.

**B** ▸ **2** Write the decimal 0.25 in words.

____twenty-five hundredths____

**M** ▸ **3** Write a number from the box to complete each model.

| 0.08 | 0.88 | 0.8 |

0.8                 0.08                0.88

©Curriculum Associates, LLC   Copying is not permitted.                Lesson 1 Understand Place Value  **3**

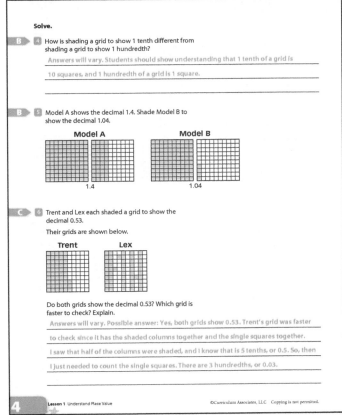

**Solve.**

**B** ▸ **4** How is shading a grid to show 1 tenth different from shading a grid to show 1 hundredth?

Answers will vary. Students should show understanding that 1 tenth of a grid is

10 squares, and 1 hundredth of a grid is 1 square.

**B** ▸ **5** Model A shows the decimal 1.4. Shade Model B to show the decimal 1.04.

**Model A**                    **Model B**

1.4                          1.04

**C** ▸ **6** Trent and Lex each shaded a grid to show the decimal 0.53.

Their grids are shown below.

**Trent**        **Lex**

Do both grids show the decimal 0.53? Which grid is faster to check? Explain.

Answers will vary. Possible answer: Yes, both grids show 0.53. Trent's grid was faster

to check since it has the shaded columns together and the single squares together.

I saw that half of the columns were shaded, and I know that is 5 tenths, or 0.5. So, then

I just needed to count the single squares. There are 3 hundredths, or 0.03.

**4**  Lesson 1 Understand Place Value                ©Curriculum Associates, LLC   Copying is not permitted.

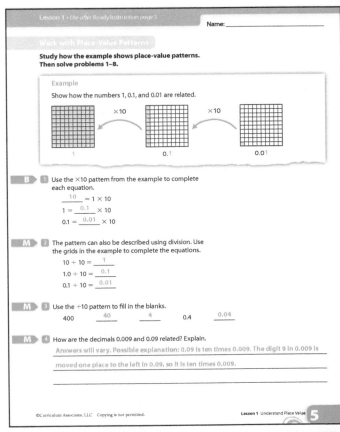

Lesson 1 • *Use after Ready Instruction page 5*

Name: _____

**Work with Place-Value Patterns**

**Study how the example shows place-value patterns. Then solve problems 1–8.**

**Example**

Show how the numbers 1, 0.1, and 0.01 are related.

×10          ×10

1          0.1          0.01

**B** ▸ **1** Use the ×10 pattern from the example to complete each equation.

____10____ = 1 × 10

1 = ____0.1____ × 10

0.1 = ____0.01____ × 10

**M** ▸ **2** The pattern can also be described using division. Use the grids in the example to complete the equations.

10 ÷ 10 = ____1____

1.0 ÷ 10 = ____0.1____

0.1 ÷ 10 = ____0.01____

**M** ▸ **3** Use the ÷10 pattern to fill in the blanks.

400   ____40____   ____4____   0.4   ____0.04____

**M** ▸ **4** How are the decimals 0.009 and 0.09 related? Explain.

Answers will vary. Possible explanation: 0.09 is ten times 0.009. The digit 9 in 0.009 is

moved one place to the left in 0.09, so it is ten times 0.009.

©Curriculum Associates, LLC   Copying is not permitted.                Lesson 1 Understand Place Value  **5**

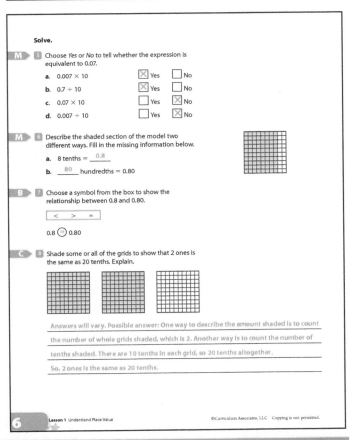

**Solve.**

**M** ▸ **5** Choose *Yes* or *No* to tell whether the expression is equivalent to 0.07.

**a.**  0.007 × 10          ☒ Yes   ☐ No

**b.**  0.7 ÷ 10             ☒ Yes   ☐ No

**c.**  0.07 × 10            ☐ Yes   ☒ No

**d.**  0.007 ÷ 10           ☐ Yes   ☒ No

**M** ▸ **6** Describe the shaded section of the model two different ways. Fill in the missing information below.

**a.**  8 tenths = ____0.8____

**b.**  ____80____ hundredths = 0.80

**B** ▸ **7** Choose a symbol from the box to show the relationship between 0.8 and 0.80.

| < | > | = |

0.8 ⊜ 0.80

**C** ▸ **8** Shade some or all of the grids to show that 2 ones is the same as 20 tenths. Explain.

Answers will vary. Possible answer: One way to describe the amount shaded is to count

the number of whole grids shaded, which is 2. Another way is to count the number of

tenths shaded. There are 10 tenths in each grid, so 20 tenths altogether.

So, 2 ones is the same as 20 tenths.

**6**  Lesson 1 Understand Place Value                ©Curriculum Associates, LLC   Copying is not permitted.

©Curriculum Associates, LLC   Copying is not permitted.

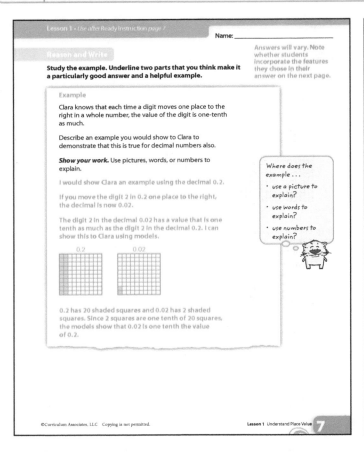

Lesson 1 · *Use after Ready Instruction page 7*

Name: _____

**Reason and Write**

**Study the example. Underline two parts that you think make it a particularly good answer and a helpful example.**

Answers will vary. Note whether students incorporate the features they chose in their answer on the next page.

**Example**

Clara knows that each time a digit moves one place to the right in a whole number, the value of the digit is one-tenth as much.

Describe an example you would show to Clara to demonstrate that this is true for decimal numbers also.

***Show your work.*** Use pictures, words, or numbers to explain.

I would show Clara an example using the decimal 0.2.

If you move the digit 2 in 0.2 one place to the right, the decimal is now 0.02.

The digit 2 in the decimal 0.02 has a value that is one tenth as much as the digit 2 in the decimal 0.2. I can show this to Clara using models.

Where does the example . . .
- use a picture to explain?
- use words to explain?
- use numbers to explain?

0.2 has 20 shaded squares and 0.02 has 2 shaded squares. Since 2 squares are one tenth of 20 squares, the models show that 0.02 is one tenth the value of 0.2.

---

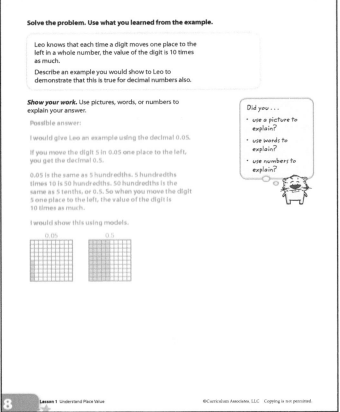

**Solve the problem. Use what you learned from the example.**

Leo knows that each time a digit moves one place to the left in a whole number, the value of the digit is 10 times as much.

Describe an example you would show to Leo to demonstrate that this is true for decimal numbers also.

***Show your work.*** Use pictures, words, or numbers to explain your answer.

Possible answer:

I would give Leo an example using the decimal 0.05.

If you move the digit 5 in 0.05 one place to the left, you get the decimal 0.5.

0.05 is the same as 5 hundredths. 5 hundredths times 10 is 50 hundredths. 50 hundredths is the same as 5 tenths, or 0.5. So when you move the digit 5 one place to the left, the value of the digit is 10 times as much.

I would show this using models.

Did you . . .
- use a picture to explain?
- use words to explain?
- use numbers to explain?

| | Key |
|---|---|
| B | Basic |
| M | Medium |
| C | Challenge |

©Curriculum Associates, LLC   Copying is not permitted.

---

Lesson 2    *Use after Ready Instruction page 9*

## Understand Powers of Ten

Name: _____

How can you multiply and divide decimals by 10?

**Study the example problem showing multiplying a decimal by 10. Then solve problems 1–6.**

**Example**

Find $0.05 \times 10$. Check your answer using a model.

When you multiply the value of a digit by 10, the digit moves one place to the left, so $0.05 \times 10 = 0.5$.

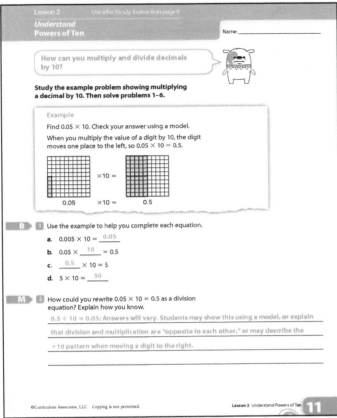

0.05    ×10 =    0.5

**B** **1** Use the example to help you complete each equation.

a. $0.005 \times 10 = \underline{0.05}$

b. $0.05 \times \underline{10} = 0.5$

c. $\underline{0.5} \times 10 = 5$

d. $5 \times 10 = \underline{50}$

**M** **2** How could you rewrite $0.05 \times 10 = 0.5$ as a division equation? Explain how you know.

$0.5 \div 10 = 0.05$; Answers will vary. Students may show this using a model, or explain

that division and multiplication are "opposite to each other," or may describe the

$\div 10$ pattern when moving a digit to the right.

©Curriculum Associates, LLC   Copying is not permitted.    Lesson 2 Understand Powers of Ten **11**

---

**12**   Lesson 2   Understand Powers of Ten

**Solve.**

**M** **3** Each grid below represents a whole. Shade Models A, B, and C to match the number and decimals.

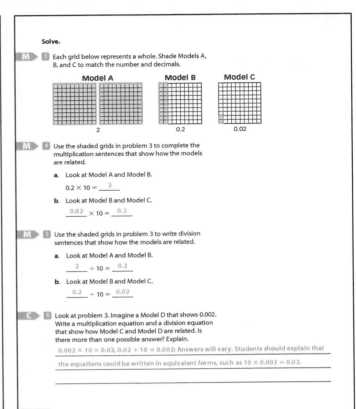

Model A          Model B          Model C

2              0.2              0.02

**M** **4** Use the shaded grids in problem 3 to complete the multiplication sentences that show how the models are related.

a. Look at Model A and Model B.

$0.2 \times 10 = \underline{2}$

b. Look at Model B and Model C.

$\underline{0.02} \times 10 = \underline{0.2}$

**M** **5** Use the shaded grids in problem 3 to write division sentences that show how the models are related.

a. Look at Model A and Model B.

$\underline{2} \div 10 = \underline{0.2}$

b. Look at Model B and Model C.

$\underline{0.2} \div 10 = \underline{0.02}$

**C** **6** Look at problem 3. Imagine a Model D that shows 0.002. Write a multiplication equation and a division equation that show how Model C and Model D are related. Is there more than one possible answer? Explain.

$0.002 \times 10 = 0.02, 0.02 \div 10 = 0.002$; Answers will vary. Students should explain that

the equations could be written in equivalent forms, such as $10 \times 0.002 = 0.02$.

©Curriculum Associates, LLC   Copying is not permitted.

---

Lesson 2 · *Use after Ready Instruction page 11*

Name: _____

## Multiply and Divide with Powers of Ten

**Study the example showing how the decimal point moves when you multiply a decimal number by a power of ten. Then solve problems 1–7.**

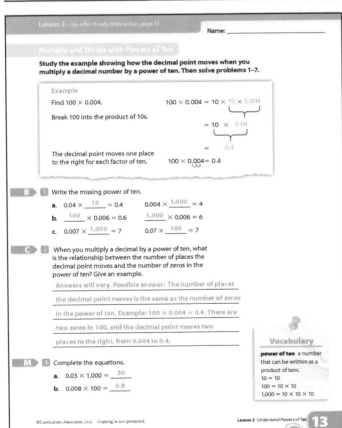

**Example**

Find $100 \times 0.004$.        $100 \times 0.004 = 10 \times 10 \times 0.004$

Break 100 into the product of 10s.

$= 10 \times 0.04$

$= 0.4$

The decimal point moves one place to the right for each factor of ten.    $100 \times 0.004 = 0.4$

**B** **1** Write the missing power of ten.

a. $0.04 \times \underline{10} = 0.4$      $0.004 \times \underline{1,000} = 4$

b. $\underline{100} \times 0.006 = 0.6$      $\underline{1,000} \times 0.006 = 6$

c. $0.007 \times \underline{1,000} = 7$      $0.07 \times \underline{100} = 7$

**C** **2** When you multiply a decimal by a power of ten, what is the relationship between the number of places the decimal point moves and the number of zeros in the power of ten? Give an example.

Answers will vary. Possible answer: The number of places

the decimal point moves is the same as the number of zeros

in the power of ten. Example: $100 \times 0.004 = 0.4$. There are

two zeros in 100, and the decimal point moves two

places to the right, from 0.004 to 0.4.

**M** **3** Complete the equations.

a. $0.03 \times 1,000 = \underline{30}$

b. $0.008 \times 100 = \underline{0.8}$

**Vocabulary**

**power of ten** a number that can be written as a product of tens.

$10 = 10$
$100 = 10 \times 10$
$1,000 = 10 \times 10 \times 10$

©Curriculum Associates, LLC   Copying is not permitted.    Lesson 2 Understand Powers of Ten **13**

---

**14**   Lesson 2   Understand Powers of Ten

**Solve.**

**M** **4** Complete the table below to show dividing by powers of ten.

| Ones | . | Tenths | Hundredths | Thousandths | |
|------|---|--------|------------|-------------|--|
| 9 | . | 0 | 0 | 0 | |
| 0 | . | 9 | 0 | 0 | $9 \div 10$ |
| 0 | . | 0 | 9 | 0 | $9 \div 100$ |
| 0 | . | 0 | 0 | 9 | $9 \div 1,000$ |

**M** **5** Write the quotient.

a. $0.03 \div 10 = \underline{0.003}$

b. $0.3 \div 100 = \underline{0.003}$

c. $3 \div 1,000 = \underline{0.003}$

**M** **6** How is the way the decimal point moves when you divide a decimal number by a power of ten the same as when you multiply? How is it different?

Answers will vary. Possible answer: The decimal point moves one place for each power

of ten when you multiply or divide. When you multiply by a power of ten you move the

decimal point to the right, but when you divide by a power of ten you move the

decimal point to the left.

**M** **7** Complete the equations showing powers of tens using exponents.

a. $8 \times 100 = 8 \times 10^2 = \underline{800}$

b. $8 \times 1,000 = 8 \times 10^3 = \underline{8,000}$

c. $2 \times \underline{10} = 2 \times 10^1 = \underline{20}$

d. $0.02 \times 100 = 0.02 \times 10^2 = \underline{2}$

**Vocabulary**

**exponent** the number in a power that tells how many times to use the base as a factor.

$10^2 \leftarrow$ exponent
$\uparrow$
base

$10^2 = 10 \times 10$, or 100

©Curriculum Associates, LLC   Copying is not permitted.

---

# Practice Lesson 2 *Understand* Powers of Ten

**Unit 1**

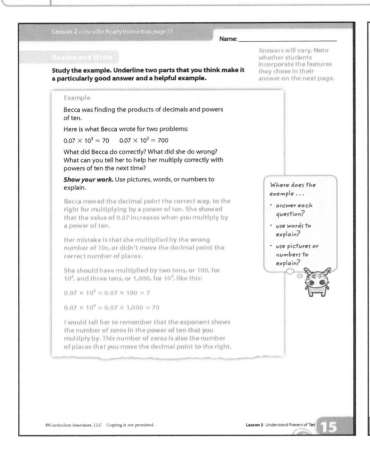

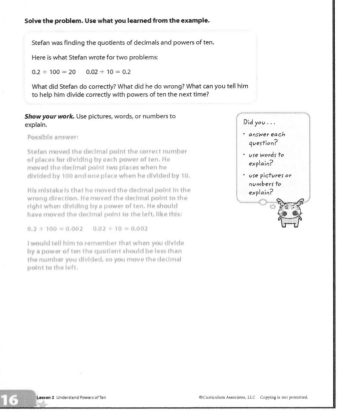

**Lesson 2** · *Use after Ready Instruction page 13*

Name: _____

Answers will vary. Note whether students incorporate the features they chose in their answer on the next page.

**Reason and Write**

**Study the example. Underline two parts that you think make it a particularly good answer and a helpful example.**

Example

Becca was finding the products of decimals and powers of ten.

Here is what Becca wrote for two problems:

$0.07 \times 10^2 = 70$    $0.07 \times 10^3 = 700$

What did Becca do correctly? What did she do wrong? What can you tell her to help her multiply correctly with powers of ten the next time?

***Show your work.*** Use pictures, words, or numbers to explain.

Becca moved the decimal point the correct way, to the right for multiplying by a power of ten. She showed that the value of 0.07 increases when you multiply by a power of ten.

Her mistake is that she multiplied by the wrong number of 10s, or didn't move the decimal point the correct number of places.

She should have multiplied by two tens, or 100, for $10^2$, and three tens, or 1,000, for $10^3$, like this:

$0.07 \times 10^2 = 0.07 \times 100 = 7$

$0.07 \times 10^3 = 0.07 \times 1,000 = 70$

I would tell her to remember that the exponent shows the number of zeros in the power of ten that you multiply by. This number of zeros is also the number of places that you move the decimal point to the right.

Where does the example . . .
• answer each question?
• use words to explain?
• use pictures or numbers to explain?

**Solve the problem. Use what you learned from the example.**

Stefan was finding the quotients of decimals and powers of ten.

Here is what Stefan wrote for two problems:

$0.2 \div 100 = 20$    $0.02 \div 10 = 0.2$

What did Stefan do correctly? What did he do wrong? What can you tell him to help him divide correctly with powers of ten the next time?

***Show your work.*** Use pictures, words, or numbers to explain.

Possible answer:

Stefan moved the decimal point the correct number of places for dividing by each power of ten. He moved the decimal point two places when he divided by 100 and one place when he divided by 10.

His mistake is that he moved the decimal point in the wrong direction. He moved the decimal point to the right when dividing by a power of ten. He should have moved the decimal point to the left, like this:

$0.2 \div 100 = 0.002$    $0.02 \div 10 = 0.002$

I would tell him to remember that when you divide by a power of ten the quotient should be less than the number you divided, so you move the decimal point to the left.

Did you . . .
• answer each question?
• use words to explain?
• use pictures or numbers to explain?

©Curriculum Associates, LLC   Copying is not permitted.    **Lesson 2** Understand Powers of Ten  **15**

**16**  **Lesson 2** Understand Powers of Ten    ©Curriculum Associates, LLC   Copying is not permitted.

| Key | |
|---|---|
| B | Basic |
| M | Medium |
| C | Challenge |

**4**  Practice and Problem Solving    Unit 1 Number and Operations in Base Ten
©Curriculum Associates, LLC   Copying is not permitted.

---

Lesson 3    *Use after Ready Instruction page 15*

## Read and Write Decimals

Name: _____

### Write Fractions as Decimals

**Study the example showing how to write a fraction as a decimal. Then solve problems 1–8.**

**Example**

Models can help you write fractions with denominators of 10 or 100 as decimals.

Each section is one tenth of the whole, or 0.1.

$3 \times \frac{1}{10}$, or $\frac{3}{10}$ is shaded.

Each square is one hundredth of the whole, or 0.01.

$45 \times \frac{1}{100}$, or $\frac{45}{100}$ is shaded.

$\frac{3}{10}$ is equivalent to 0.3.     $\frac{45}{100}$ is equivalent to 0.45.

**B  1** Write the amount shaded as a fraction. Then write the fraction as a decimal.

$82 \times \frac{1}{100}$ is shaded.

$\frac{82}{100}$ is equivalent to __0.82__.

**M  2** Shade the model to show 5 tenths. Then write a fraction and a decimal to describe the amount shaded.

$\frac{5}{10}$, or __0.5__ is shaded.

**B  3** Write a fraction and a decimal to represent 17 hundredths.

$\frac{17}{100}$ and __0.17__

©Curriculum Associates, LLC  Copying is not permitted.     **Lesson 3** Read and Write Decimals   **19**

---

**20**   **Lesson 3** Read and Write Decimals     ©Curriculum Associates, LLC  Copying is not permitted.

**Solve.**

**M  4** How many places after the decimal point does the equivalent decimal have if:

   **a.** the denominator of the fraction is 10? __1__

   **b.** the denominator of the fraction is 100? __2__

**C  5** Look at your answers to problem 4. Explain the reasoning you used to find the answers.

Answers will vary. Possible answer: If the denominator of the fraction is 10, the fraction is an amount in tenths. Tenths is the first place after the decimal point.

If the denominator of the fraction is 100, the fraction describes an amount in hundredths. Hundredths is two places after the decimal point.

**M  6** Shade the model to show 4 hundredths. Then write a fraction and a decimal to describe the amount shaded.

$\frac{4}{100}$, or __0.04__ is shaded.

**M  7** Choose either *Yes* or *No* to tell if the expression or number represents 7 hundredths.

   **a.** $7 \times \frac{1}{10}$    ☐ Yes   ☒ No

   **b.** $7 \times \frac{1}{100}$    ☒ Yes   ☐ No

   **c.** 0.70    ☐ Yes   ☒ No

   **d.** 0.07    ☒ Yes   ☐ No

**C  8** Explain how using a model can help you write a fraction with a denominator of 10 or 100 as a decimal.

Answers will vary. Possible answer: If you use a model like the place-value blocks that can be used to show both fractions and decimals, you can first shade the model to show the fraction amount. Then you can think about what decimal amount the model shows and write the decimal.

---

Lesson 3 • *Use after Ready Instruction page 17*

Name: _____

### Read a Decimal

**Study the example problem showing how to read a decimal. Then solve problems 1–7.**

**Example**

To read a decimal, you name the place value of the smallest-sized unit, and tell how many of those units there are.

| Ones | . | Tenths | Hundredths | Thousandths |
|------|---|--------|------------|-------------|
| 0    | . | 0      | 7          | 3           |

The least place value of 0.073 is thousandths.

There are 73 thousandths.

To read the decimal 0.073, say: *seventy-three thousandths*.

**B  1** Write the decimal 0.24 in the place-value chart.

| Ones | . | Tenths | Hundredths | Thousandths |
|------|---|--------|------------|-------------|
| 0    | . | 2      | 4          |             |

**B  2** Using the chart in problem 1, what is the least place value of 0.24?

hundredths

**M  3** How do you read the decimal 0.24?

twenty-four hundredths

**M  4** Write the word form of each decimal.

   **a.** 0.8 __eight tenths__

   **b.** 0.08 __eight hundredths__

   **c.** 0.008 __eight thousandths__

©Curriculum Associates, LLC  Copying is not permitted.     **Lesson 3** Read and Write Decimals   **21**

---

**22**   **Lesson 3** Read and Write Decimals     ©Curriculum Associates, LLC  Copying is not permitted.

**Solve.**

**C  5** The two grids show the same amount shaded. Is the word form of the decimals the same? Explain.

0.4 is shaded.     0.40 is shaded.

Answers will vary. Possible answer: No. The fractional part used to describe the amount shaded is different, so the name is different. The word form of 0.4 is four tenths. The word form of 0.40 is forty hundredths.

**M  6** Write the expanded form of 0.68 with decimals.

$0.68 = 0.6 + $ __0.08__

$\quad = $ __6__ $\times 0.1 + 8 \times$ __0.01__

**M  7** Write the expanded form of 0.031 with fractions.

$0.031 = $ ⬚3 $\times \frac{1}{100} + $ ⬚1 $\times \frac{1}{1,000}$

$\quad = \frac{3}{100} + \frac{1}{1,000}$

$\quad = \frac{30}{1,000} + \frac{1}{1,000}$

$\quad = \frac{31}{1,000}$

**Vocabulary**

**expanded form** a way to show the value of each digit in a number.

For example, $34.56 = (3 \times 10) + (4 \times 1) + \left(5 \times \frac{1}{10}\right) + \left(6 \times \frac{1}{100}\right)$

©Curriculum Associates, LLC    Copying is not permitted.

Name: _____

### Write a Mixed Number as a Decimal

Study the example showing a number written in multiple forms. Then solve problems 1–6.

| Example | |
|---|---|
| words | one and forty-six thousandths |
| mixed number | $1\frac{46}{1,000}$ |
| expanded form | $1 + \frac{46}{1,000}$<br>$1 + \frac{40}{1,000} + \frac{6}{1,000}$<br>$1 + \frac{4}{100} + \frac{6}{1,000}$ |
| decimal | 1.046 |

**B** **1** In the example, what does the 0 in 1.046 mean?

Answers will vary. Students should indicate that there are 0 tenths.

_____

**M** **2** Fill in the missing information in the table below.

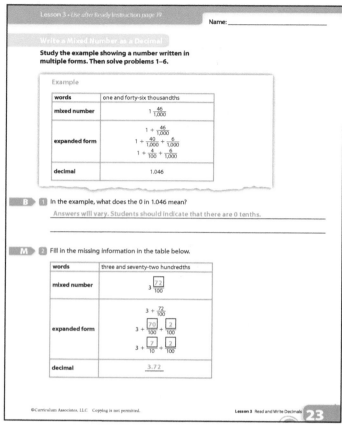

| words | three and seventy-two hundredths |
|---|---|
| mixed number | $3\boxed{\frac{72}{100}}$ |
| expanded form | $3 + \frac{72}{100}$<br>$3 + \boxed{\frac{70}{100}} + \boxed{\frac{2}{100}}$<br>$3 + \boxed{\frac{7}{10}} + \boxed{\frac{2}{100}}$ |
| decimal | 3.72 |

---

**Solve.**

**M** **3** Fill in the blanks to write numbers and words to show the values of the digits.

Four and seventy-two hundredths is ___4___ ones and ___72___ hundredths. 72 hundredths is ___70___ hundredths and ___2___ hundredths, or 7 ___tenths___ and 2 ___hundredths___ .

**M** **4** Write the decimal four and seventy-two hundredths in the place-value chart and then write it in decimal form.

| Ones | . | Tenths | Hundredths | Thousandths |
|---|---|---|---|---|
| 4 | . | 7 | 2 | |

Four and seventy-two hundredths is written ___4.72___ .

**C** **5** When a decimal is written in word form, what indicates that the equivalent form is a mixed number and not a fraction? Explain.

Answers will vary. Possible answer: When the word form has a whole number followed

by the word *and*, it is a mixed number; otherwise it is a fraction.

**C** **6** The length of an Eastern Gray Tree Frog tadpole can be as long as five and twenty-two hundredths centimeters. What is this length written as a decimal?

***Show your work.***

Possible student work:

Five and twenty-two hundredths    $5\frac{22}{100}$

$5 + \frac{22}{100}$

$5 + \frac{20}{100} + \frac{2}{100}$

$5 + \frac{2}{10} + \frac{2}{100}$

Solution: ___5.22 centimeters___

---

Name: _____

### Read and Write Decimals

**Solve the problems.**

**B** **1** Sonya measured her pet mouse from the tip of its nose to the tip of its tail. Her mouse is fourteen hundredths of a meter long. Which of the following expresses this length as a decimal?

*How many decimal places will this number have?*

A  0.014      C  1.4

**(B)** 0.14      D  14.00

**M** **2** Choose either *Yes* or *No* to tell if each of the following represents 0.87.

*What are the place values of each digit in 0.87?*

a. $\frac{8}{10} + \frac{7}{100}$    ☒ Yes ☐ No

b. $\frac{8}{100} + \frac{7}{100}$    ☐ Yes ☒ No

c. 87 hundredths    ☒ Yes ☐ No

d. eighty-seven hundredths    ☒ Yes ☐ No

**C** **3** $3 \times 10 + 2 \times 1 + 6 \times \frac{1}{100} + 4 \times \frac{1}{1,000}$ is the expanded form of which decimal?

*Which decimal places are represented in the expanded form?*

A  3.2064      C  32.604

**(B)** 32.064      D  320.064

Santo chose **C** as the correct answer. How did he get that answer?

Possible explanation: Santo wrote the 6 and

0 digits in the wrong places. The zero should be

written in the tenths place and the 6 should be

written in the hundredths place.

---

**Solve.**

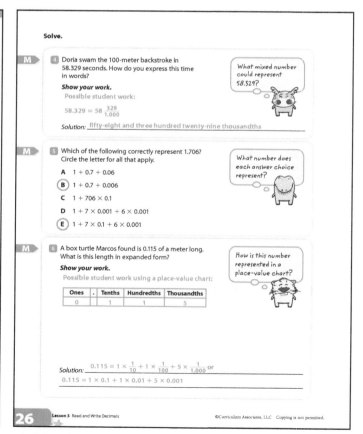

**M** **4** Doria swam the 100-meter backstroke in 58.329 seconds. How do you express this time in words?

*What mixed number could represent 58.329?*

***Show your work.***

Possible student work:

$58.329 = 58\frac{329}{1,000}$

Solution: ___fifty-eight and three hundred twenty-nine thousandths___

**M** **5** Which of the following correctly represent 1.706? Circle the letter for all that apply.

*What number does each answer choice represent?*

A  $1 + 0.7 + 0.06$

**(B)** $1 + 0.7 + 0.006$

C  $1 + 706 \times 0.1$

D  $1 + 7 \times 0.001 + 6 \times 0.001$

**(E)** $1 + 7 \times 0.1 + 6 \times 0.001$

**M** **6** A box turtle Marcos found is 0.115 of a meter long. What is this length in expanded form?

*How is this number represented in a place-value chart?*

***Show your work.***

Possible student work using a place-value chart:

| Ones | . | Tenths | Hundredths | Thousandths |
|---|---|---|---|---|
| 0 | . | 1 | 1 | 5 |

Solution: $0.115 = 1 \times \frac{1}{10} + 1 \times \frac{1}{100} + 5 \times \frac{1}{1,000}$ or

$0.115 = 1 \times 0.1 + 1 \times 0.01 + 5 \times 0.001$

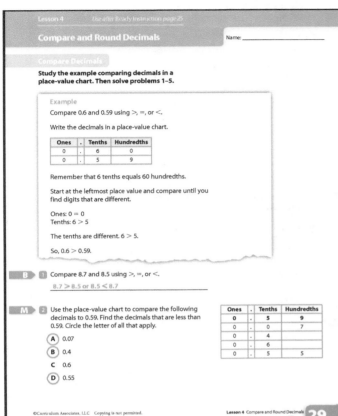

Lesson 4    *Use after Ready Instruction page 25*

**Compare and Round Decimals**

Name: _____

**Compare Decimals**

**Study the example comparing decimals in a place-value chart. Then solve problems 1–5.**

**Example**

Compare 0.6 and 0.59 using >, =, or <.

Write the decimals in a place-value chart.

| Ones | . | Tenths | Hundredths |
|------|---|--------|------------|
| 0 | . | 6 | 0 |
| 0 | . | 5 | 9 |

Remember that 6 tenths equals 60 hundredths.

Start at the leftmost place value and compare until you find digits that are different.

Ones: 0 = 0
Tenths: 6 > 5

The tenths are different. 6 > 5.

So, 0.6 > 0.59.

**B** **1** Compare 8.7 and 8.5 using >, =, or <.

8.7 > 8.5 or 8.5 < 8.7

**M** **2** Use the place-value chart to compare the following decimals to 0.59. Find the decimals that are less than 0.59. Circle the letter of all that apply.

| Ones | . | Tenths | Hundredths |
|------|---|--------|------------|
| 0 | . | 5 | 9 |
| 0 | . | 0 | 7 |
| 0 | . | 4 | |
| 0 | . | 6 | |
| 0 | . | 5 | 5 |

(A) 0.07

(B) 0.4

C 0.6

(D) 0.55

©Curriculum Associates, LLC   Copying is not permitted.     **Lesson 4** Compare and Round Decimals   **29**

---

**Solve.**

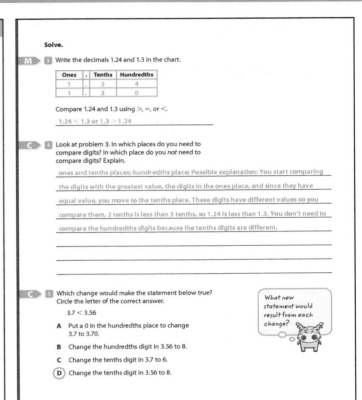

**M** **3** Write the decimals 1.24 and 1.3 in the chart.

| Ones | . | Tenths | Hundredths |
|------|---|--------|------------|
| 1 | . | 2 | 4 |
| 1 | . | 3 | 0 |

Compare 1.24 and 1.3 using >, =, or <.

1.24 < 1.3 or 1.3 > 1.24

**C** **4** Look at problem 3. In which places do you need to compare digits? In which place do you *not* need to compare digits? Explain.

ones and tenths places; hundredths place; Possible explanation: You start comparing

the digits with the greatest value, the digits in the ones place, and since they have

equal value, you move to the tenths place. These digits have different values so you

compare them. 2 tenths is less than 3 tenths, so 1.24 is less than 1.3. You don't need to

compare the hundredths digits because the tenths digits are different.

_____

_____

_____

**C** **5** Which change would make the statement below true? Circle the letter of the correct answer.

3.7 < 3.56

> *What new statement would result from each change?*

**A** Put a 0 in the hundredths place to change 3.7 to 3.70.

**B** Change the hundredths digit in 3.56 to 8.

**C** Change the tenths digit in 3.7 to 6.

(D) Change the tenths digit in 3.56 to 8.

**30**   **Lesson 4** Compare and Round Decimals     ©Curriculum Associates, LLC   Copying is not permitted.

---

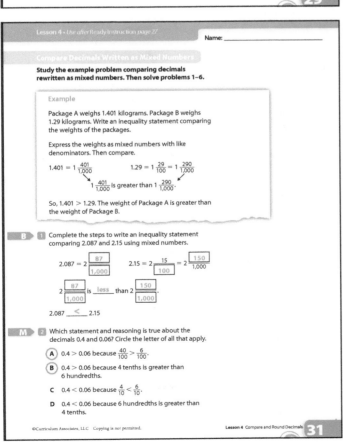

Lesson 4 • *Use after Ready Instruction page 27*

Name: _____

**Compare Decimals Written as Mixed Numbers**

**Study the example problem comparing decimals rewritten as mixed numbers. Then solve problems 1–6.**

**Example**

Package A weighs 1.401 kilograms. Package B weighs 1.29 kilograms. Write an inequality statement comparing the weights of the packages.

Express the weights as mixed numbers with like denominators. Then compare.

$1.401 = 1\frac{401}{1,000}$      $1.29 = 1\frac{29}{100} = 1\frac{290}{1,000}$

$1\frac{401}{1,000}$ is greater than $1\frac{290}{1,000}$

So, 1.401 > 1.29. The weight of Package A is greater than the weight of Package B.

**B** **1** Complete the steps to write an inequality statement comparing 2.087 and 2.15 using mixed numbers.

$2.087 = 2\frac{87}{1,000}$    $2.15 = 2\frac{15}{100} = 2\frac{150}{1,000}$

$2\frac{87}{1,000}$ is $\underline{less}$ than $2\frac{150}{1,000}$.

2.087 $\underline{<}$ 2.15

**M** **2** Which statement and reasoning is true about the decimals 0.4 and 0.06? Circle the letter of all that apply.

(A) 0.4 > 0.06 because $\frac{40}{100} > \frac{6}{100}$.

(B) 0.4 > 0.06 because 4 tenths is greater than 6 hundredths.

**C** 0.4 < 0.06 because $\frac{4}{10} < \frac{6}{10}$.

**D** 0.4 < 0.06 because 6 hundredths is greater than 4 tenths.

©Curriculum Associates, LLC   Copying is not permitted.     **Lesson 4** Compare and Round Decimals   **31**

---

**Solve.**

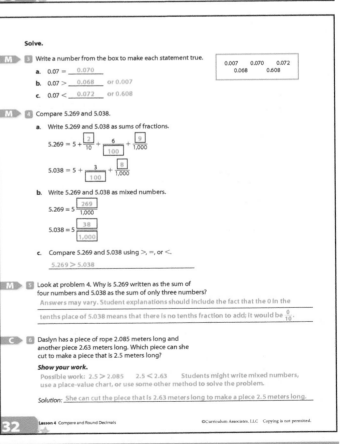

**M** **3** Write a number from the box to make each statement true.

| 0.007 | 0.070 | 0.072 |
|-------|-------|-------|
| 0.068 | | 0.608 |

**a.** 0.07 = $\underline{0.070}$

**b.** 0.07 > $\underline{0.068}$   or 0.007

**c.** 0.07 < $\underline{0.072}$   or 0.608

**M** **4** Compare 5.269 and 5.038.

**a.** Write 5.269 and 5.038 as sums of fractions.

$5.269 = 5 + \frac{2}{10} + \frac{6}{100} + \frac{9}{1,000}$

$5.038 = 5 + \frac{3}{100} + \frac{8}{1,000}$

**b.** Write 5.269 and 5.038 as mixed numbers.

$5.269 = 5\frac{269}{1,000}$

$5.038 = 5\frac{38}{1,000}$

**c.** Compare 5.269 and 5.038 using >, =, or <.

5.269 > 5.038

**M** **5** Look at problem 4. Why is 5.269 written as the sum of four numbers and 5.038 as the sum of only three numbers?

Answers may vary. Student explanations should include the fact that the 0 in the

tenths place of 5.038 means that there is no tenths fraction to add; it would be $\frac{0}{10}$.

**C** **6** Daslyn has a piece of rope 2.085 meters long and another piece 2.63 meters long. Which piece can she cut to make a piece that is 2.5 meters long?

**Show your work.**

Possible work: 2.5 > 2.085    2.5 < 2.63     Students might write mixed numbers,

use a place-value chart, or use some other method to solve the problem.

*Solution:* She can cut the piece that is 2.63 meters long to make a piece 2.5 meters long.

**32**   **Lesson 4** Compare and Round Decimals     ©Curriculum Associates, LLC   Copying is not permitted.

©Curriculum Associates, LLC   Copying is not permitted.

---

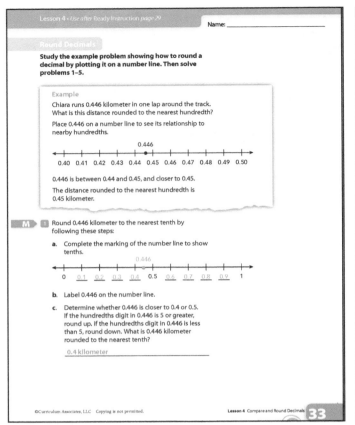

Lesson 4 · Use after Ready Instruction page 29    Name: _____

**Round Decimals**

**Study the example problem showing how to round a decimal by plotting it on a number line. Then solve problems 1–5.**

Example

Chiara runs 0.446 kilometer in one lap around the track. What is this distance rounded to the nearest hundredth?

Place 0.446 on a number line to see its relationship to nearby hundredths.

0.446
0.40 0.41 0.42 0.43 0.44 0.45 0.46 0.47 0.48 0.49 0.50

0.446 is between 0.44 and 0.45, and closer to 0.45.

The distance rounded to the nearest hundredth is 0.45 kilometer.

**M 1** Round 0.446 kilometer to the nearest tenth by following these steps:

a. Complete the marking of the number line to show tenths.

0.446
0  0.1  0.2  0.3  0.4  0.5  0.6  0.7  0.8  0.9  1

b. Label 0.446 on the number line.

c. Determine whether 0.446 is closer to 0.4 or 0.5. If the hundredths digit in 0.446 is 5 or greater, round up. If the hundredths digit in 0.446 is less than 5, round down. What is 0.446 kilometer rounded to the nearest tenth?

0.4 kilometer

©Curriculum Associates, LLC  Copying is not permitted.    Lesson 4 Compare and Round Decimals  **33**

---

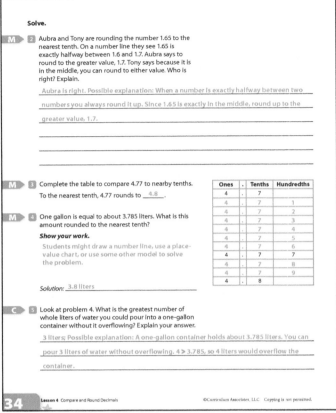

**34**  Lesson 4 Compare and Round Decimals

**Solve.**

**M 2** Aubra and Tony are rounding the number 1.65 to the nearest tenth. On a number line they see 1.65 is exactly halfway between 1.6 and 1.7. Aubra says to round to the greater value, 1.7. Tony says because it is in the middle, you can round to either value. Who is right? Explain.

Aubra is right. Possible explanation: When a number is exactly halfway between two numbers you always round it up. Since 1.65 is exactly in the middle, round up to the greater value, 1.7.

**M 3** Complete the table to compare 4.77 to nearby tenths. To the nearest tenth, 4.77 rounds to __4.8__ .

| Ones | . | Tenths | Hundredths |
|------|---|--------|------------|
| 4 | . | 7 | |
| 4 | . | 7 | 1 |
| 4 | . | 7 | 2 |
| 4 | . | 7 | 3 |
| 4 | . | 7 | 4 |
| 4 | . | 7 | 5 |
| 4 | . | 7 | 6 |
| 4 | . | 7 | 7 |
| 4 | . | 7 | 8 |
| 4 | . | 7 | 9 |
| 4 | . | 8 | |

**M 4** One gallon is equal to about 3.785 liters. What is this amount rounded to the nearest tenth?

**Show your work.**

Students might draw a number line, use a place-value chart, or use some other model to solve the problem.

Solution: __3.8 liters__

**C 5** Look at problem 4. What is the greatest number of whole liters of water you could pour into a one-gallon container without it overflowing? Explain your answer.

3 liters; Possible explanation: A one-gallon container holds about 3.785 liters. You can pour 3 liters of water without overflowing. 4 > 3.785, so 4 liters would overflow the container.

©Curriculum Associates, LLC  Copying is not permitted.

---

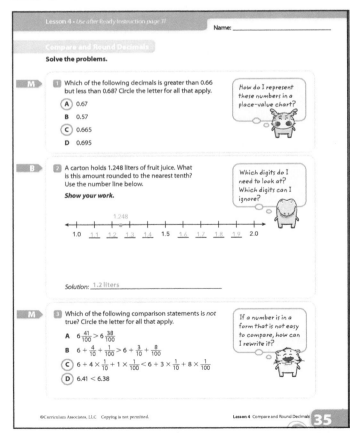

Lesson 4 · Use after Ready Instruction page 31    Name: _____

**Compare and Round Decimals**

**Solve the problems.**

**M 1** Which of the following decimals is greater than 0.66 but less than 0.68? Circle the letter for all that apply.

A 0.67
B 0.57
C 0.665
D 0.695

*How do I represent these numbers in a place-value chart?*

**B 2** A carton holds 1.248 liters of fruit juice. What is this amount rounded to the nearest tenth? Use the number line below.

**Show your work.**

1.248
1.0  1.1  1.2  1.3  1.4  1.5  1.6  1.7  1.8  1.9  2.0

*Which digits do I need to look at? Which digits can I ignore?*

Solution: __1.2 liters__

**M 3** Which of the following comparison statements is *not* true? Circle the letter for all that apply.

A  $6\frac{41}{100} > 6\frac{38}{100}$
B  $6 + \frac{4}{10} + \frac{1}{100} > 6 + \frac{3}{10} + \frac{8}{100}$
C  $6 + 4 \times \frac{1}{10} + 1 \times \frac{1}{100} < 6 + 3 \times \frac{1}{10} + 8 \times \frac{1}{100}$
D  6.41 < 6.38

*If a number is in a form that is not easy to compare, how can I rewrite it?*

©Curriculum Associates, LLC  Copying is not permitted.    Lesson 4 Compare and Round Decimals  **35**

---

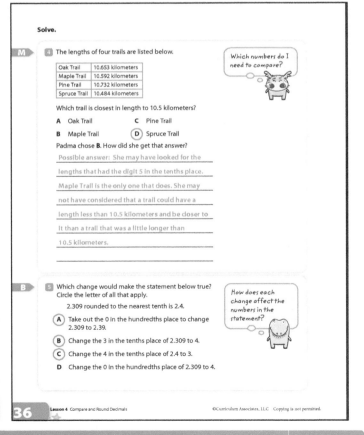

**36**  Lesson 4 Compare and Round Decimals

**Solve.**

**M 4** The lengths of four trails are listed below.

| Oak Trail | 10.653 kilometers |
| Maple Trail | 10.592 kilometers |
| Pine Trail | 10.732 kilometers |
| Spruce Trail | 10.484 kilometers |

*Which numbers do I need to compare?*

Which trail is closest in length to 10.5 kilometers?

A  Oak Trail        C  Pine Trail
B  Maple Trail      D  Spruce Trail

Padma chose **B**. How did she get that answer?

Possible answer: She may have looked for the lengths that had the digit 5 in the tenths place. Maple Trail is the only one that does. She may not have considered that a trail could have a length less than 10.5 kilometers and be closer to it than a trail that was a little longer than 10.5 kilometers.

**B 5** Which change would make the statement below true? Circle the letter of all that apply.

2.309 rounded to the nearest tenth is 2.4.

A  Take out the 0 in the hundredths place to change 2.309 to 2.39.
B  Change the 3 in the tenths place of 2.309 to 4.
C  Change the 4 in the tenths place of 2.4 to 3.
D  Change the 0 in the hundredths place of 2.309 to 4.

*How does each change affect the numbers in the statement?*

©Curriculum Associates, LLC  Copying is not permitted.

---

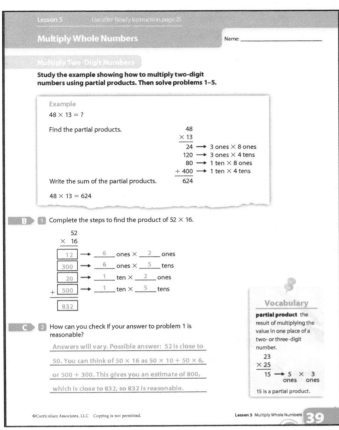

Lesson 5          Use after Ready Instruction page 35

## Multiply Whole Numbers

Name: _____

**Multiply Two-Digit Numbers**

**Study the example showing how to multiply two-digit numbers using partial products. Then solve problems 1–5.**

Example

$48 \times 13 = ?$

Find the partial products.

$$\begin{array}{r} 48 \\ \times\ 13 \\ \hline 24 \rightarrow 3\ \text{ones} \times 8\ \text{ones} \\ 120 \rightarrow 3\ \text{ones} \times 4\ \text{tens} \\ 80 \rightarrow 1\ \text{ten} \times 8\ \text{ones} \\ +\ 400 \rightarrow 1\ \text{ten} \times 4\ \text{tens} \end{array}$$

Write the sum of the partial products.     624

$48 \times 13 = 624$

**B** **1** Complete the steps to find the product of $52 \times 16$.

$$\begin{array}{r} 52 \\ \times\ 16 \\ \hline \boxed{12} \rightarrow \underline{6}\ \text{ones} \times \underline{2}\ \text{ones} \\ \boxed{300} \rightarrow \underline{6}\ \text{ones} \times \underline{5}\ \text{tens} \\ \boxed{20} \rightarrow \underline{1}\ \text{ten} \times \underline{2}\ \text{ones} \\ +\ \boxed{500} \rightarrow \underline{1}\ \text{ten} \times \underline{5}\ \text{tens} \\ \hline \boxed{832} \end{array}$$

**C** **2** How can you check if your answer to problem 1 is reasonable?

Answers will vary. Possible answer: 52 is close to

50. You can think of $50 \times 16$ as $50 \times 10 + 50 \times 6$,

or $500 + 300$. This gives you an estimate of 800,

which is close to 832, so 832 is reasonable.

**Vocabulary**

**partial product** the result of multiplying the value in one place of a two- or three-digit number.

$$\begin{array}{r} 23 \\ \times\ 25 \\ \hline 15 \rightarrow 5 \times 3 \\ \text{ones\ ones} \end{array}$$

15 is a partial product.

©Curriculum Associates, LLC   Copying is not permitted.     Lesson 5 Multiply Whole Numbers **39**

**40** Lesson 5 Multiply Whole Numbers

**Solve.**

**M** **3** You can also use an area model to multiply.

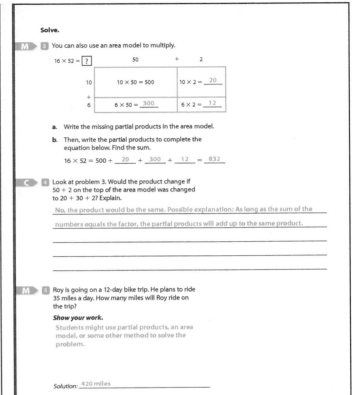

$16 \times 52 = \boxed{?}$

| | 50 | + | 2 |
|---|---|---|---|
| 10 | $10 \times 50 = 500$ | | $10 \times 2 = \underline{20}$ |
| + 6 | $6 \times 50 = \underline{300}$ | | $6 \times 2 = \underline{12}$ |

a. Write the missing partial products in the area model.

b. Then, write the partial products to complete the equation below. Find the sum.

$16 \times 52 = 500 + \underline{20} + \underline{300} + \underline{12} = \underline{832}$

**C** **4** Look at problem 3. Would the product change if $50 + 2$ on the top of the area model was changed to $20 + 30 + 2$? Explain.

No, the product would be the same. Possible explanation: As long as the sum of the

numbers equals the factor, the partial products will add up to the same product.

_____

_____

_____

**M** **5** Roy is going on a 12-day bike trip. He plans to ride 35 miles a day. How many miles will Roy ride on the trip?

**Show your work.**

Students might use partial products, an area model, or some other method to solve the problem.

Solution: _420 miles_

©Curriculum Associates, LLC   Copying is not permitted.

---

Lesson 5 • Use after Ready Instruction page 37

Name: _____

**Multiply Three-Digit Numbers**

**Study the example showing how to multiply a three-digit number by a two-digit number using the distributive property. Then solve problems 1–3.**

Example

Find $132 \times 26$.

Use the distributive property.     $132 \times 26 = 132(20 + 6)$
$= (132 \times 20) + (132 \times 6)$

Find the partial products.

$$\begin{array}{r} 132 \\ \times\ 20 \\ \hline 40\ (20 \times 2) \\ 600\ (20 \times 30) \\ +\ 2{,}000\ (20 \times 100) \\ \hline 2{,}640 \end{array} \qquad \begin{array}{r} 132 \\ \times\ 6 \\ \hline 12\ (6 \times 2) \\ 180\ (6 \times 30) \\ +\ 600\ (6 \times 100) \\ \hline 792 \end{array}$$

Write the sum of the partial products.     $2{,}640 + 792 = 3{,}432$

$132 \times 26 = 3{,}432$

**B** **1** Complete the steps to find $253 \times 34$.

$253 \times 34 = 253(30 + 4) = (\underline{253} \times 30) + (\underline{253} \times 4)$

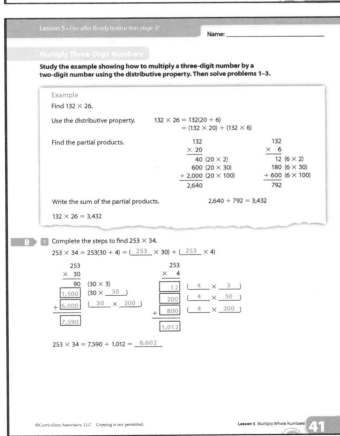

$$\begin{array}{r} 253 \\ \times\ 30 \\ \hline 90\ (30 \times 3) \\ \boxed{1{,}500}\ (30 \times \underline{50}) \\ +\ \boxed{6{,}000}\ (\underline{30} \times \underline{200}) \\ \hline \boxed{7{,}590} \end{array} \qquad \begin{array}{r} 253 \\ \times\ 4 \\ \hline \boxed{12}\ (\underline{4} \times \underline{3}) \\ \boxed{200}\ (\underline{4} \times \underline{50}) \\ +\ \boxed{800}\ (\underline{4} \times \underline{200}) \\ \hline \boxed{1{,}012} \end{array}$$

$253 \times 34 = 7{,}590 + 1{,}012 = \underline{8{,}602}$

©Curriculum Associates, LLC   Copying is not permitted.     Lesson 5 Multiply Whole Numbers **41**

**42** Lesson 5 Multiply Whole Numbers

**Solve.**

**M** **2** You can also use an area model to find the product of $253 \times 34$.

a. Write the missing partial products in the area model.

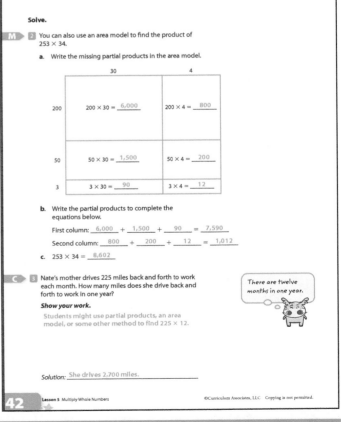

| | 30 | 4 |
|---|---|---|
| 200 | $200 \times 30 = \underline{6{,}000}$ | $200 \times 4 = \underline{800}$ |
| 50 | $50 \times 30 = \underline{1{,}500}$ | $50 \times 4 = \underline{200}$ |
| 3 | $3 \times 30 = \underline{90}$ | $3 \times 4 = \underline{12}$ |

b. Write the partial products to complete the equations below.

First column: $\underline{6{,}000} + \underline{1{,}500} + \underline{90} = \underline{7{,}590}$

Second column: $\underline{800} + \underline{200} + \underline{12} = \underline{1{,}012}$

c. $253 \times 34 = \underline{8{,}602}$

**C** **3** Nate's mother drives 225 miles back and forth to work each month. How many miles does she drive back and forth to work in one year?

**Show your work.**

Students might use partial products, an area model, or some other method to find $225 \times 12$.

> There are twelve months in one year.

Solution: _She drives 2,700 miles._

©Curriculum Associates, LLC   Copying is not permitted.

©Curriculum Associates, LLC     Copying is not permitted.

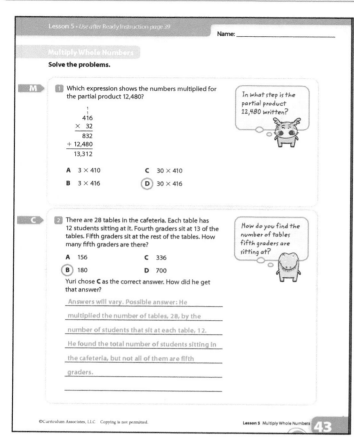

Lesson 5 · Use after Ready Instruction page 39

Name: _____

**Multiply Whole Numbers**

**Solve the problems.**

**M** **1** Which expression shows the numbers multiplied for the partial product 12,480?

```
    1
    1
   416
 ×  32
 ─────
   832
+ 12,480
 ──────
 13,312
```

*In what step is the partial product 12,480 written?*

A  3 × 410

C  30 × 410

B  3 × 416

(D)  30 × 416

**C** **2** There are 28 tables in the cafeteria. Each table has 12 students sitting at it. Fourth graders sit at 13 of the tables. Fifth graders sit at the rest of the tables. How many fifth graders are there?

*How do you find the number of tables fifth graders are sitting at?*

A  156

C  336

(B)  180

D  700

Yuri chose **C** as the correct answer. How did he get that answer?

Answers will vary. Possible answer: He

multiplied the number of tables, 28, by the

number of students that sit at each table, 12.

He found the total number of students sitting in

the cafeteria, but not all of them are fifth

graders.

_____

©Curriculum Associates, LLC  Copying is not permitted.

**Lesson 5** Multiply Whole Numbers **43**

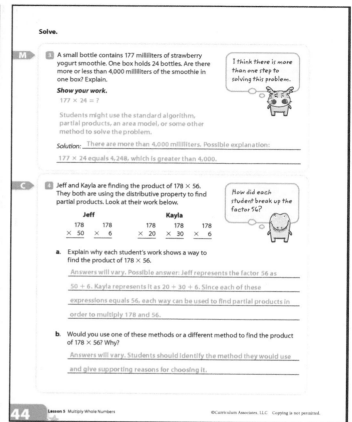

**44** **Lesson 5** Multiply Whole Numbers

Solve.

**M** **3** A small bottle contains 177 milliliters of strawberry yogurt smoothie. One box holds 24 bottles. Are there more or less than 4,000 milliliters of the smoothie in one box? Explain.

*I think there is more than one step to solving this problem.*

**Show your work.**

177 × 24 = ?

Students might use the standard algorithm, partial products, an area model, or some other method to solve the problem.

Solution: ___There are more than 4,000 milliliters. Possible explanation:___

177 × 24 equals 4,248, which is greater than 4,000.

**C** **4** Jeff and Kayla are finding the product of 178 × 56. They both are using the distributive property to find partial products. Look at their work below.

*How did each student break up the factor 56?*

| Jeff | | Kayla | | |
|------|------|------|------|------|
| 178 | 178 | 178 | 178 | 178 |
| × 50 | × 6 | × 20 | × 30 | × 6 |

**a.** Explain why each student's work shows a way to find the product of 178 × 56.

Answers will vary. Possible answer: Jeff represents the factor 56 as

50 + 6. Kayla represents it as 20 + 30 + 6. Since each of these

expressions equals 56, each way can be used to find partial products in

order to multiply 178 and 56.

**b.** Would you use one of these methods or a different method to find the product of 178 × 56? Why?

Answers will vary. Students should identify the method they would use

and give supporting reasons for choosing it.

©Curriculum Associates, LLC  Copying is not permitted.

| | Key |
|---|---|
| B | Basic |
| M | Medium |
| C | Challenge |

©Curriculum Associates, LLC  Copying is not permitted.

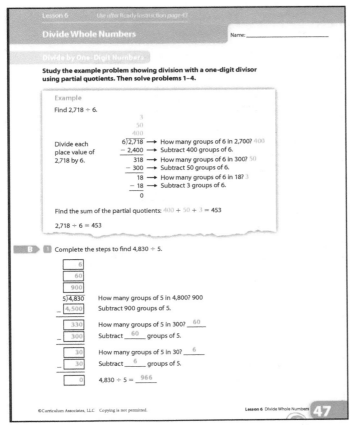

Lesson 6    Use after Ready Instruction page 47

### Divide Whole Numbers

Name: _____

#### Divide by One-Digit Numbers

**Study the example problem showing division with a one-digit divisor using partial quotients. Then solve problems 1–4.**

Example

Find 2,718 ÷ 6.

Divide each place value of 2,718 by 6.

$$\begin{array}{r} 3 \\ 50 \\ 400 \\ 6\overline{)2{,}718} \end{array}$$ → How many groups of 6 in 2,700? 400
− 2,400 → Subtract 400 groups of 6.
318 → How many groups of 6 in 300? 50
− 300 → Subtract 50 groups of 6.
18 → How many groups of 6 in 18? 3
− 18 → Subtract 3 groups of 6.

Find the sum of the partial quotients: 400 + 50 + 3 = 453

2,718 ÷ 6 = 453

**B** **1** Complete the steps to find 4,830 ÷ 5.

| 6 |
| 60 |
| 900 |

5)4,830     How many groups of 5 in 4,800? 900
− 4,500     Subtract 900 groups of 5.
330     How many groups of 5 in 300? _60_
− 300     Subtract _60_ groups of 5.
30     How many groups of 5 in 30? _6_
− 30     Subtract _6_ groups of 5.
0     4,830 ÷ 5 = _966_

©Curriculum Associates, LLC   Copying is not permitted.     Lesson 6 Divide Whole Numbers **47**

---

**48** Lesson 6 Divide Whole Numbers     ©Curriculum Associates, LLC   Copying is not permitted.

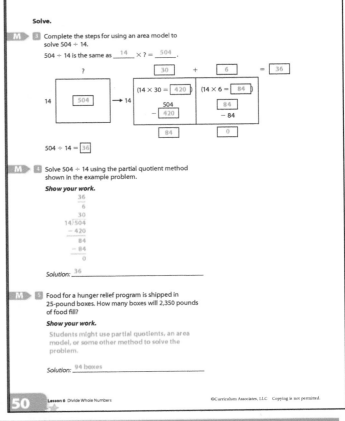

**Solve.**

**C** **2** Quinn and Jewel are finding the quotient of 336 ÷ 8. Look at their work to the right.

How are Quinn's and Jewel's ways of finding the quotient similar? How are they different?

Answers will vary. Possible answer: Both students are using partial quotients to find the answer. The sum of the partial quotients for each student is the correct answer, 42. Quinn did the division using three partial quotients; Jewel used two.

| Quinn | Jewel |
|---|---|
| 2 | 2 |
| 10 | 40 |
| 30 | 8)336 |
| 8)336 | − 320 |
| − 240 | 16 |
| 96 | − 16 |
| − 80 | 0 |
| 16 | |
| − 16 | |
| 0 | |

**M** **3** A game store has 2,540 video games on 4 racks. Each rack holds the same number of video games. How many video games are on each rack?

**Show your work.**

2,540 ÷ 4 = ?

Students might use partial quotients, an area model, or some other method to solve the problem.

Solution: _635 video games_

**M** **4** A sports team donates 157 tickets to a sporting event, with tickets to be shared equally among 9 classrooms. How many tickets does each classroom receive? How many tickets are left over?

**Show your work.**

157 ÷ 9 = ?

Students might use partial quotients, an area model, or some other method to solve the problem.

Solution: Each classroom receives _17_ tickets.

There are _4_ tickets left over.

---

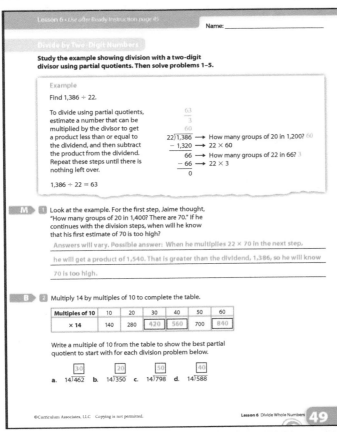

Lesson 6 • Use after Ready Instruction page 49

Name: _____

#### Divide by Two-Digit Numbers

**Study the example showing division with a two-digit divisor using partial quotients. Then solve problems 1–5.**

Example

Find 1,386 ÷ 22.

To divide using partial quotients, estimate a number that can be multiplied by the divisor to get a product less than or equal to the dividend, and then subtract the product from the dividend. Repeat these steps until there is nothing left over.

$$\begin{array}{r} 63 \\ 3 \\ 60 \\ 22\overline{)1{,}386} \end{array}$$ → How many groups of 20 in 1,200? 60
− 1,320 → 22 × 60
66 → How many groups of 22 in 66? 3
− 66 → 22 × 3
0

1,386 ÷ 22 = 63

**M** **1** Look at the example. For the first step, Jaime thought, "How many groups of 20 in 1,400? There are 70." If he continues with the division steps, when will he know that his first estimate of 70 is too high?

Answers will vary. Possible answer: When he multiplies 22 × 70 in the next step, he will get a product of 1,540. That is greater than the dividend, 1,386, so he will know 70 is too high.

**B** **2** Multiply 14 by multiples of 10 to complete the table.

| Multiples of 10 | 10 | 20 | 30 | 40 | 50 | 60 |
|---|---|---|---|---|---|---|
| × 14 | 140 | 280 | 420 | 560 | 700 | 840 |

Write a multiple of 10 from the table to show the best partial quotient to start with for each division problem below.

**a.** 30  14)462     **b.** 20  14)350     **c.** 50  14)798     **d.** 40  14)588

©Curriculum Associates, LLC   Copying is not permitted.     Lesson 6 Divide Whole Numbers **49**

---

**50** Lesson 6 Divide Whole Numbers     ©Curriculum Associates, LLC   Copying is not permitted.

**Solve.**

**M** **3** Complete the steps for using an area model to solve 504 ÷ 14.

504 ÷ 14 is the same as _14_ × ? = _504_.

? 

14 | 504 → 14

30 + 6 = 36

(14 × 30 = 420)   (14 × 6 = 84)

504        84
− 420     − 84
84        0

504 ÷ 14 = 36

**M** **4** Solve 504 ÷ 14 using the partial quotient method shown in the example problem.

**Show your work.**

$$\begin{array}{r} 36 \\ 6 \\ 30 \\ 14\overline{)504} \\ − 420 \\ \hline 84 \\ − 84 \\ \hline 0 \end{array}$$

Solution: _36_

**M** **5** Food for a hunger relief program is shipped in 25-pound boxes. How many boxes will 2,350 pounds of food fill?

**Show your work.**

Students might use partial quotients, an area model, or some other method to solve the problem.

Solution: _94 boxes_

---

©Curriculum Associates, LLC    Copying is not permitted.

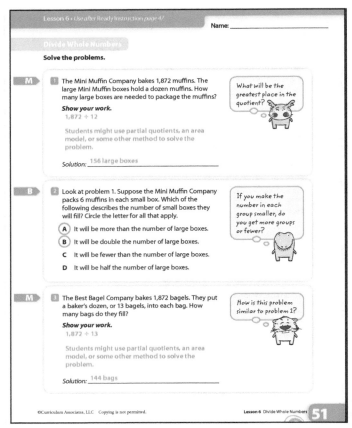

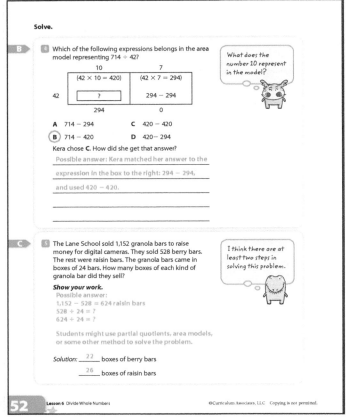

©Curriculum Associates, LLC    Copying is not permitted.

| Key | |
| --- | --- |
| B | Basic |
| M | Medium |
| C | Challenge |

---

Lesson 7          *Use after Ready Instruction page 51*

## Add and Subtract Decimals

Name: _____

### Add and Subtract Whole Numbers

**Study the example showing subtracting whole numbers using regrouping. Then solve problems 1–6.**

> **Example**
>
> Find 8,305 − 4,267.
>
> Write the problem          8,305      3 hundreds = 2 hundreds + 10 tens
> vertically.               − 4,267
> Align places and
> regroup as needed.          8,305     10 tens = 9 tens + 10 ones
>                           − 4,267     5 ones + 10 ones = 15 ones
>
> Subtract.                   8,305
>                           − 4,267
>                             4,038      So, 8,305 − 4,267 = 4,038.

**B 1** Which of the equations represents regrouping needed for the problem shown? Circle the letter for all that apply.

52,134
− 36,091

A   3 tens = 2 tens + 10 ones

(B)  1 hundred = 0 hundreds + 10 tens

C   2 thousands = 1 thousand + 10 hundreds

(D)  5 ten thousands = 4 ten thousands + 10 thousands

**M 2** Find the difference for the subtraction problem in problem 1.

**Show your work.**

Students might use an algorithm, place-value chart, or some other method to solve the problem.

Solution: 16,043

©Curriculum Associates, LLC   Copying is not permitted.          Lesson 7  Add and Subtract Decimals  **55**

---

**Solve.**

**M 3** You can also show regrouping above addition problems. The addition to the right is partially completed. Why is there a 1 above the hundreds place?

627,643
+ 236,083
726

Answers may vary. Possible answer: Because 4 tens + 8 tens = 12 tens = 1 hundred +

2 tens. You show the 1 hundred over the hundreds place.

**B 4** Look at problem 3.

a.  Estimate the sum.

Possible answer: 600,000 + 200,000 = 800,000

b.  Find the sum. _863,726_

c.  Is your answer reasonable? Explain.

Possible explanation: Yes, 863,726 is close to 800,000.

Use the information in the chart to solve problems 5 and 6.

| Mountain (Continent) | Elevation (feet) |
|---|---|
| Everest (Asia) | 29,035 |
| McKinley (North America) | 20,237 |
| Kosciuszko (Australia) | 7,310 |

**M 5** How much higher is the summit of Mt. McKinley than the summit of Mt. Kosciuszko?

**Show your work.**

Students might use an algorithm, place-value chart, or some other method to solve the problem.

Solution: _12,927 feet higher_

**C 6** How much higher is the summit of Mt. Everest than the combined elevations of Mt. McKinley and Mt. Kosciuszko?

**Show your work.**

This is a two-step problem. Students need to find the sum of the elevations of Mts. McKinley and Kosciuszko and subtract that from the elevation of Mt. Everest.

Students might use an algorithm, place-value chart, or some other method to solve the problem.

Solution: _1,488 feet higher_

**56**  Lesson 7  Add and Subtract Decimals          ©Curriculum Associates, LLC   Copying is not permitted.

---

Lesson 7 • *Use after Ready Instruction page 53*

Name: _____

### Add Decimals to Hundredths

**Study the example problem showing decimal addition using a place-value chart. Then solve problems 1–5.**

> **Example**
>
> Alana walks 3.45 miles before lunch and 5.18 miles after lunch. How many miles does she walk in all?
>
> | Ones | . | Tenths | Hundredths |
> |---|---|---|---|
> | 3 | . | 4 | 5 |
> | 5 | . | 1 | 8 |
>
> 3 ones + 5 ones = 8 ones
> 4 tenths + 1 tenth = 5 tenths
> 5 hundredths + 8 hundredths = 13 hundredths
>
> Sum = 8 ones + 5 tenths + 13 hundredths
>      = 8 ones + 6 tenths + 3 hundredths
>
> Alana walks 8.63 miles in all.

**B 1** Look at the example problem. Suppose Alana walks 6.6 miles the next day. Complete the steps below to find the number of miles she walks in two days.

| Ones | . | Tenths | Hundredths |
|---|---|---|---|
| 8 | . | 6 | 3 |
| 6 | . | 6 | 0 |

Sum = 14 ones + _12_ tenths + _3_ hundredths

= _15_ ones + 2 tenths + 3 hundredths

= _1_ ten + _5_ ones + _2_ tenths + _3_ hundredths

Alana walks _15.23_ miles in two days.

©Curriculum Associates, LLC   Copying is not permitted.          Lesson 7  Add and Subtract Decimals  **57**

---

**Solve.**

**M 2** You can also add decimals by writing the problem vertically, lining up the decimal points to keep track of place values.

14.52
+ 22.29
1

The problem to the right is partially completed. Explain why there is a 1 above the tenths place.

Possible answer: 2 hundredths + 9 hundredths = 11 hundredths;

11 hundredths = 1 tenth and 1 hundredth. The 1 represents the regrouped 1 tenth.

**M 3** Find the sum for the addition problem in problem 2. Tell whether each statement about it is *True* or *False*.

a.  It is more than 36.          ☒ True  ☐ False

b.  It is closer to 37 than 36.   ☒ True  ☐ False

c.  It is 36.71.                  ☐ True  ☒ False

d.  It is 36.81.                  ☒ True  ☐ False

**M 4** The size 4 soccer ball Sean's team uses should weigh no more than 0.37 kilogram, and no less than 0.31 kilogram. A soccer bag has two balls in it. What is the most they could weigh together? The least?

**Show your work.**

Students might use equations, a place-value chart, number line, or some other method to solve the problem.

Solution: _0.74 kg; 0.62 kg_

**C 5** Look at problem 4. Will three soccer balls weigh more than 1 kilogram? Explain.

Possible answer: They may or may not. The most three balls would weigh is

0.74 + 0.37, or 1.11 kilograms. The least three balls would weigh is 0.62 + 0.31, or

0.93 kilogram.

**58**  Lesson 7  Add and Subtract Decimals          ©Curriculum Associates, LLC   Copying is not permitted.

©Curriculum Associates, LLC   Copying is not permitted.

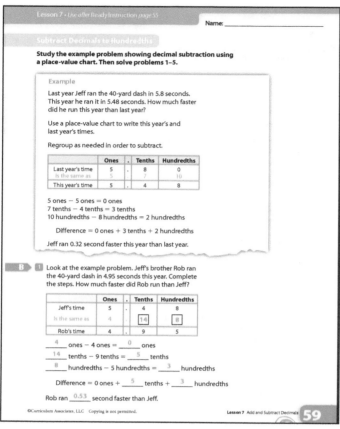

Lesson 7 · *Use after Ready Instruction page 55*

Name: _____

**Subtract Decimals to Hundredths**

**Study the example problem showing decimal subtraction using a place-value chart. Then solve problems 1–5.**

Example

Last year Jeff ran the 40-yard dash in 5.8 seconds. This year he ran it in 5.48 seconds. How much faster did he run this year than last year?

Use a place-value chart to write this year's and last year's times.

Regroup as needed in order to subtract.

| | Ones | . | Tenths | Hundredths |
|---|---|---|---|---|
| Last year's time | 5 | . | 8 | 0 |
| is the same as | 5 | . | 7 | 10 |
| This year's time | 5 | . | 4 | 8 |

5 ones − 5 ones = 0 ones
7 tenths − 4 tenths = 3 tenths
10 hundredths − 8 hundredths = 2 hundredths

Difference = 0 ones + 3 tenths + 2 hundredths

Jeff ran 0.32 second faster this year than last year.

**B** **1** Look at the example problem. Jeff's brother Rob ran the 40-yard dash in 4.95 seconds this year. Complete the steps. How much faster did Rob run than Jeff?

| | Ones | . | Tenths | Hundredths |
|---|---|---|---|---|
| Jeff's time | 5 | . | 4 | 8 |
| Is the same as | 4 | . | 14 | 8 |
| Rob's time | 4 | . | 9 | 5 |

__4__ ones − 4 ones = __0__ ones

__14__ tenths − 9 tenths = __5__ tenths

__8__ hundredths − 5 hundredths = __3__ hundredths

Difference = 0 ones + __5__ tenths + __3__ hundredths

Rob ran __0.53__ second faster than Jeff.

©Curriculum Associates, LLC   Copying is not permitted.          Lesson 7 Add and Subtract Decimals **59**

---

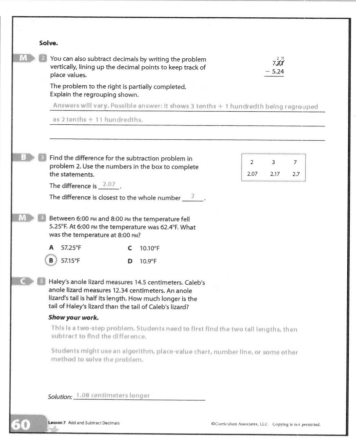

**Solve.**

**M** **2** You can also subtract decimals by writing the problem vertically, lining up the decimal points to keep track of place values.

$$\begin{array}{r} \overset{2\ 11}{7.\cancel{3}\cancel{1}} \\ -\ 5.24 \end{array}$$

The problem to the right is partially completed. Explain the regrouping shown.

Answers will vary. Possible answer: It shows 3 tenths + 1 hundredth being regrouped

as 2 tenths + 11 hundredths.

**B** **3** Find the difference for the subtraction problem in problem 2. Use the numbers in the box to complete the statements.

| 2 | 3 | 7 |
|---|---|---|
| 2.07 | 2.17 | 2.7 |

The difference is __2.07__.

The difference is closest to the whole number __2__.

**M** **4** Between 6:00 PM and 8:00 PM the temperature fell 5.25°F. At 6:00 PM the temperature was 62.4°F. What was the temperature at 8:00 PM?

A   57.25°F          C   10.10°F

**B**   57.15°F          D   10.9°F

**C** **5** Haley's anole lizard measures 14.5 centimeters. Caleb's anole lizard measures 12.34 centimeters. An anole lizard's tail is half its length. How much longer is the tail of Haley's lizard than the tail of Caleb's lizard?

**Show your work.**

This is a two-step problem. Students need to first find the two tail lengths, then subtract to find the difference.

Students might use an algorithm, place-value chart, number line, or some other method to solve the problem.

Solution: __1.08 centimeters longer__

**60** Lesson 7 Add and Subtract Decimals          ©Curriculum Associates, LLC   Copying is not permitted.

---

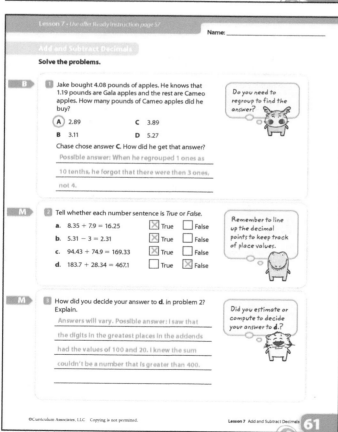

Lesson 7 · *Use after Ready Instruction page 57*

Name: _____

**Add and Subtract Decimals**

**Solve the problems.**

**B** **1** Jake bought 4.08 pounds of apples. He knows that 1.19 pounds are Gala apples and the rest are Cameo apples. How many pounds of Cameo apples did he buy?

*Do you need to regroup to find the answer?*

**A** 2.89          C   3.89

B   3.11          D   5.27

Chase chose answer **C**. How did he get that answer?

Possible answer: When he regrouped 1 ones as

10 tenths, he forgot that there were then 3 ones,

not 4.

**M** **2** Tell whether each number sentence is *True* or *False*.

*Remember to line up the decimal points to keep track of place values.*

a.   8.35 + 7.9 = 16.25          ☒ True  ☐ False

b.   5.31 − 3 = 2.31            ☒ True  ☐ False

c.   94.43 + 74.9 = 169.33        ☒ True  ☐ False

d.   183.7 + 28.34 = 467.1        ☐ True  ☒ False

**M** **3** How did you decide your answer to **d.** in problem 2? Explain.

*Did you estimate or compute to decide your answer to d.?*

Answers will vary. Possible answer: I saw that

the digits in the greatest places in the addends

had the values of 100 and 20. I knew the sum

couldn't be a number that is greater than 400.

©Curriculum Associates, LLC   Copying is not permitted.          Lesson 7 Add and Subtract Decimals **61**

---

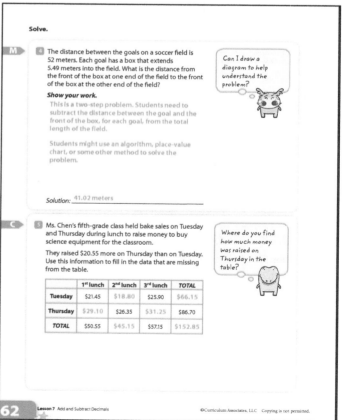

**Solve.**

**M** **4** The distance between the goals on a soccer field is 52 meters. Each goal has a box that extends 5.49 meters into the field. What is the distance from the front of the box at one end of the field to the front of the box at the other end of the field?

*Can I draw a diagram to help understand the problem?*

**Show your work.**

This is a two-step problem. Students need to subtract the distance between the goal and the front of the box, for each goal, from the total length of the field.

Students might use an algorithm, place-value chart, or some other method to solve the problem.

Solution: __41.02 meters__

**C** **5** Ms. Chen's fifth-grade class held bake sales on Tuesday and Thursday during lunch to raise money to buy science equipment for the classroom.

They raised $20.55 more on Thursday than on Tuesday. Use this information to fill in the data that are missing from the table.

*Where do you find how much money was raised on Thursday in the table?*

| | 1st lunch | 2nd lunch | 3rd lunch | TOTAL |
|---|---|---|---|---|
| Tuesday | $21.45 | $18.80 | $25.90 | $66.15 |
| Thursday | $29.10 | $26.35 | $31.25 | $86.70 |
| TOTAL | $50.55 | $45.15 | $57.15 | $152.85 |

**62** Lesson 7 Add and Subtract Decimals          ©Curriculum Associates, LLC   Copying is not permitted.

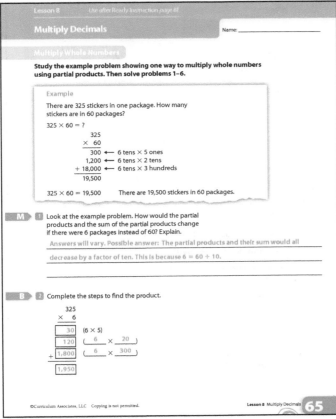

Lesson 8    Use after Ready Instruction page 61

**Multiply Decimals**    Name: _____

**Multiply Whole Numbers**

Study the example problem showing one way to multiply whole numbers using partial products. Then solve problems 1–6.

Example

There are 325 stickers in one package. How many stickers are in 60 packages?

325 × 60 = ?

```
      325
   ×   60
      300  ← 6 tens × 5 ones
    1,200  ← 6 tens × 2 tens
 + 18,000  ← 6 tens × 3 hundreds
   19,500
```

325 × 60 = 19,500    There are 19,500 stickers in 60 packages.

**M** 1 Look at the example problem. How would the partial products and the sum of the partial products change if there were 6 packages instead of 60? Explain.

Answers will vary. Possible answer: The partial products and their sum would all

decrease by a factor of ten. This is because 6 = 60 ÷ 10.

**B** 2 Complete the steps to find the product.

```
      325
    ×   6
     30    (6 × 5)
    120    ( 6 × 20 )
 + 1,800   ( 6 × 300 )
   1,950
```

---

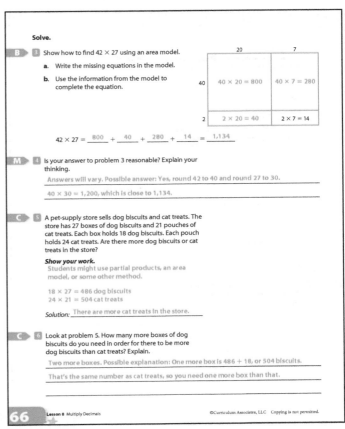

Solve.

**B** 3 Show how to find 42 × 27 using an area model.

a. Write the missing equations in the model.

b. Use the information from the model to complete the equation.

|     | 20 | 7 |
|-----|----|----|
| 40  | 40 × 20 = 800 | 40 × 7 = 280 |
| 2   | 2 × 20 = 40 | 2 × 7 = 14 |

42 × 27 = __800__ + __40__ + __280__ + __14__ = __1,134__

**M** 4 Is your answer to problem 3 reasonable? Explain your thinking.

Answers will vary. Possible answer: Yes, round 42 to 40 and round 27 to 30.

40 × 30 = 1,200, which is close to 1,134.

**C** 5 A pet-supply store sells dog biscuits and cat treats. The store has 27 boxes of dog biscuits and 21 pouches of cat treats. Each box holds 18 dog biscuits. Each pouch holds 24 cat treats. Are there more dog biscuits or cat treats in the store?

**Show your work.**
Students might use partial products, an area model, or some other method.

18 × 27 = 486 dog biscuits
24 × 21 = 504 cat treats

Solution: There are more cat treats in the store.

**C** 6 Look at problem 5. How many more boxes of dog biscuits do you need in order for there to be more dog biscuits than cat treats? Explain.

Two more boxes. Possible explanation: One more box is 486 + 18, or 504 biscuits.

That's the same number as cat treats, so you need one more box than that.

---

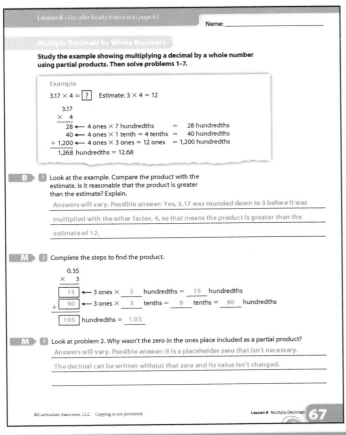

Lesson 8 · Use after Ready Instruction page 63    Name: _____

**Multiply Decimals by Whole Numbers**

Study the example showing multiplying a decimal by a whole number using partial products. Then solve problems 1–7.

Example

3.17 × 4 = [?]    Estimate: 3 × 4 = 12

```
     3.17
   ×    4
      28  ← 4 ones × 7 hundredths   =   28 hundredths
      40  ← 4 ones × 1 tenth = 4 tenths  =   40 hundredths
 + 1,200  ← 4 ones × 3 ones = 12 ones    = 1,200 hundredths
   1,268 hundredths = 12.68
```

**B** 1 Look at the example. Compare the product with the estimate. Is it reasonable that the product is greater than the estimate? Explain.

Answers will vary. Possible answer: Yes, 3.17 was rounded down to 3 before it was

multiplied with the other factor, 4, so that means the product is greater than the

estimate of 12.

**M** 2 Complete the steps to find the product.

```
     0.35
   ×    3
     15   ← 3 ones × 5 hundredths = 15 hundredths
 +   90   ← 3 ones × 3 tenths = 9 tenths = 90 hundredths
    105 hundredths = 1.05
```

**M** 3 Look at problem 2. Why wasn't the zero in the ones place included as a partial product?

Answers will vary. Possible answer: It is a placeholder zero that isn't necessary.

The decimal can be written without that zero and its value isn't changed.

---

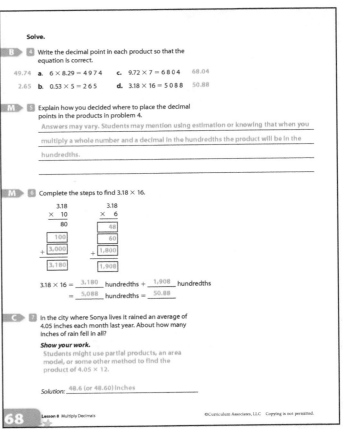

Solve.

**B** 4 Write the decimal point in each product so that the equation is correct.

49.74 a. 6 × 8.29 = 4 9 7 4    c. 9.72 × 7 = 6 8 0 4    68.04

2.65 b. 0.53 × 5 = 2 6 5    d. 3.18 × 16 = 5 0 8 8    50.88

**M** 5 Explain how you decided where to place the decimal points in the products in problem 4.

Answers may vary. Students may mention using estimation or knowing that when you

multiply a whole number and a decimal in the hundredths the product will be in the

hundredths.

**M** 6 Complete the steps to find 3.18 × 16.

```
     3.18         3.18
   ×  10        ×    6
     80           48
    100           60
 + 3,000       + 1,800
   3,180         1,908
```

3.18 × 16 = __3,180__ hundredths + __1,908__ hundredths
          = __5,088__ hundredths = __50.88__

**C** 7 In the city where Sonya lives it rained an average of 4.05 inches each month last year. About how many inches of rain fell in all?

**Show your work.**
Students might use partial products, an area model, or some other method to find the product of 4.05 × 12.

Solution: 48.6 (or 48.60) inches

©Curriculum Associates, LLC    Copying is not permitted.

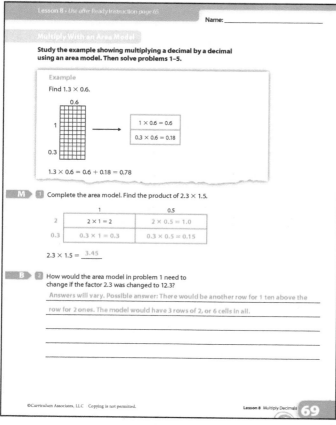

Lesson 8 • Use after Ready Instruction page 66

Name: _____

**Multiply With an Area Model**

Study the example showing multiplying a decimal by a decimal using an area model. Then solve problems 1–5.

Example
Find 1.3 × 0.6.

$1 \times 0.6 = 0.6$
$0.3 \times 0.6 = 0.18$

$1.3 \times 0.6 = 0.6 + 0.18 = 0.78$

**M** 1 Complete the area model. Find the product of 2.3 × 1.5.

| | 1 | 0.5 |
|---|---|---|
| 2 | 2 × 1 = 2 | 2 × 0.5 = 1.0 |
| 0.3 | 0.3 × 1 = 0.3 | 0.3 × 0.5 = 0.15 |

2.3 × 1.5 = __3.45__

**B** 2 How would the area model in problem 1 need to change if the factor 2.3 was changed to 12.3?

Answers will vary. Possible answer: There would be another row for 1 ten above the row for 2 ones. The model would have 3 rows of 2, or 6 cells in all.

---

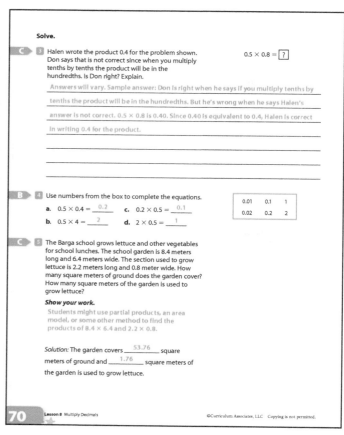

**Solve.**

**C** 3 Halen wrote the product 0.4 for the problem shown. Don says that is not correct since when you multiply tenths by tenths the product will be in the hundredths. Is Don right? Explain.

$0.5 \times 0.8 = \boxed{?}$

Answers will vary. Sample answer: Don is right when he says if you multiply tenths by tenths the product will be in the hundredths. But he's wrong when he says Halen's answer is not correct. 0.5 × 0.8 is 0.40. Since 0.40 is equivalent to 0.4, Halen is correct in writing 0.4 for the product.

**B** 4 Use numbers from the box to complete the equations.

a. 0.5 × 0.4 = __0.2__    c. 0.2 × 0.5 = __0.1__

b. 0.5 × 4 = __2__    d. 2 × 0.5 = __1__

| 0.01 | 0.1 | 1 |
|---|---|---|
| 0.02 | 0.2 | 2 |

**C** 5 The Barga school grows lettuce and other vegetables for school lunches. The school garden is 8.4 meters long and 6.4 meters wide. The section used to grow lettuce is 2.2 meters long and 0.8 meter wide. How many square meters of ground does the garden cover? How many square meters of the garden is used to grow lettuce?

**Show your work.**

Students might use partial products, an area model, or some other method to find the products of 8.4 × 6.4 and 2.2 × 0.8.

*Solution:* The garden covers __53.76__ square meters of ground and __1.76__ square meters of the garden is used to grow lettuce.

---

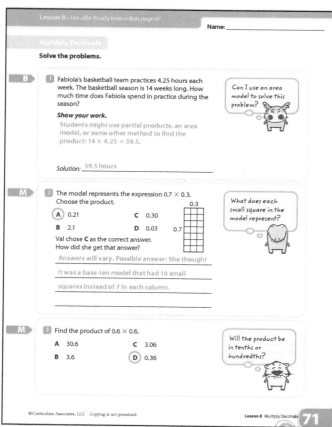

Lesson 8 • Use after Ready Instruction page 67

Name: _____

**Multiply Decimals**

**Solve the problems.**

**B** 1 Fabiola's basketball team practices 4.25 hours each week. The basketball season is 14 weeks long. How much time does Fabiola spend in practice during the season?

**Show your work.**

Students might use partial products, an area model, or some other method to find the product: 14 × 4.25 = 59.5.

*Can I use an area model to solve this problem?*

*Solution:* __59.5 hours__

**M** 2 The model represents the expression 0.7 × 0.3. Choose the product.

(A) 0.21    C 0.30
B 2.1    D 0.03

Val chose **C** as the correct answer. How did she get that answer?

*What does each small square in the model represent?*

Answers will vary. Possible answer: She thought it was a base-ten model that had 10 small squares instead of 7 in each column.

**M** 3 Find the product of 0.6 × 0.6.

A 30.6    C 3.06
B 3.6    (D) 0.36

*Will the product be in tenths or hundredths?*

---

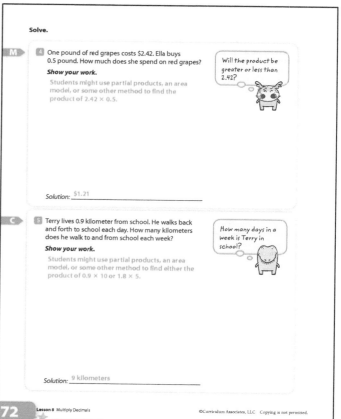

**Solve.**

**M** 4 One pound of red grapes costs $2.42. Ella buys 0.5 pound. How much does she spend on red grapes?

**Show your work.**

Students might use partial products, an area model, or some other method to find the product of 2.42 × 0.5.

*Will the product be greater or less than 2.42?*

*Solution:* __$1.21__

**C** 5 Terry lives 0.9 kilometer from school. He walks back and forth to school each day. How many kilometers does he walk to and from school each week?

**Show your work.**

Students might use partial products, an area model, or some other method to find either the product of 0.9 × 10 or 1.8 × 5.

*How many days in a week is Terry in school?*

*Solution:* __9 kilometers__

Lesson 9     *Use after Ready Instruction page 71*

## Divide Decimals

Name: _____

### Divide Whole Numbers

**Study the example problem showing how to use a bar model to represent division. Then solve problems 1–5.**

**Example**

Stands at the Lincoln Football Field seat 320 people. They are divided into 4 equal sections. How many people can sit in each section?

320 ÷ 4 = ?
You can represent this division problem with a bar model.

320 seats

To find 320 ÷ 4, think 4 × ? = 320.

320 = 32 tens     4 × 8 tens = 32 tens
               4 × 80     = 320

320 ÷ 4 = 80     80 people can sit in each section.

**M** **1** Look at the example. How would the quotient change if the total number of seats was 3,200 instead of 320? Explain.

Answers will vary. Possible answer: The quotient would be ten times greater, or

8 hundreds. 3,200 is 32 hundreds. 4 × 8 hundreds = 32 hundreds, so 3,200 ÷ 4 = 800.

**B** **2** Rewrite each division problem as a multiplication problem and solve.

a. 490 ÷ 7 = ?     7 × ? = 490     490 ÷ 7 = 70

b. 2,400 ÷ 12 = ?     12 × ? = 2,400     2,400 ÷ 12 = 200

c. 350 ÷ 50 = ?     50 × ? = 350     350 ÷ 50 = 7

d. 5,400 ÷ 90 = ?     90 × ? = 5,400     5,400 ÷ 90 = 60

©Curriculum Associates, LLC   Copying is not permitted.     **Lesson 9** Divide Decimals **75**

---

**Solve.**

**M** **3** Choose *Yes* or *No* to tell whether the expression represents the number 40.

a. 1,600 ÷ 4     ☐ Yes   ☒ No

b. 120 ÷ 3     ☒ Yes   ☐ No

c. 480 ÷ 12     ☒ Yes   ☐ No

d. 280 ÷ 70     ☐ Yes   ☒ No

**M** **4** A large drink dispenser used at a school field day holds 640 ounces of lemonade. How many glasses of lemonade can be poured from the dispenser if each glass holds 8 ounces?

**Show your work.**

8 × ? = 640
8 × 80 = 640
640 ÷ 8 = 80

Solution: 80 glasses

**C** **5** Each costume for a dance group in a talent show requires 2 yards of black material and 3 yards of red material. The dance group has 30 yards of black material and 60 yards of red material. What is the greatest number of costumes they can make? Explain.

**Show your work.**

Students might use a bar model, rewrite as a multiplication equation, or use another method to find 30 ÷ 2 = 15 (black material) and 60 ÷ 3 = 20 (red material).

Solution: 15 costumes. Possible explanation: They have enough black material for

15 costumes and enough red material to make 20 costumes. Since each costume

requires both colors, the greatest number of costumes they can make is 15.

**76** **Lesson 9** Divide Decimals     ©Curriculum Associates, LLC   Copying is not permitted.

---

Lesson 9 • *Use after Ready Instruction page 73*

Name: _____

### Divide a Decimal by a Whole Number

**Study the example problem showing one way to divide a decimal by a whole number. Then solve problems 1–5.**

**Example**

The temperature rose 4.8 degrees in 6 hours. If the temperature rose by an equal amount each hour, how many degrees did it rise each hour?

You can represent this with a bar model.

4.8 degrees

To find 4.8 ÷ 6, think 6 × ? = 4.8.

4.8 = 48 tenths     6 × 8 tenths = 48 tenths
6 × 0.8 = 4.8
4.8 ÷ 6 = 0.8

The temperature rose 0.8 degree each hour.

**B** **1** Look at the example problem. Suppose the temperature had risen 5.4 degrees in 6 hours. Complete the steps to solve 5.4 ÷ 6.

a. 5.4 ÷ 6   Think: 6 × ? = 5.4

b. 5.4 = 54 tenths     6 × ? = 54 tenths

c. 6 × 9 tenths = 54 tenths

d. 5.4 ÷ 6 = 0.9

**B** **2** Use numbers from the box. Write the number of tenths and hundredths in each decimal.

| 3.5 | 0.79 | 0.35 |
|---|---|---|
| | 350 | 35 |
| 7.9 | 79 | 790 |

3.5 = 35 tenths     3.5 = 350 hundredths

0.79 = 7.9 tenths     0.79 = 79 hundredths

©Curriculum Associates, LLC   Copying is not permitted.     **Lesson 9** Divide Decimals **77**

---

**Solve.**

**M** **3** Complete the steps for using an area model to solve 1.56 ÷ 12.

1.56 ÷ 12 is the same as 12 × ? = 1.56 .

1.56 = 156 hundredths

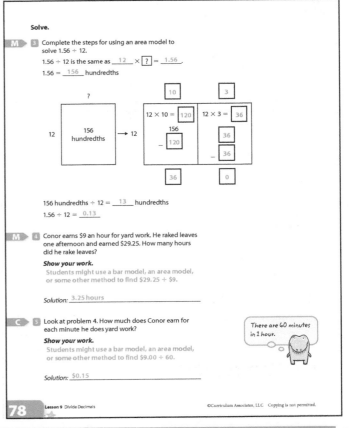

156 hundredths ÷ 12 = 13 hundredths

1.56 ÷ 12 = 0.13

**M** **4** Conor earns $9 an hour for yard work. He raked leaves one afternoon and earned $29.25. How many hours did he rake leaves?

**Show your work.**

Students might use a bar model, an area model, or some other method to find $29.25 ÷ $9.

Solution: 3.25 hours

**C** **5** Look at problem 4. How much does Conor earn for each minute he does yard work?

**Show your work.**

Students might use a bar model, an area model, or some other method to find $9.00 ÷ 60.

Solution: $0.15

There are 60 minutes in 1 hour.

**78** **Lesson 9** Divide Decimals     ©Curriculum Associates, LLC   Copying is not permitted.

©Curriculum Associates, LLC    Copying is not permitted.

# Practice Lesson 9 Divide Decimals

Unit 1

---

Lesson 9 • Use after Ready Instruction page 75

Name: _____

## Divide by Tenths

**Study the example showing one way to divide a decimal by a decimal. Then solve problems 1–7.**

**Example**

What is 2.1 ÷ 0.7?

You can represent this problem with decimal grids.

Each large square represents 1 whole.

To find 2.1 ÷ 0.7, think 0.7 × ? = 2.1.

The lines separate groups of 0.7.

2.1 = 21 tenths
0.7 = 7 tenths

In words: 7 tenths × ? = 21 tenths
7 tenths × 3 = 21 tenths

2.1 ÷ 0.7 = 3

**B** 1 Look at the example. How is the quotient, 3, represented by the grids?

Answers will vary. Possible answer: It is represented by the 3 groups you make when you divide 2.1, or 21 tenths, into groups of 7 tenths.

**M** 2 What other expressions are represented by the decimal grids in the example problem? Circle the letter of all that apply.

(A) 0.7 × 3      C  0.7 ÷ 3
(B) 3 × 0.7      (D) 2.1 ÷ 3

**B** 3 How many grids would you need to represent the problem 4.5 ÷ 0.5? Explain.

5 grids. Possible explanation: In order to represent 4.5 I would use 4 decimal grids to represent 4, and 1 more to represent 0.5, for a total of 5 grids.

©Curriculum Associates, LLC   Copying is not permitted.

Lesson 9 Divide Decimals **79**

---

**80** Lesson 9 Divide Decimals

**Solve.**

**B** 4 Complete the steps to solve 4.5 ÷ 0.5.

a. 4.5 ÷ 0.5  Think: _0.5_ × [?] = _4.5_

b. 4.5 = _45_ tenths and 0.5 = _5_ tenths

c. 5 tenths × _9_ = 45 tenths

d. 4.5 ÷ 0.5 = _9_

**M** 5 Rewrite each division problem as a multiplication problem and solve.

a. 6.3 ÷ 0.9 = [?]    _0.9_ × [?] = _6.3_    6.3 ÷ 0.9 = _7_

b. 3.2 ÷ 0.4 = [?]    _0.4_ × [?] = _3.2_    3.2 ÷ 0.4 = _8_

c. 1.8 ÷ 0.3 = [?]    _0.3_ × [?] = _1.8_    1.8 ÷ 0.3 = _6_

d. 2.4 ÷ 1.2 = [?]    _1.2_ × [?] = _2.4_    2.4 ÷ 1.2 = _2_

**M** 6 The Razdan family drinks 0.5 gallon of milk a day. Will 2.5 gallons of milk last them more than 1 week? Explain.

**Show your work.**

Students might use decimal grids, rewrite as a multiplication equation, or use another method to find 2.5 ÷ 0.5.

Solution: _No. Possible explanation: 2.5 ÷ 0.5 = 5 and 5 < 7, so 2.5 gallons will only last 5 days, not more than 1 week._

**C** 7 Mrs. Lang is hanging drawings for the school art show across a wall that is 2.8 meters wide. She determines each picture, along with the space needed around each picture, will take up 0.4 meter along the wall. How many pictures can she hang in one row across the wall?

**Show your work.**

Students might use decimal grids, rewrite as a multiplication equation, or some other method to find 2.8 ÷ 0.4.

Solution: _7 pictures_

©Curriculum Associates, LLC   Copying is not permitted.

---

Lesson 9 • Use after Ready Instruction page 77

Name: _____

## Divide by Hundredths

**Study the example showing one way to divide by hundredths. Then solve problems 1–6.**

**Example**

1.8 ÷ 0.04 = ?

Identify the least place. Write each decimal to the least place.

0.04 = 4 hundredths
1.8 = 180 hundredths

180 hundredths ÷ 4 hundredths = 45
1.8 ÷ 0.04 = 45

Divide as you would with whole numbers, using partial quotients or another method.

```
      45
       5
      40
  4)180
  −160
    20
   −20
     0
```

**B** 1 Complete the steps to solve 1.02 ÷ 0.06.

a. 1.02 ÷ 0.06

b. 1.02 = _102_ hundredths
   0.06 = _6_ hundredths

c. 102 ÷ 6 = _17_

d. 1.02 ÷ 0.06 = _17_

**M** 2 Did you use partial quotients or another method to divide 102 by 6 in problem 1? Explain.

Answers will vary. Possible answer: I used mental math. I thought of 102 as 60 + 42. That's (6 × 10) + (6 × 7), or 6 × 17. So, 102 ÷ 6 = 17.

**B** 3 Check your answer to problem 1 by writing the decimals in a multiplication equation.

_0.06_ × _17_ = _1.02_

©Curriculum Associates, LLC   Copying is not permitted.

Lesson 9 Divide Decimals **81**

---

**82** Lesson 9 Divide Decimals

**Solve.**

**M** 4 Choose *True* or *False* for each equation.

a. 1.23 = 123 hundredths    [X] True  [ ] False

b. 0.5 = 50 hundredths       [X] True  [ ] False

c. 74 hundredths = 7.4        [ ] True  [X] False

d. 1,088 hundredths = 10.88  [X] True  [ ] False

**M** 5 Jaden buys 1.15 pounds of cheese at the deli counter. If each slice is 0.05 pound, how many slices of cheese does she buy?

**Show your work.**

Students might use partial quotients, rewrite as a multiplication equation, or use another method to find 1.15 ÷ 0.05.

Solution: _23 slices_

**C** 6 Ray feeds his dog 0.12 kilogram of dry dog food each day. He wants to buy the smallest bag that has enough food to feed his dog for one month. Should he buy the bag that has 1.8 kilograms, 2.4 kilograms, or 4.2 kilograms of dog food?

**Show your work.**

Students might use partial quotients, rewrite as multiplication equations, or use another method to find 1.8 ÷ 0.12 = 15, 2.4 ÷ 0.12 = 20, and 4.2 ÷ 0.12 = 35.

Solution: _the bag that has 4.2 kilograms_

©Curriculum Associates, LLC   Copying is not permitted.

---

**18** Practice and Problem Solving

Unit 1 Number and Operations in Base Ten

©Curriculum Associates, LLC   Copying is not permitted.

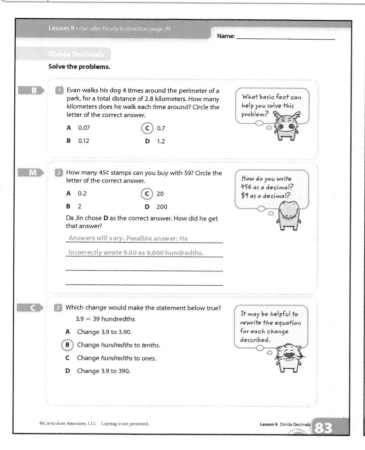

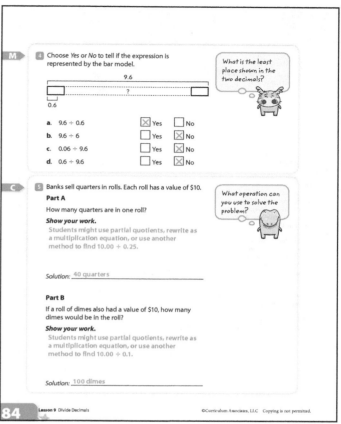

©Curriculum Associates, LLC　Copying is not permitted.

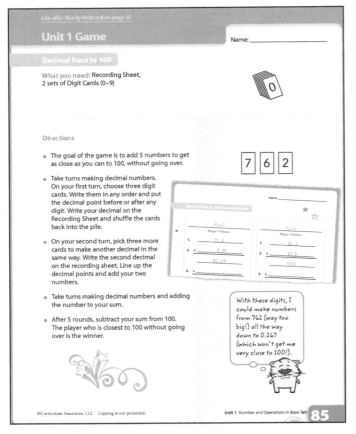

## STEP BY STEP

| CCSS Focus - 5.NBT.B.7, 5.NBT.A.3   *Embedded SMPs* - 2, 6, 7, 8 <br> **Objective:** Add and subtract decimals. | **Materials** For each pair: Recording Sheet (TR 1), 2 sets of 0-9 Digit Cards (TR 2) |
|---|---|

- The goal of the game is to add 5 numbers to get as close as you can to 100, without going over.

- Players should shuffle the digit cards and place them facedown in a pile. Players will take turns drawing three digit cards to make a decimal number.

- On a player's first turn, he/she will pick three digit cards to make a decimal number. They will put the three digits in any order and decide where to place the decimal point. They can place the decimal point before or after any digit. Players record their decimal on the Recording Sheet and shuffle the digit cards back in the pile.

- On a player's second turn, he/she will pick three new cards to make another decimal in the same way. They will write the second decimal on the recording sheet, line up the decimal points, and add the two numbers.

- Now players take turns picking digit cards to make another decimal number and adding the new number to their old sum.

- After 5 turns, the players will subtract their total from 100, to determine who is closest to 100 without going over. If a player goes over 100, they lose.

- Model one complete round for students before they play. Discuss strategies for placing the decimal point. Encourage students to use estimation to decide what decimal to make.

**Vary the Game** Play to 1,000 instead of to 100. How does this change the strategy?

**Challenge** Start at 200 and play "backwards" to 100. Players must subtract decimals to reach their goal.

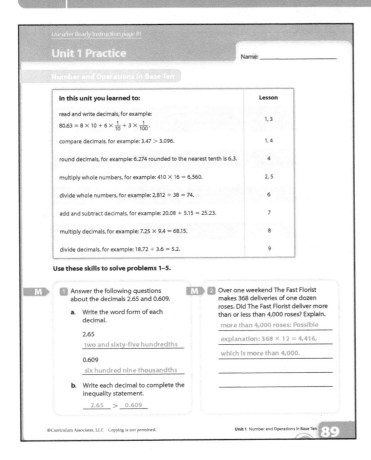

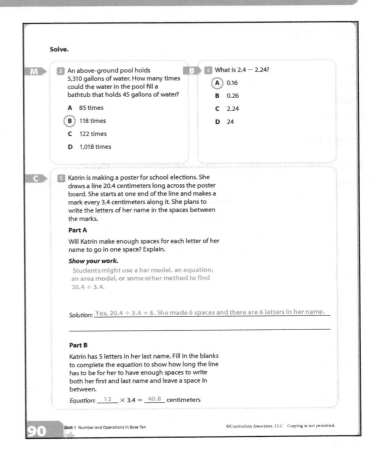

# TEACHER NOTES

**Common Core Standards:** 5.NBT.A.4, 5.NBT.B.7
**Standards for Mathematical Practice:** 1, 2, 4, 5, 6, 7, 8
**DOK:** 3
**Materials:** None

### About the Task

To complete this task, students solve a multi-step problem that involves estimating, adding, subtracting, and multiplying with decimals. The task requires them to use their estimates to plan their purchases; develop plans for purchasing multiple items; calculate the tax; and compare the results against a given budget.

### Getting Started

Read the problem aloud with students and go over the checklist. Have them identify the goal and list the steps needed to buy the props. One approach is to first outline the main tasks: price the dinnerware, price the utensils, price the chairs, calculate the tax, check that the plan is within budget. You may need to explain that tax is an amount of money that is added to the total cost of the items they bought. **(SMP 1, 2)**

### Completing the Task

Students start by estimating which items to buy. They should round the money amounts to estimate. However, students may find that they get a better estimate for the cloth seat chairs by using number sense to estimate. These chairs cost nearly $25, and they may recognize that 3 × $25 is $75. If they round, they may end up with an estimate of $20 per chair or $60 for three chairs, which is the same as the rounded estimates for the other chairs. The less costly items can be rounded to the nearest dollar. **(SMP 5, 6)**

As students price each group of items, they must multiply the price per item by 3. Some students may struggle with calculating the tax. There are three steps. First, multiply the total cost by 0.05; this is the tax. Then write the tax as dollars and cents. Finally, add the tax to the total cost. Encourage students to share their plans and explain how they meet the criteria. Discuss which plan they prefer and why. **(SMP 7, 8)**

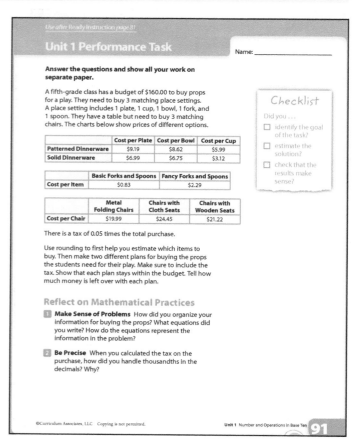

### Extension

If some students have more time to spend on this problem, you can have them solve this extension:

The class has decided to buy a more expensive set of dinnerware. Plates cost $9.97, bowls $9.25, and cups $7.02. Make a plan to buy these and still get the other items they need. How much money is left?

©Curriculum Associates, LLC Copying is not permitted.

## SAMPLE RESPONSES AND RUBRIC

**4-Point Solution**

Round dinnerware and utensil prices to the nearest dollar and multiply by 3. Patterned dinnerware: $9 plate + $9 bowl + $6 cup = $24 per setting, a total of $72. Solid dinnerware: $7 plate + $7 bowl + $3 cup = $17 per setting, a total of $51. Basic utensils: $6. Fancy utensils: $12. Round metal and wooden chair prices to the nearest $10, which is $20 each or $60 for three. Cloth chairs cost almost $25, so it's $75 for three. To get cloth chairs I could get solid dinnerware and basic utensils in order to have money for tax. With less expensive chairs I might be able to get patterned dinnerware.

1. **patterned dinnerware:** $3 \times (9.19 + 8.62 + 5.99) = 71.40$; **basic utensils:** $3 \times (0.83 + 0.83) = 4.98$; **wooden chairs:** $3 \times 21.22 = 63.66$. Cost is $71.40 + 4.98 + 63.66 = 140.04$ and tax is $0.05 \times 140.04 = 7.002$, which rounds to $7.00. Add $7.00 to $140.04. The total is $147.04 with $12.96 left.

2. **solid dinnerware:** $3 \times (6.99 + 6.75 + 3.12) = 50.58$; **basic utensils:** $3 \times (0.83 + 0.83) = 4.98$; **cloth chairs:** $3 \times 24.45 = 73.35$. Cost is $50.58 + 4.98 + 73.35 = 128.91$ and tax is $0.05 \times 128.91 = 6.4455$, which rounds to $6.45. Add $6.45 to $128.91. The total is $135.36 with $24.64 left.

## REFLECT ON MATHEMATICAL PRACTICES

1. Students should estimate first and then calculate. Equations should show the cost per item multiplied by 3 where appropriate. **(SMP 1)**

2. Students should recognize that 0.001 is $\frac{1}{10}$ of 0.01 (one cent), and that they have to round to the nearest hundredth. **(SMP 6)**

## SCORING RUBRIC

**4 points**  The student has completed all parts of the problem and shows understanding of the problem. Estimates use rounding correctly and help lead to a plan. Calculations are complete, including tax, and show how much money is left.

**3 points**  The student has completed all parts of the problem, with one or two errors. Possible errors might include incorrect calculations, missing tax cost, or the student may not show how much money is left.

**2 points**  The student has attempted all parts of the problem, with a number of errors. Estimates may be incorrect and/or may not be used in planning. Calculations may be incomplete or incorrect, or may not show how much money is left.

**1 point**  The student has not completed all parts of the problem. There are several errors. Estimates may be incorrect or missing. Calculations may be incomplete or incorrect, or may not show how much money is left. Tax is calculated incorrectly or is not calculated at all.

## SOLUTION TO THE EXTENSION

**Possible Solutions:**

**new dinnerware:** $3 \times (9.97 + 9.25 + 7.02) = 78.72$; **basic utensils:** $3 \times (0.83 + 0.83) = 4.98$; **folding chairs:** $3 \times 19.99 = 59.97$. Total is $78.72 + 4.98 + 59.97 = 143.67$ and tax is $0.05 \times 152.43 = 7.1835$, which rounds to $7.18. Add $7.18 to $143.67. The total is $150.85 with $9.15 left.

©Curriculum Associates, LLC   Copying is not permitted.

Lesson 10    *Use after Ready Instruction page 87*

## Add and Subtract Fractions

Name: _____

### Find Equivalent Fractions

**Study the example showing how you can use models and multiplication to find equivalent fractions. Then solve problems 1–7.**

> **Example**
>
> The model is divided into 4 equal parts.
> The shaded section shows the fraction $\frac{1}{4}$.
>
> $\frac{1}{4}$
>
> You can divide the same whole into 2 times as many equal parts. There are 2 times as many parts shaded.
>
> $\frac{1 \times 2}{4 \times 2} = \frac{2}{8}$
>
> You can divide the same whole into 3 times as many equal parts. There are 3 times as many parts shaded.
>
> $\frac{1 \times 3}{4 \times 3} = \frac{3}{12}$
>
> The fractions $\frac{1}{4}$, $\frac{2}{8}$, and $\frac{3}{12}$ are equivalent because they each show the same shaded part of a whole.

**B** **1** Look at the model to the right. $\frac{3}{5}$ of the whole is shaded. Divide the model into a different number of equal parts to find an equivalent fraction. Complete the equation.

$\frac{3}{5} = \frac{6}{10}$

**B** **2** Write the missing numbers to describe the equivalent fraction you found in problem 1.

There are ___2___ times as many equal parts.

There are ___2___ times as many shaded parts.

$\frac{3 \times 2}{5 \times 2} = \frac{6}{10}$

©Curriculum Associates, LLC   Copying is not permitted.

**Lesson 10** Add and Subtract Fractions **103**

---

**104** **Lesson 10** Add and Subtract Fractions

**Solve.**

**M** **3** Shade the model to show $\frac{2}{3}$. Then divide the model to show 6 equal parts.

**M** **4** Look at the model in problem 3. Write the missing numbers to show the equivalent fraction you formed by dividing it into 6 equal parts.

$\frac{2 \times 2}{3 \times 2} = \frac{4}{6}$

**M** **5** Explain how you can multiply to find equivalent fractions.

Answers will vary. Students should show an understanding that the numerator and

denominator of a fraction is multiplied by the same number in order to find an

equivalent fraction.

**C** **6** Choose *Yes* or *No* to tell whether the fraction is equivalent to $\frac{2}{5}$.

$\frac{2 \times ?}{5 \times ?} = \boxed{\phantom{0}}$

a. $\frac{4}{10}$  ☒ Yes  ☐ No

b. $\frac{5}{8}$  ☐ Yes  ☒ No

c. $\frac{6}{15}$  ☒ Yes  ☐ No

d. $\frac{6}{20}$  ☐ Yes  ☒ No

e. $\frac{10}{25}$  ☒ Yes  ☐ No

**M** **7** How did you determine whether a fraction was equivalent to $\frac{2}{5}$ in problem 6? Explain.

Answers will vary. Students may indicate a preference for one method or the other

(using models or multiplying) or explain they use some combination of both methods.

©Curriculum Associates, LLC   Copying is not permitted.

---

Lesson 10 · *Use after Ready Instruction page 89*

Name: _____

### Add Fractions with Unlike Denominators

**Study the example showing one way to add fractions with unlike denominators. Then solve problems 1–4.**

> **Example**
>
> What is $\frac{3}{4} + 1\frac{1}{6}$?
>
> To add fractions, the size of the parts must be the same. Write each addend as an equivalent fraction with a common denominator.
>
> $\frac{3}{4}$  +  1  $\frac{1}{6}$
>
> Identify a common multiple of the denominators, 4 and 6: 12. Divide models into 12 equal parts.
>
> Write the equivalent fractions.
>
> $\frac{3}{4} = \frac{9}{12}$ and $1\frac{1}{6} = 1\frac{2}{12}$
>
> $\frac{9}{12}$  +  1  $\frac{2}{12}$
>
> Find the sum.  $\frac{3}{4} + 1\frac{1}{6} = \frac{9}{12} + 1\frac{2}{12} = 1\frac{11}{12}$

**M** **1** The example uses 12 as the common multiple of 4 and 6.

a. Name a different common multiple of 4 and 6.

   Possible answer: 24

b. Using the common multiple from part **a.**, how would the models be different? How would they be the same?

   Possible answer: There would be twice as many equal parts in each model, and

   each part would be smaller. The areas shaded would be the same.

c. Use the common multiple from part **a.** as the common denominator to write equivalent fractions for $\frac{3}{4}$ and $1\frac{1}{6}$.

   $\frac{3}{4} = \frac{18}{24}$      $1\frac{1}{6} = 1\frac{4}{24}$

©Curriculum Associates, LLC   Copying is not permitted.

**Lesson 10** Add and Subtract Fractions **105**

---

**106** **Lesson 10** Add and Subtract Fractions

**Solve.**

**M** **2** One way to find a common denominator is by multiplying the denominators of the two fractions together and using the product as the common denominator.

Use this method to find a common denominator for each pair of fractions. Write the equivalent fractions.

a. $1\frac{3}{5} = 1\frac{12}{20}$      $1\frac{3}{4} = 1\frac{15}{20}$

b. $2\frac{1}{2} = 2\frac{5}{10}$      $\frac{4}{5} = \frac{8}{10}$

c. $\frac{3}{8} = \frac{18}{48}$      $\frac{1}{6} = \frac{8}{48}$

**M** **3** Show how to add $2\frac{1}{2} + \frac{4}{5}$ using the number line below.

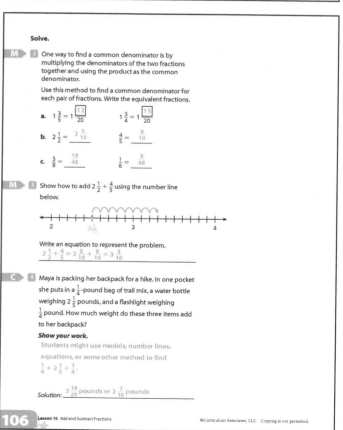

Write an equation to represent the problem.

$2\frac{1}{2} + \frac{4}{5} = 2\frac{5}{10} + \frac{8}{10} = 3\frac{3}{10}$

**C** **4** Maya is packing her backpack for a hike. In one pocket she puts in a $\frac{1}{4}$-pound bag of trail mix, a water bottle weighing $2\frac{1}{5}$ pounds, and a flashlight weighing $\frac{1}{4}$ pound. How much weight do these three items add to her backpack?

***Show your work.***

Students might use models, number lines,

equations, or some other method to find

$\frac{1}{4} + 2\frac{1}{5} + \frac{1}{4}$.

*Solution:* $2\frac{14}{20}$ pounds or $2\frac{7}{10}$ pounds

©Curriculum Associates, LLC   Copying is not permitted.

# Practice Lesson 10 Add and Subtract Fractions

---

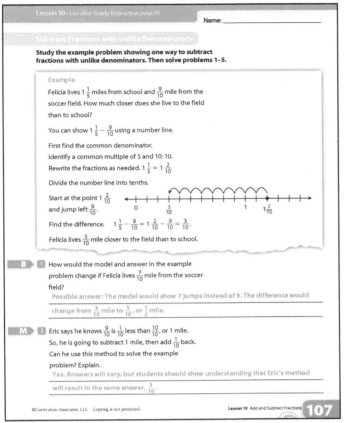

**Lesson 10 · Use after Ready Instruction page 91**

Name: _____

### Subtract Fractions with Unlike Denominators

**Study the example problem showing one way to subtract fractions with unlike denominators. Then solve problems 1–5.**

**Example**

Felicia lives $1\frac{1}{5}$ miles from school and $\frac{9}{10}$ mile from the soccer field. How much closer does she live to the field than to school?

You can show $1\frac{1}{5} - \frac{9}{10}$ using a number line.

First find the common denominator.

Identify a common multiple of 5 and 10: 10.

Rewrite the fractions as needed. $1\frac{1}{5} = 1\frac{2}{10}$

Divide the number line into tenths.

Start at the point $1\frac{2}{10}$ and jump left $\frac{9}{10}$.

Find the difference. $1\frac{1}{5} - \frac{9}{10} = 1\frac{2}{10} - \frac{9}{10} = \frac{3}{10}$.

Felicia lives $\frac{3}{10}$ mile closer to the field than to school.

**B** **1** How would the model and answer in the example problem change if Felicia lives $\frac{7}{10}$ mile from the soccer field?

Possible answer: The model would show 7 jumps instead of 9. The difference would change from $\frac{3}{10}$ mile to $\frac{5}{10}$, or $\frac{1}{2}$ mile.

**M** **2** Eric says he knows $\frac{9}{10}$ is $\frac{1}{10}$ less than $\frac{10}{10}$, or 1 mile. So, he is going to subtract 1 mile, then add $\frac{1}{10}$ back. Can he use this method to solve the example problem? Explain.

Yes. Answers will vary, but students should show understanding that Eric's method will result in the same answer, $\frac{3}{10}$.

©Curriculum Associates, LLC  Copying is not permitted.

Lesson 10 Add and Subtract Fractions **107**

---

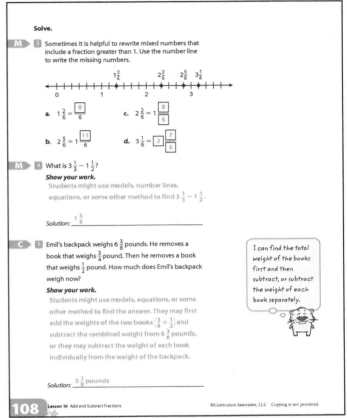

**108** Lesson 10 Add and Subtract Fractions

**Solve.**

**M** **3** Sometimes it is helpful to rewrite mixed numbers that include a fraction greater than 1. Use the number line to write the missing numbers.

$1\frac{2}{6}$  $2\frac{2}{6}$  $2\frac{5}{6}$  $3\frac{1}{6}$

a. $1\frac{2}{6} = \frac{\boxed{8}}{6}$   c. $2\frac{2}{6} = 1\frac{\boxed{8}}{6}$

b. $2\frac{5}{6} = 1\frac{\boxed{11}}{6}$   d. $3\frac{1}{6} = 2\frac{\boxed{7}}{6}$

**M** **4** What is $3\frac{1}{3} - 1\frac{1}{2}$?
**Show your work.**

Students might use models, number lines, equations, or some other method to find $3\frac{1}{3} - 1\frac{1}{2}$.

Solution: $1\frac{5}{6}$

**C** **5** Emil's backpack weighs $6\frac{3}{8}$ pounds. He removes a book that weighs $\frac{3}{4}$ pound. Then he removes a book that weighs $\frac{1}{2}$ pound. How much does Emil's backpack weigh now?
**Show your work.**

Students might use models, equations, or some other method to find the answer. They may first add the weights of the two books $\left(\frac{3}{4} + \frac{1}{2}\right)$ and subtract the combined weight from $6\frac{3}{8}$ pounds, or they may subtract the weight of each book individually from the weight of the backpack.

Solution: $5\frac{1}{8}$ pounds

> I can find the total weight of the books first and then subtract, or subtract the weight of each book separately.

©Curriculum Associates, LLC  Copying is not permitted.

---

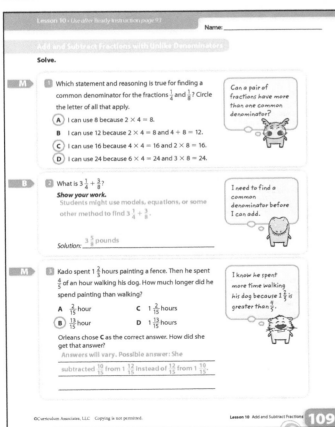

**Lesson 10 · Use after Ready Instruction page 93**

Name: _____

### Add and Subtract Fractions with Unlike Denominators

**Solve.**

**M** **1** Which statement and reasoning is true for finding a common denominator for the fractions $\frac{1}{4}$ and $\frac{1}{8}$? Circle the letter of all that apply.

A  I can use 8 because $2 \times 4 = 8$.
B  I can use 12 because $2 \times 4 = 8$ and $4 + 8 = 12$.
C  I can use 16 because $4 \times 4 = 16$ and $2 \times 8 = 16$.
D  I can use 24 because $6 \times 4 = 24$ and $3 \times 8 = 24$.

> Can a pair of fractions have more than one common denominator?

**B** **2** What is $3\frac{1}{4} + \frac{3}{8}$?
**Show your work.**

Students might use models, equations, or some other method to find $3\frac{1}{4} + \frac{3}{8}$.

Solution: $3\frac{5}{8}$ pounds

> I need to find a common denominator before I can add.

**M** **3** Kado spent $1\frac{2}{3}$ hours painting a fence. Then he spent $\frac{4}{5}$ of an hour walking his dog. How much longer did he spend painting than walking?

A  $\frac{2}{15}$ hour   C  $1\frac{2}{15}$ hours
B  $\frac{13}{15}$ hour   D  $1\frac{13}{15}$ hours

Orleans chose **C** as the correct answer. How did she get that answer?

Answers will vary. Possible answer: She subtracted $\frac{10}{15}$ from $1\frac{12}{15}$ instead of $\frac{12}{15}$ from $1\frac{10}{15}$.

> I know he spent more time walking his dog because $1\frac{2}{3}$ is greater than $\frac{4}{5}$.

©Curriculum Associates, LLC  Copying is not permitted.

Lesson 10 Add and Subtract Fractions **109**

---

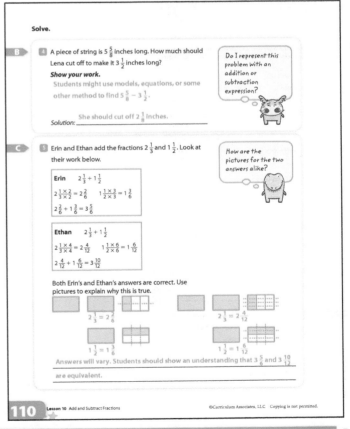

**110** Lesson 10 Add and Subtract Fractions

**Solve.**

**B** **4** A piece of string is $5\frac{5}{8}$ inches long. How much should Lena cut off to make it $3\frac{1}{2}$ inches long?
**Show your work.**

Students might use models, equations, or some other method to find $5\frac{5}{8} - 3\frac{1}{2}$.

Solution: She should cut off $2\frac{1}{8}$ inches.

> Do I represent this problem with an addition or subtraction expression?

**C** **5** Erin and Ethan add the fractions $2\frac{1}{3}$ and $1\frac{1}{2}$. Look at their work below.

**Erin**  $2\frac{1}{3} + 1\frac{1}{2}$

$2\frac{1 \times 2}{3 \times 2} = 2\frac{2}{6}$   $1\frac{1 \times 3}{2 \times 3} = 1\frac{3}{6}$

$2\frac{2}{6} + 1\frac{3}{6} = 3\frac{5}{6}$

**Ethan**  $2\frac{1}{3} + 1\frac{1}{2}$

$2\frac{1 \times 4}{3 \times 4} = 2\frac{4}{12}$   $1\frac{1 \times 6}{2 \times 6} = 1\frac{6}{12}$

$2\frac{4}{12} + 1\frac{6}{12} = 3\frac{10}{12}$

Both Erin's and Ethan's answers are correct. Use pictures to explain why this is true.

$2\frac{1}{3} = 2\frac{2}{6}$   $2\frac{1}{3} = 2\frac{4}{12}$

$1\frac{1}{2} = 1\frac{3}{6}$   $1\frac{1}{2} = 1\frac{6}{12}$

Answers will vary. Students should show an understanding that $3\frac{5}{6}$ and $3\frac{10}{12}$ are equivalent.

> How are the pictures for the two answers alike?

©Curriculum Associates, LLC  Copying is not permitted.

---

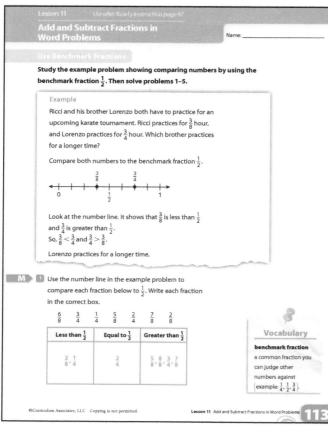

Lesson 11    *Use after Ready Instruction page 97*

## Add and Subtract Fractions in Word Problems

Name: _____

### Use Benchmark Fractions

Study the example problem showing comparing numbers by using the benchmark fraction $\frac{1}{2}$. Then solve problems 1–5.

**Example**

Ricci and his brother Lorenzo both have to practice for an upcoming karate tournament. Ricci practices for $\frac{3}{8}$ hour, and Lorenzo practices for $\frac{3}{4}$ hour. Which brother practices for a longer time?

Compare both numbers to the benchmark fraction $\frac{1}{2}$.

Look at the number line. It shows that $\frac{3}{8}$ is less than $\frac{1}{2}$ and $\frac{3}{4}$ is greater than $\frac{1}{2}$.

So, $\frac{3}{8} < \frac{3}{4}$ and $\frac{3}{4} > \frac{3}{8}$.

Lorenzo practices for a longer time.

**M** **1** Use the number line in the example problem to compare each fraction below to $\frac{1}{2}$. Write each fraction in the correct box.

$$\frac{6}{8} \quad \frac{3}{8} \quad \frac{1}{4} \quad \frac{5}{8} \quad \frac{2}{4} \quad \frac{7}{8} \quad \frac{2}{8}$$

| Less than $\frac{1}{2}$ | Equal to $\frac{1}{2}$ | Greater than $\frac{1}{2}$ |
|---|---|---|
| $\frac{2}{8}$, $\frac{1}{4}$ | $\frac{2}{4}$ | $\frac{5}{8}$, $\frac{6}{8}$, $\frac{3}{4}$, $\frac{7}{8}$ |

**Vocabulary**

**benchmark fraction** a common fraction you can judge other numbers against (example: $\frac{1}{4}$, $\frac{1}{2}$, $\frac{3}{4}$).

©Curriculum Associates, LLC   Copying is not permitted.

Lesson 11  Add and Subtract Fractions in Word Problems  **113**

---

**114**  Lesson 11  Add and Subtract Fractions in Word Problems

**Solve.**

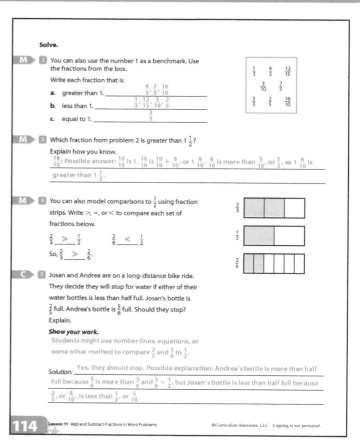

**M** **2** You can also use the number 1 as a benchmark. Use the fractions from the box.

Write each fraction that is

a. greater than 1. ___$\frac{4}{3}$, $\frac{7}{5}$, $\frac{16}{10}$___

b. less than 1. ___$\frac{1}{3}$, $\frac{12}{15}$, $\frac{3}{10}$, $\frac{2}{5}$___

c. equal to 1. ___$\frac{3}{3}$___

| $\frac{1}{3}$ | $\frac{4}{3}$ | $\frac{12}{15}$ |
|---|---|---|
| | $\frac{3}{10}$ | $\frac{7}{5}$ |
| $\frac{3}{3}$ | $\frac{2}{5}$ | $\frac{16}{10}$ |

**M** **3** Which fraction from problem 2 is greater than $1\frac{1}{2}$? Explain how you know.

$\frac{16}{10}$; Possible answer: $\frac{10}{10}$ is 1. $\frac{16}{10}$ is $\frac{10}{10} + \frac{6}{10}$, or $1\frac{6}{10}$. $\frac{6}{10}$ is more than $\frac{5}{10}$, or $\frac{1}{2}$, so $1\frac{6}{10}$ is greater than $1\frac{1}{2}$.

**M** **4** You can also model comparisons to $\frac{1}{2}$ using fraction strips. Write >, =, or < to compare each set of fractions below.

$\frac{2}{3} \; > \; \frac{1}{2}$          $\frac{2}{6} \; < \; \frac{1}{2}$

So, $\frac{2}{3} \; > \; \frac{2}{6}$.

**C** **5** Josan and Andrea are on a long-distance bike ride. They decide they will stop for water if either of their water bottles is less than half full. Josan's bottle is $\frac{2}{5}$ full. Andrea's bottle is $\frac{5}{6}$ full. Should they stop? Explain.

**Show your work.**

Students might use number lines, equations, or some other method to compare $\frac{2}{5}$ and $\frac{5}{6}$ to $\frac{1}{2}$.

Solution: ___Yes, they should stop. Possible explanation: Andrea's bottle is more than half full because $\frac{5}{6}$ is more than $\frac{3}{6}$ and $\frac{3}{6} = \frac{1}{2}$, but Josan's bottle is less than half full because $\frac{2}{5}$, or $\frac{4}{10}$, is less than $\frac{1}{2}$, or $\frac{5}{10}$.___

©Curriculum Associates, LLC   Copying is not permitted.

---

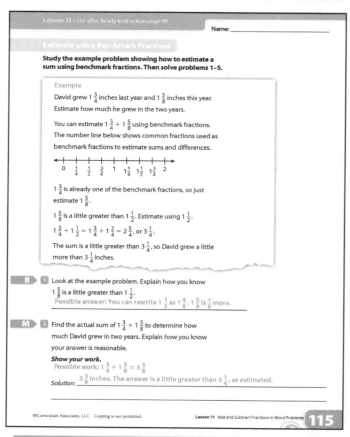

Lesson 11 • *Use after Ready Instruction page 99*

Name: _____

### Estimate using Benchmark Fractions

Study the example problem showing how to estimate a sum using benchmark fractions. Then solve problems 1–5.

**Example**

David grew $1\frac{3}{4}$ inches last year and $1\frac{5}{8}$ inches this year. Estimate how much he grew in the two years.

You can estimate $1\frac{3}{4} + 1\frac{5}{8}$ using benchmark fractions. The number line below shows common fractions used as benchmark fractions to estimate sums and differences.

$1\frac{3}{4}$ is already one of the benchmark fractions, so just estimate $1\frac{5}{8}$.

$1\frac{5}{8}$ is a little greater than $1\frac{1}{2}$. Estimate using $1\frac{1}{2}$.

$1\frac{3}{4} + 1\frac{1}{2} = 1\frac{3}{4} + 1\frac{2}{4} = 2\frac{5}{4}$, or $3\frac{1}{4}$.

The sum is a little greater than $3\frac{1}{4}$, so David grew a little more than $3\frac{1}{4}$ inches.

**B** **1** Look at the example problem. Explain how you know $1\frac{5}{8}$ is a little greater than $1\frac{1}{2}$.

Possible answer: You can rewrite $1\frac{1}{2}$ as $1\frac{4}{8}$. $1\frac{5}{8}$ is $\frac{1}{8}$ more.

**M** **2** Find the actual sum of $1\frac{3}{4} + 1\frac{5}{8}$ to determine how much David grew in two years. Explain how you know your answer is reasonable.

**Show your work.**

Possible work: $1\frac{3}{4} + 1\frac{5}{8} = 3\frac{3}{8}$

Solution: ___$3\frac{3}{8}$ inches. The answer is a little greater than $3\frac{1}{4}$, as estimated.___

©Curriculum Associates, LLC   Copying is not permitted.

Lesson 11  Add and Subtract Fractions in Word Problems  **115**

---

**116**  Lesson 11  Add and Subtract Fractions in Word Problems

**Solve.**

Irene makes $4\frac{2}{3}$ cups of pancake batter. She splits the batter into 2 bowls. She mixes blueberries into $2\frac{1}{4}$ cups of batter and walnuts into the rest of the batter.

**C** **3** Estimate how much of the batter has walnuts in it. Explain your estimate.

Estimates and explanations will vary, but the estimate should be about $2\frac{1}{2}$ cups.

**M** **4** Find the actual amount of batter that has walnuts in it. Explain how you know your answer is reasonable.

**Show your work.**

Students might use fraction strips, equations, or some other method to subtract $2\frac{1}{4}$ from $4\frac{2}{3}$.

Solution: ___$2\frac{5}{12}$ cups. Explanations will vary but should indicate that the answer $2\frac{5}{12}$ is close to the estimate from problem 3.___

**M** **5** Irene makes a second batch of $3\frac{1}{4}$ cups of pancake batter. She wants to know how much more batter she made in the first batch. She estimates that the difference between the sizes of the two batches $4\frac{2}{3} - 3\frac{1}{4}$ is $2\frac{1}{2}$. Explain why this estimate is *not* reasonable.

Answers will vary. Possible answer: If $4\frac{2}{3} - 3\frac{1}{4} = 2\frac{1}{2}$ is true, then $3\frac{1}{4} + 2\frac{1}{2} = 4\frac{2}{3}$ would also be true. But $3 + 2 = 5$, so $3\frac{1}{4} + 2\frac{1}{2}$ is greater than 5.

©Curriculum Associates, LLC   Copying is not permitted.

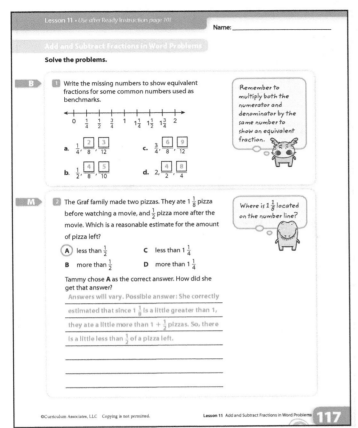

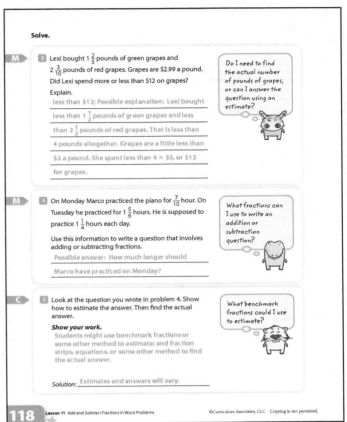

**Key**

| B | Basic |
|---|---|
| M | Medium |
| C | Challenge |

---

Lesson 12    *Use after Ready Instruction page 105*

### Fractions as Division

Name: _____

#### Write a Fraction as a Mixed Number

**Study the example problem showing how to write a fraction greater than 1 as a mixed number. Then solve problems 1–5.**

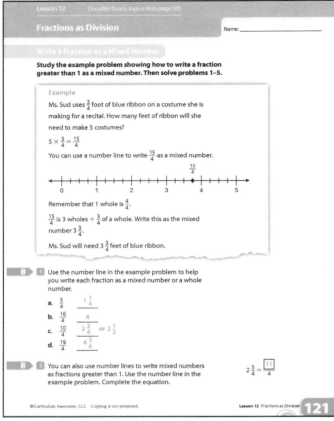

> **Example**
>
> Ms. Sud uses $\frac{3}{4}$ foot of blue ribbon on a costume she is making for a recital. How many feet of ribbon will she need to make 5 costumes?
>
> $5 \times \frac{3}{4} = \frac{15}{4}$
>
> You can use a number line to write $\frac{15}{4}$ as a mixed number.
>
> Remember that 1 whole is $\frac{4}{4}$.
>
> $\frac{15}{4}$ is 3 wholes + $\frac{3}{4}$ of a whole. Write this as the mixed number $3\frac{3}{4}$.
>
> Ms. Sud will need $3\frac{3}{4}$ feet of blue ribbon.

**B** **1** Use the number line in the example problem to help you write each fraction as a mixed number or a whole number.

a. $\frac{5}{4}$    $1\frac{1}{4}$

b. $\frac{16}{4}$    $4$

c. $\frac{10}{4}$    $2\frac{2}{4}$ or $2\frac{1}{2}$

d. $\frac{19}{4}$    $4\frac{3}{4}$

**B** **2** You can also use number lines to write mixed numbers as fractions greater than 1. Use the number line in the example problem. Complete the equation.

$2\frac{3}{4} = \frac{\boxed{11}}{4}$

---

**Solve.**

**M** **3** Write a mixed number and a fraction greater than 1 for each point on the number line.

a. $1\frac{1}{6}$ , $\frac{7}{6}$

b. $1\frac{4}{6}$ , $\frac{10}{6}$

c. $2\frac{5}{6}$ , $\frac{17}{6}$

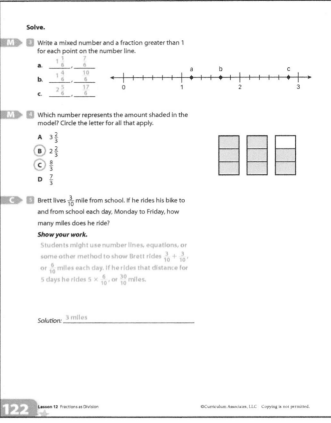

**M** **4** Which number represents the amount shaded in the model? Circle the letter for all that apply.

A   $3\frac{2}{3}$

(B)   $2\frac{2}{3}$

(C)   $\frac{8}{3}$

D   $\frac{7}{3}$

**C** **5** Brett lives $\frac{3}{10}$ mile from school. If he rides his bike to and from school each day, Monday to Friday, how many miles does he ride?

**Show your work.**

Students might use number lines, equations, or some other method to show Brett rides $\frac{3}{10} + \frac{3}{10}$, or $\frac{6}{10}$ miles each day. If he rides that distance for 5 days he rides $5 \times \frac{6}{10}$, or $\frac{30}{10}$ miles.

Solution: ___3 miles___

---

Lesson 12 · *Use after Ready Instruction page 107*

Name: _____

#### Find Fraction Quotients

**Study the example problem showing whole number division with a fraction quotient. Then solve problems 1–5.**

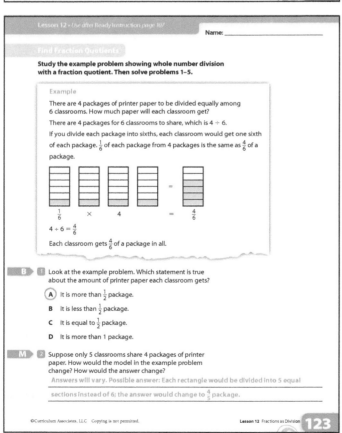

> **Example**
>
> There are 4 packages of printer paper to be divided equally among 6 classrooms. How much paper will each classroom get?
>
> There are 4 packages for 6 classrooms to share, which is $4 \div 6$.
>
> If you divide each package into sixths, each classroom would get one sixth of each package. $\frac{1}{6}$ of each package from 4 packages is the same as $\frac{4}{6}$ of a package.
>
> $\frac{1}{6}$ × 4 = $\frac{4}{6}$
>
> $4 \div 6 = \frac{4}{6}$
>
> Each classroom gets $\frac{4}{6}$ of a package in all.

**B** **1** Look at the example problem. Which statement is true about the amount of printer paper each classroom gets?

(A) It is more than $\frac{1}{2}$ package.

B   It is less than $\frac{1}{2}$ package.

C   It is equal to $\frac{1}{2}$ package.

D   It is more than 1 package.

**M** **2** Suppose only 5 classrooms share 4 packages of printer paper. How would the model in the example problem change? How would the answer change?

Answers will vary. Possible answer: Each rectangle would be divided into 5 equal

sections instead of 6; the answer would change to $\frac{4}{5}$ package.

---

**Solve.**

**M** **3** Trish is taking care of the Han family's dogs. The Hans leave 7 cans of dog food for the 3 days they'll be away. How much food will the dogs get each day if Trish feeds them an equal amount each day?

**Show your work.**

Students might use number lines, equations, or some other method to show the quotient of $7 \div 3$.

Solution: $\frac{7}{3}$, or $2\frac{1}{3}$ cans

**C** **4** Look at problem 3. How many more cans of dog food would Trish need if she needed to feed the dogs 3 cans each day? Explain.

2 more cans; Possible explanation: 2 more cans would make 9 cans, and $\frac{9}{3} = 3$.

_____

_____

_____

_____

**M** **5** Gus is making 48 ounces of spiced cider. If he serves an equal amount to 7 people, will each person get more than 1 cup of cider or less than 1 cup?

> I know that 1 cup is the same as 8 ounces.

**Show your work.**

Students might use fraction models, equations, or some other method to show $48 \div 7 = \frac{48}{7}$ or $7\frac{1}{7}$. $7\frac{1}{7}$ ounces < 8 ounces

Solution: ___less than 1 cup___

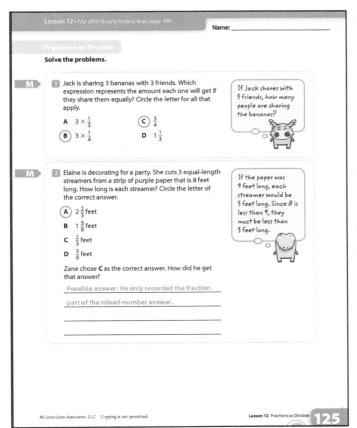

Fractions as Division

**Solve the problems.**

**M**  ① Jack is sharing 3 bananas with 3 friends. Which expression represents the amount each one will get if they share them equally? Circle the letter for all that apply.

**A** $3 \times \frac{1}{3}$        **C** $\frac{3}{4}$

**B** $3 \times \frac{1}{4}$        **D** $1\frac{1}{3}$

*If Jack shares with 3 friends, how many people are sharing the bananas?*

**M**  ② Elaine is decorating for a party. She cuts 3 equal-length streamers from a strip of purple paper that is 8 feet long. How long is each streamer? Circle the letter of the correct answer.

**A** $2\frac{2}{3}$ feet

**B** $1\frac{3}{8}$ feet

**C** $\frac{2}{3}$ feet

**D** $\frac{3}{8}$ feet

Zane chose **C** as the correct answer. How did he get that answer?

Possible answer: He only recorded the fraction

part of the mixed-number answer.

_____

_____

*If the paper was 9 feet long, each streamer would be 3 feet long. Since 8 is less than 9, they must be less than 3 feet long.*

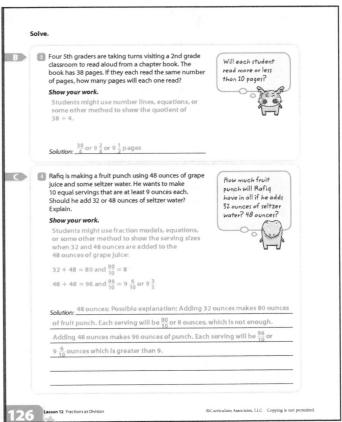

**Solve.**

**B**  ③ Four 5th graders are taking turns visiting a 2nd grade classroom to read aloud from a chapter book. The book has 38 pages. If they each read the same number of pages, how many pages will each one read?

**Show your work.**

Students might use number lines, equations, or some other method to show the quotient of 38 ÷ 4.

*Will each student read more or less than 10 pages?*

Solution: $\frac{38}{4}$ or $9\frac{2}{4}$ or $9\frac{1}{2}$ pages

**C**  ④ Rafiq is making a fruit punch using 48 ounces of grape juice and some seltzer water. He wants to make 10 equal servings that are at least 9 ounces each. Should he add 32 or 48 ounces of seltzer water? Explain.

**Show your work.**

Students might use fraction models, equations, or some other method to show the serving sizes when 32 and 48 ounces are added to the 48 ounces of grape juice:

$32 + 48 = 80$ and $\frac{80}{10} = 8$

$48 + 48 = 96$ and $\frac{96}{10} = 9\frac{6}{10}$ or $9\frac{3}{5}$

*How much fruit punch will Rafiq have in all if he adds 32 ounces of seltzer water? 48 ounces?*

Solution: 48 ounces; Possible explanation: Adding 32 ounces makes 80 ounces

of fruit punch. Each serving will be $\frac{80}{10}$ or 8 ounces, which is not enough.

Adding 48 ounces makes 96 ounces of punch. Each serving will be $\frac{96}{10}$ or

$9\frac{6}{10}$ ounces which is greater than 9.

_____

_____

|  | **Key** |
|---|---|
| B | Basic |
| M | Medium |
| C | Challenge |

---

Lesson 13    *Use after Ready Instruction page 113*

**Understand**
**Products of Fractions**

Name: _____

How do you multiply a fraction by a whole number?

**Study the example showing multiplying a fraction by a whole number. Then solve problems 1–8.**

> **Example**
>
> Find $4 \times \frac{2}{3}$.
>
> $4 \times \frac{2}{3}$ can be modeled as 4 groups of $\frac{2}{3}$.
>
> 4 $\times$ $\frac{2}{3}$ = $\frac{8}{3}$ or $2\frac{2}{3}$
>
> You can count eight shaded $\frac{1}{3}$ parts. Eight $\frac{1}{3}$ parts, or $\frac{8}{3}$, is the same as $2\frac{2}{3}$.
>
> $4 \times \frac{2}{3} = 2\frac{2}{3}$

**B** ▸ **1** Explain how you can model $3 \times \frac{2}{4}$.

   Possible answer: $3 \times \frac{2}{4}$ is 3 groups of $\frac{2}{4}$.

**M** ▸ **2** Draw a model to show $3 \times \frac{2}{4}$.
   Possible student work:

**B** ▸ **3** How many fourths are shaded in your model in problem 2? ___6___

**M** ▸ **4** $3 \times \frac{2}{4} = $ ___$\frac{6}{4}$ or $1\frac{2}{4}$ or $1\frac{1}{2}$___

©Curriculum Associates, LLC   Copying is not permitted.

Lesson 13 Understand Products of Fractions **129**

---

**130** Lesson 13 Understand Products of Fractions

**Solve.**

**M** ▸ **5** What might a model for $3 \times \frac{3}{5}$ look like? How many fifths would be shaded in all?

   Answers will vary. Possible answer: It might be 3 rectangles, each shaded to show $\frac{3}{5}$;

   There would be 9 fifths shaded in all.

**M** ▸ **6** Fill in the blanks to write a multiplication problem for the model shown to the right.

   $\boxed{6} \times \frac{1}{5} = \boxed{\frac{6}{5}}$ or $1\frac{1}{5}$

**M** ▸ **7** You can also use a number line to multiply a fraction by a whole number.

   Label the number line below and use it to show $3 \times \frac{3}{5}$.

   $3 \times \frac{3}{5} = $ ___$\frac{9}{5}$ or $1\frac{4}{5}$___

**C** ▸ **8** Tristan jogs a route that is $\frac{7}{10}$ mile. If he wants to jog between 2 and 3 miles, how many times should he plan to run the route? Circle the letter for all that apply.

   **A** 2 times

   **B** 3 times

   **C** 4 times

   **D** 5 times

©Curriculum Associates, LLC   Copying is not permitted.

---

Lesson 13 • *Use after Ready Instruction page 115*

Name: _____

**Multiply a Fraction by a Fraction**

**Study the example showing multiplying a fraction by a fraction. Then solve problems 1–6.**

> **Example**
>
> Use an area model to find the product $\frac{2}{3} \times \frac{3}{5}$.
>
> Each row is $\frac{1}{3}$ of the whole.
> Each column is $\frac{1}{5}$ of the whole.
> The whole is divided into 15 equal parts.
>
> The dark gray parts show $\frac{2}{3}$ of $\frac{3}{5}$.
> 6 out of 15 parts of the whole are shaded dark gray, so the dark gray shows $\frac{6}{15}$.
>
> $\frac{2}{3} \times \frac{3}{5} = \frac{6}{15}$

**B** ▸ **1** Why are fifteenths shown in the example model?

   Answers will vary. Possible answer: Since the whole is divided into fifths and then

   thirds, you get fifteenths.

**M** ▸ **2** Use the area model in the example to write the product.

   $\frac{1}{3} \times \frac{3}{5} = $ ___$\frac{3}{15}$___

   $\frac{2}{3} \times \frac{4}{5} = $ ___$\frac{8}{15}$___

   $\frac{3}{3} \times \frac{2}{5} = $ ___$\frac{6}{15}$___

**M** ▸ **3** Choose *Yes* or *No* to tell whether the denominator of each product is twelfths.

   a. $\frac{1}{2} \times \frac{1}{6}$   ☒ Yes  ☐ No

   b. $\frac{3}{4} \times \frac{2}{2}$   ☐ Yes  ☒ No

   c. $\frac{1}{4} \times \frac{2}{3}$   ☒ Yes  ☐ No

   d. $\frac{5}{6} \times \frac{2}{2}$   ☒ Yes  ☐ No

> The denominator of the product is the same as the product of the denominators of the factors.

©Curriculum Associates, LLC   Copying is not permitted.

Lesson 13 Understand Products of Fractions **131**

---

**132** Lesson 13 Understand Products of Fractions

**Solve.**

**M** ▸ **4** The number line shows $\frac{1}{2} \times \frac{3}{4}$.

   a. Each fourth on the number line is divided into how many equal parts? ___2___

   b. Each of these parts is what fraction of the whole?
      ___$\frac{1}{8}$___

   c. How many eighths of the whole are shaded?
      ___3___

   d. $\frac{1}{2} \times \frac{3}{4} = $ ___$\frac{3}{8}$___

**M** ▸ **5** Use the area model. Write the product.

   a. $\frac{1}{3} \times \frac{1}{3} = $ ___$\frac{1}{9}$___

   b. $\frac{1}{3} \times \frac{2}{3} = $ ___$\frac{2}{9}$___

   c. $\frac{2}{3} \times \frac{2}{3} = $ ___$\frac{4}{9}$___

   d. $\frac{3}{3} \times \frac{2}{3} = $ ___$\frac{6}{9}$___

   e. $\frac{3}{3} \times \frac{3}{3} = $ ___$\frac{9}{9}$ or 1___

**C** ▸ **6** Choose whether the statement is *True* or *False* for the product of $\frac{2}{4} \times \frac{3}{5}$.

   a. The denominator is 20.   ☒ True  ☐ False

   b. The denominator is 9.   ☐ True  ☒ False

   c. The product is less than either factor.   ☒ True  ☐ False

   d. The product is greater than either factor.   ☐ True  ☒ False

©Curriculum Associates, LLC   Copying is not permitted.

---

# Practice Lesson 13 *Understand* Products of Fractions

**Unit 2**

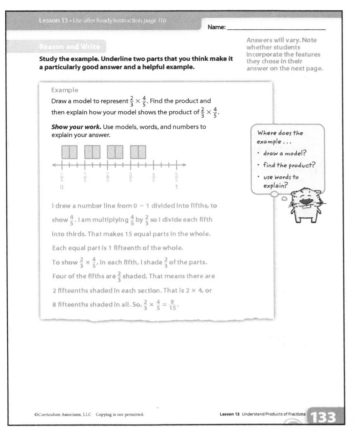

Lesson 13 • *Use after Ready Instruction page 116*

Name: _____

**Reason and Write**

**Study the example. Underline two parts that you think make it a particularly good answer and a helpful example.**

*Answers will vary. Note whether students incorporate the features they chose in their answer on the next page.*

Example

Draw a model to represent $\frac{2}{3} \times \frac{4}{5}$. Find the product and then explain how your model shows the product of $\frac{2}{3} \times \frac{4}{5}$.

***Show your work.*** Use models, words, and numbers to explain your answer.

I drew a number line from 0 − 1 divided into fifths, to show $\frac{4}{5}$. I am multiplying $\frac{4}{5}$ by $\frac{2}{3}$ so I divide each fifth into thirds. That makes 15 equal parts in the whole.

Each equal part is 1 fifteenth of the whole.

To show $\frac{2}{3} \times \frac{4}{5}$, in each fifth, I shade $\frac{2}{3}$ of the parts.

Four of the fifths are $\frac{2}{3}$ shaded. That means there are 2 fifteenths shaded in each section. That is 2 × 4, or 8 fifteenths shaded in all. So, $\frac{2}{3} \times \frac{4}{5} = \frac{8}{15}$.

> Where does the example . . .
> • *draw a model?*
> • *find the product?*
> • *use words to explain?*

©Curriculum Associates, LLC   Copying is not permitted.

**Lesson 13** Understand Products of Fractions  **133**

---

**Solve the problem. Use what you learned from the model.**

Draw a model to represent $\frac{3}{4} \times \frac{3}{5}$. Find the product and then explain how your model shows the product of $\frac{3}{4} \times \frac{3}{5}$.

***Show your work.*** Use models, words, and numbers to explain your answer.

Possible answer:

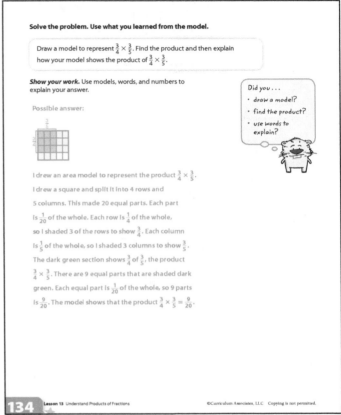

I drew an area model to represent the product $\frac{3}{4} \times \frac{3}{5}$. I drew a square and split it into 4 rows and 5 columns. This made 20 equal parts. Each part is $\frac{1}{20}$ of the whole. Each row is $\frac{1}{4}$ of the whole, so I shaded 3 of the rows to show $\frac{3}{4}$. Each column is $\frac{1}{5}$ of the whole, so I shaded 3 columns to show $\frac{3}{5}$. The dark green section shows $\frac{3}{4}$ of $\frac{3}{5}$, the product $\frac{3}{4} \times \frac{3}{5}$. There are 9 equal parts that are shaded dark green. Each equal part is $\frac{1}{20}$ of the whole, so 9 parts is $\frac{9}{20}$. The model shows that the product $\frac{3}{4} \times \frac{3}{5} = \frac{9}{20}$.

> Did you . . .
> • *draw a model?*
> • *find the product?*
> • *use words to explain?*

**134**  **Lesson 13** Understand Products of Fractions

©Curriculum Associates, LLC   Copying is not permitted.

---

| Key | |
|---|---|
| B | Basic |
| M | Medium |
| C | Challenge |

Practice and Problem Solving

Unit 2 Number and Operations—Fractions  **31**

©Curriculum Associates, LLC   Copying is not permitted.

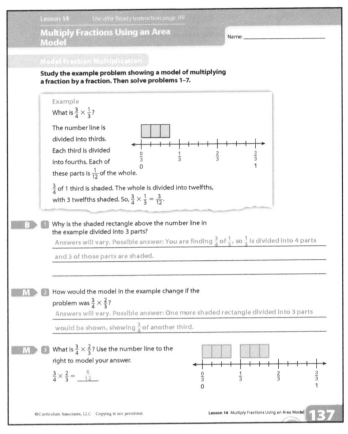

**Multiply Fractions Using an Area Model**

Name: _____

**Model Fraction Multiplication**

Study the example problem showing a model of multiplying a fraction by a fraction. Then solve problems 1–7.

**Example**

What is $\frac{3}{4} \times \frac{1}{3}$?

The number line is divided into thirds. Each third is divided into fourths. Each of these parts is $\frac{1}{12}$ of the whole.

$\frac{3}{4}$ of 1 third is shaded. The whole is divided into twelfths, with 3 twelfths shaded. So, $\frac{3}{4} \times \frac{1}{3} = \frac{3}{12}$.

**B 1** Why is the shaded rectangle above the number line in the example divided into 3 parts?

Answers will vary. Possible answer: You are finding $\frac{3}{4}$ of $\frac{1}{3}$, so $\frac{1}{3}$ is divided into 4 parts and 3 of those parts are shaded.

**M 2** How would the model in the example change if the problem was $\frac{3}{4} \times \frac{2}{3}$?

Answers will vary. Possible answer: One more shaded rectangle divided into 3 parts would be shown, showing $\frac{3}{4}$ of another third.

**M 3** What is $\frac{3}{4} \times \frac{2}{3}$? Use the number line to the right to model your answer.

$\frac{3}{4} \times \frac{2}{3} = \frac{6}{12}$

---

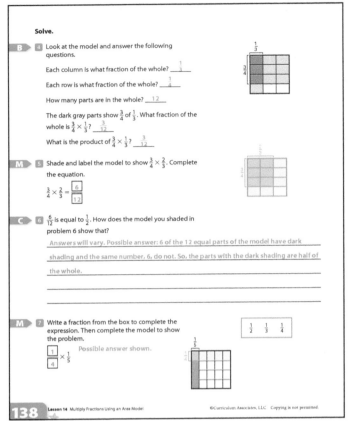

**Solve.**

**B 4** Look at the model and answer the following questions.

Each column is what fraction of the whole? $\frac{1}{3}$

Each row is what fraction of the whole? $\frac{1}{4}$

How many parts are in the whole? 12

The dark gray parts show $\frac{3}{4}$ of $\frac{1}{3}$. What fraction of the whole is $\frac{3}{4} \times \frac{1}{3}$? $\frac{3}{12}$

What is the product of $\frac{3}{4} \times \frac{1}{3}$? $\frac{3}{12}$

**M 5** Shade and label the model to show $\frac{3}{4} \times \frac{2}{3}$. Complete the equation.

$\frac{3}{4} \times \frac{2}{3} = \frac{6}{12}$

**C 6** $\frac{6}{12}$ is equal to $\frac{1}{2}$. How does the model you shaded in problem 6 show that?

Answers will vary. Possible answer: 6 of the 12 equal parts of the model have dark shading and the same number, 6, do not. So, the parts with the dark shading are half of the whole.

**M 7** Write a fraction from the box to complete the expression. Then complete the model to show the problem.

$\boxed{1 \atop 4} \times \frac{1}{5}$    Possible answer shown.

| $\frac{1}{2}$ | $\frac{1}{3}$ | $\frac{1}{4}$ |

---

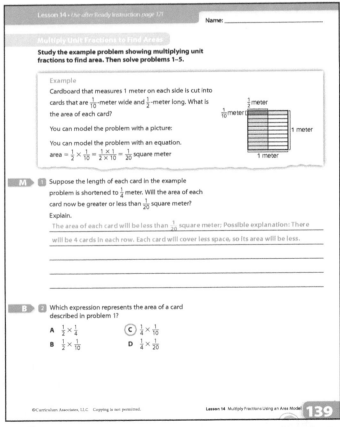

Name: _____

**Multiply Unit Fractions to Find Areas**

Study the example problem showing multiplying unit fractions to find area. Then solve problems 1–5.

**Example**

Cardboard that measures 1 meter on each side is cut into cards that are $\frac{1}{10}$-meter wide and $\frac{1}{2}$-meter long. What is the area of each card?

You can model the problem with a picture:

You can model the problem with an equation.

area $= \frac{1}{2} \times \frac{1}{10} = \frac{1 \times 1}{2 \times 10} = \frac{1}{20}$ square meter

**M 1** Suppose the length of each card in the example problem is shortened to $\frac{1}{4}$ meter. Will the area of each card now be greater or less than $\frac{1}{20}$ square meter? Explain.

The area of each card will be less than $\frac{1}{20}$ square meter; Possible explanation: There will be 4 cards in each row. Each card will cover less space, so its area will be less.

**B 2** Which expression represents the area of a card described in problem 1?

A $\frac{1}{2} \times \frac{1}{4}$          C $\frac{1}{4} \times \frac{1}{10}$

B $\frac{1}{2} \times \frac{1}{10}$          D $\frac{1}{4} \times \frac{1}{20}$

---

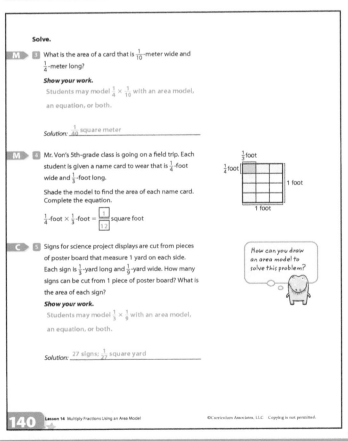

**Solve.**

**M 3** What is the area of a card that is $\frac{1}{10}$-meter wide and $\frac{1}{4}$-meter long?

**Show your work.**

Students may model $\frac{1}{4} \times \frac{1}{10}$ with an area model, an equation, or both.

*Solution:* $\frac{1}{40}$ square meter

**M 4** Mr. Von's 5th-grade class is going on a field trip. Each student is given a name card to wear that is $\frac{1}{4}$-foot wide and $\frac{1}{3}$-foot long.

Shade the model to find the area of each name card. Complete the equation.

$\frac{1}{4}$-foot $\times \frac{1}{3}$-foot $= \frac{1}{12}$ square foot

**C 5** Signs for science project displays are cut from pieces of poster board that measure 1 yard on each side. Each sign is $\frac{1}{3}$-yard long and $\frac{1}{9}$-yard wide. How many signs can be cut from 1 piece of poster board? What is the area of each sign?

**Show your work.**

Students may model $\frac{1}{3} \times \frac{1}{9}$ with an area model, an equation, or both.

How can you draw an area model to solve this problem?

*Solution:* 27 signs; $\frac{1}{27}$ square yard

---

---

Lesson 14 · *Use after Ready Instruction page 123*

Name: _____

**Multiply Fractions Greater than One**

**Study the example problem showing multiplying fractions greater than 1. Then solve problems 1–6.**

Example
What is the area of a rectangle that is $\frac{1}{2}$-yard wide and $\frac{4}{3}$-yards long?

This area model shows $\frac{1}{2}$ yard $\times \frac{1}{3}$ yard $= \frac{1}{6}$ square yard.

This model uses the same $\frac{1}{6}$-square yard parts to show an area that is $\frac{1}{2}$ yard $\times \frac{4}{3}$ yards.

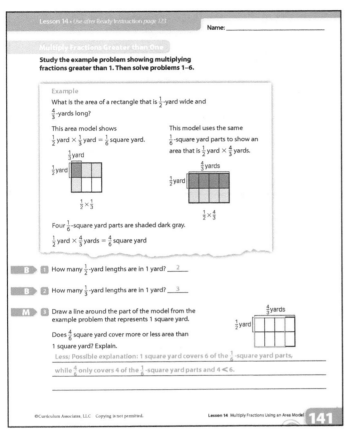

Four $\frac{1}{6}$-square yard parts are shaded dark gray.

$\frac{1}{2}$ yard $\times \frac{4}{3}$ yards $= \frac{4}{6}$ square yard

**B** ☐1 How many $\frac{1}{2}$-yard lengths are in 1 yard? __2__

**B** ☐2 How many $\frac{1}{3}$-yard lengths are in 1 yard? __3__

**M** ☐3 Draw a line around the part of the model from the example problem that represents 1 square yard.

Does $\frac{4}{6}$ square yard cover more or less area than 1 square yard? Explain.

Less; Possible explanation: 1 square yard covers 6 of the $\frac{1}{6}$-square yard parts, while $\frac{4}{6}$ only covers 4 of the $\frac{1}{6}$-square yard parts and 4 < 6.

©Curriculum Associates, LLC   Copying is not permitted.

Lesson 14 Multiply Fractions Using an Area Model **141**

---

**142** Lesson 14 Multiply Fractions Using an Area Model   ©Curriculum Associates, LLC   Copying is not permitted.

**Solve.**

**M** ☐4 Danah has a strawberry patch in her garden. Its border is $\frac{4}{5}$-meters wide and $\frac{3}{2}$-meters long. What is the area of Danah's strawberry patch?
**Show your work.**

Students may model $\frac{4}{5} \times \frac{3}{2}$ with an area model, or an equation, or both.

Solution: $\frac{12}{10}$ square meters _____

**M** ☐5 Danah is planting a second strawberry patch and wants it to have an area of exactly 1 square meter. Which of the following could be the width and length of its borders? Circle the letter for all that apply.

A  $\frac{1}{2}$-meter wide and $\frac{3}{2}$-meters long

Ⓑ  $\frac{2}{3}$-meter wide and $\frac{3}{2}$-meters long

Ⓒ  $\frac{4}{5}$-meter wide and $\frac{5}{4}$-meters long

Ⓓ  $\frac{2}{3}$-meter wide and $\frac{6}{4}$-meters long

*If I find the area of each different shape strawberry patch, I can figure out which options have an area of 1 square meter.*

**C** ☐6 Look at problem 5. If Danah wants her strawberry patch to be exactly 1 square meter, can the length of her strawberry patch be greater than 1 meter? Explain.

Yes; Possible explanation: B, C, and D all have lengths greater than 1 meter and their areas are exactly 1 square meter.

---

Lesson 14 · *Use after Ready Instruction page 125*

Name: _____

**Multiply Fractions to Find Area**

**Solve the problems.**

**M** ☐1 Owen has a square sheet of paper that measures 1 foot on each side. He folds the paper vertically and horizontally so that it makes equal sections. The model shows the unfolded paper. Which expression represents the area of 1 section?

*If each side of the paper is 1-foot long, how wide is each section? How long?*

A  $\frac{1}{3} \times \frac{1}{3}$ square feet

B  $\frac{2}{1} \times \frac{1}{3}$ square foot

Ⓒ  $\frac{1}{2} \times \frac{1}{3}$ square foot

D  $\frac{3}{1} \times \frac{1}{2}$ square foot

**M** ☐2 What is the area of a rectangle with a length of $\frac{7}{5}$ meter and a width of $\frac{5}{10}$ meter?

Ⓐ  $\frac{35}{50}$ square meter

B  $\frac{14}{20}$ square meter

C  $\frac{12}{15}$ square meter

D  $\frac{12}{10}$ square meters

*If I draw a model that is 1 square meter divided into fifths and tenths, what is the area of each small part?*

Patsy chose **C** as the correct answer. How did she get that answer?

Answers will vary. Possible answer: Patsy added the numerator and denominator of the fractions $\frac{7}{5}$ and $\frac{5}{10}$. She should have multiplied the numerators and denominators.

©Curriculum Associates, LLC   Copying is not permitted.

Lesson 14 Multiply Fractions Using an Area Model **143**

---

**144** Lesson 14 Multiply Fractions Using an Area Model   ©Curriculum Associates, LLC   Copying is not permitted.

**Solve.**

**M** ☐3 Each expression below shows the length and width of a rectangle in yards. Write each expression in the correct box according to the area it represents.

$\frac{2}{3} \times \frac{3}{5}$   $\frac{2}{3} \times \frac{3}{3}$   $\frac{1}{2} \times \frac{9}{10}$

$\frac{1}{4} \times \frac{4}{1}$   $\frac{1}{4} \times \frac{5}{3}$   $\frac{4}{3} \times \frac{6}{8}$

*How do the numerator and denominator compare in a fraction less than 1? A fraction equal to 1? A fraction greater than 1?*

| Area less than 1 square yard | Area equal to 1 square yard | Area greater than 1 square yard |
|---|---|---|
| $\frac{2}{3} \times \frac{3}{5}$ | $\frac{4}{3} \times \frac{6}{8}$ | $\frac{2}{3} \times \frac{5}{3}$ |
| $\frac{1}{4} \times \frac{5}{3}$ | $\frac{1}{4} \times \frac{4}{1}$ | |
| $\frac{1}{2} \times \frac{9}{10}$ | | |

**C** ☐4 Pick one of the expressions from problem 3. Draw an area model to represent the expression.

$\frac{4}{3}$ yard $\times \frac{6}{8}$ yard

Possible student work shown.

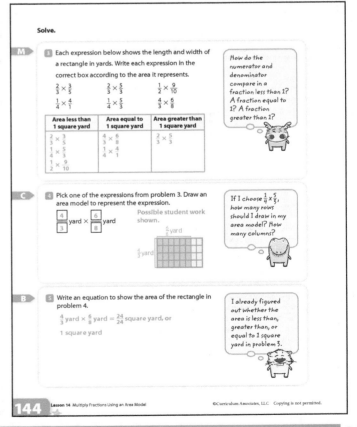

*If I choose $\frac{1}{4} \times \frac{5}{3}$, how many rows should I draw in my area model? How many columns?*

**B** ☐5 Write an equation to show the area of the rectangle in problem 4.

$\frac{4}{3}$ yard $\times \frac{6}{8}$ yard $= \frac{24}{24}$ square yard, or 1 square yard

*I already figured out whether the area is less than, greater than, or equal to 1 square yard in problem 3.*

---

©Curriculum Associates, LLC    Copying is not permitted.

---

Lesson 15    *Use after Ready Instruction page 129*

**Understand Multiplication as Scaling**

Name: _____

*How can you use area models to multiply fractions less than 1 and greater than 1?*

**Study the example showing one way to multiply by fractions less than 1 and greater than 1. Then solve problems 1–7.**

Example

Multiply $\frac{4}{5}$ by a fraction less than 1.

$\frac{2}{3} \times \frac{4}{5}$

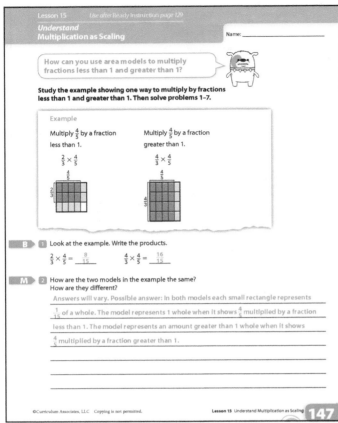

Multiply $\frac{4}{5}$ by a fraction greater than 1.

$\frac{4}{3} \times \frac{4}{5}$

**B ▶ 1** Look at the example. Write the products.

$\frac{2}{3} \times \frac{4}{5} = \frac{8}{15}$        $\frac{4}{3} \times \frac{4}{5} = \frac{16}{15}$

**M ▶ 2** How are the two models in the example the same? How are they different?

Answers will vary. Possible answer: In both models each small rectangle represents

$\frac{1}{15}$ of a whole. The model represents 1 whole when it shows $\frac{4}{5}$ multiplied by a fraction

less than 1. The model represents an amount greater than 1 whole when it shows

$\frac{4}{5}$ multiplied by a fraction greater than 1.

---

**Solve.**

**M ▶ 3** You can also use area models to show multiplying by a fraction equal to 1. Use the area model to show $\frac{3}{3} \times \frac{4}{5}$. Then complete the equation.

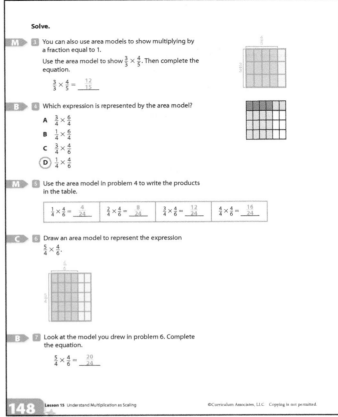

$\frac{3}{3} \times \frac{4}{5} = \frac{12}{15}$

**B ▶ 4** Which expression is represented by the area model?

A $\frac{3}{4} \times \frac{6}{4}$

B $\frac{1}{4} \times \frac{6}{4}$

C $\frac{3}{4} \times \frac{4}{6}$

Ⓓ $\frac{1}{4} \times \frac{4}{6}$

**M ▶ 5** Use the area model in problem 4 to write the products in the table.

| $\frac{1}{4} \times \frac{4}{6} = \frac{4}{24}$ | $\frac{2}{4} \times \frac{4}{6} = \frac{8}{24}$ | $\frac{3}{4} \times \frac{4}{6} = \frac{12}{24}$ | $\frac{4}{4} \times \frac{4}{6} = \frac{16}{24}$ |

**C ▶ 6** Draw an area model to represent the expression $\frac{5}{4} \times \frac{4}{6}$.

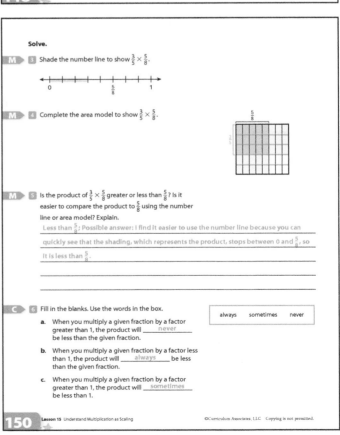

**B ▶ 7** Look at the model you drew in problem 6. Complete the equation.

$\frac{5}{4} \times \frac{4}{6} = \frac{20}{24}$

---

Lesson 15 • *Use after Ready Instruction page 131*

Name: _____

**Compare Factors and Products**

**Study the example showing how to use a number line to multiply by fractions less than 1 and greater than 1. Then solve problems 1–6.**

Example

Multiply $\frac{2}{5}$ by a fraction less than 1.

$\frac{1}{2} \times \frac{2}{5} = \frac{1}{5}$

Break $\frac{2}{5}$ into 2 equal parts. Each part is $\frac{1}{5}$. Shade 1 part.

Multiply $\frac{2}{5}$ by a fraction greater than 1.

$\frac{3}{2} \times \frac{2}{5} = \frac{3}{5}$

Break $\frac{2}{5}$ into 2 equal parts. Each part is $\frac{1}{5}$. Shade 3 parts.

**B ▶ 1** When you multiply a whole number by a fraction less than 1, the product is less than the whole number. Does the example showing $\frac{1}{2} \times \frac{2}{5}$ support a similar rule when multiplying a fraction by a fraction less than 1? Explain.

Answers will vary. Possible answer: Yes, $\frac{1}{2}$ is less than 1 and the product, $\frac{1}{5}$, is less

than $\frac{2}{5}$.

**B ▶ 2** When you multiply a whole number by a fraction greater than 1, the product is greater than the whole number. Does the example showing $\frac{3}{2} \times \frac{2}{5}$ support a similar rule when multiplying a fraction by a fraction greater than 1? Explain.

Answers will vary. Possible answer: Yes, $\frac{3}{2}$ is greater than 1 and the product, $\frac{3}{5}$, is

greater than $\frac{2}{5}$.

---

**Solve.**

**M ▶ 3** Shade the number line to show $\frac{3}{5} \times \frac{5}{8}$.

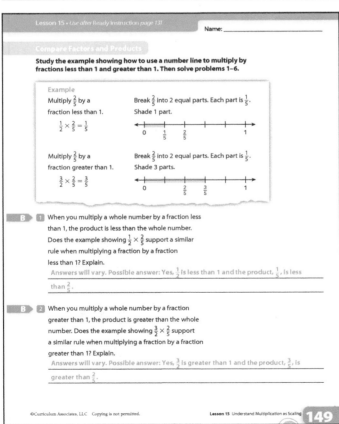

**M ▶ 4** Complete the area model to show $\frac{3}{5} \times \frac{5}{8}$.

**M ▶ 5** Is the product of $\frac{3}{5} \times \frac{5}{8}$ greater or less than $\frac{5}{8}$? Is it easier to compare the product to $\frac{5}{8}$ using the number line or area model? Explain.

Less than $\frac{5}{8}$; Possible answer: I find it easier to use the number line because you can

quickly see that the shading, which represents the product, stops between 0 and $\frac{5}{8}$, so

it is less than $\frac{5}{8}$.

**C ▶ 6** Fill in the blanks. Use the words in the box.

| always | sometimes | never |

a. When you multiply a given fraction by a factor greater than 1, the product will __never__ be less than the given fraction.

b. When you multiply a given fraction by a factor less than 1, the product will __always__ be less than the given fraction.

c. When you multiply a given fraction by a factor greater than 1, the product will __sometimes__ be less than 1.

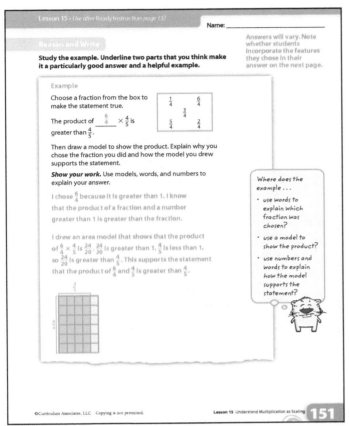

Lesson 15 · *Use after Ready Instruction page 137*

**Reason and Write**

Name: _____

Answers will vary. Note whether students incorporate the features they chose in their answer on the next page.

**Study the example. Underline two parts that you think make it a particularly good answer and a helpful example.**

**Example**

Choose a fraction from the box to make the statement true.

The product of $\frac{6}{4}$ × $\frac{4}{5}$ is greater than $\frac{4}{5}$.

| | |
|---|---|
| $\frac{1}{4}$ | $\frac{6}{4}$ |
| $\frac{3}{4}$ | |
| $\frac{5}{4}$ | $\frac{2}{4}$ |

Then draw a model to show the product. Explain why you chose the fraction you did and how the model you drew supports the statement.

***Show your work.*** Use models, words, and numbers to explain your answer.

I chose $\frac{6}{4}$ because it is greater than 1. I know that the product of a fraction and a number greater than 1 is greater than the fraction.

I drew an area model that shows that the product of $\frac{6}{4}$ × $\frac{4}{5}$ is $\frac{24}{20}$. $\frac{24}{20}$ is greater than 1. $\frac{4}{5}$ is less than 1, so $\frac{24}{20}$ is greater than $\frac{4}{5}$. This supports the statement that the product of $\frac{6}{4}$ and $\frac{4}{5}$ is greater than $\frac{4}{5}$.

Where does the example . . .
- use words to explain which fraction was chosen?
- use a model to show the product?
- use numbers and words to explain how the model supports the statement?

©Curriculum Associates, LLC   Copying is not permitted.

Lesson 15 Understand Multiplication as Scaling **151**

---

152   Lesson 15 Understand Multiplication as Scaling

**Solve the problem. Use what you learned from the example.**

Choose a fraction from the box to make the statement true.

The product of $\frac{2}{4}$ × $\frac{4}{5}$ is less than $\frac{4}{5}$.

| | |
|---|---|
| $\frac{1}{4}$ | $\frac{6}{4}$ |
| $\frac{3}{4}$ | |
| $\frac{5}{4}$ | $\frac{2}{4}$ |

Then draw a model to show the product. Explain why you chose the fraction you did and how the model you drew supports the statement.

***Show your work.*** Use models, words, and numbers to explain your answer.

Possible answer:

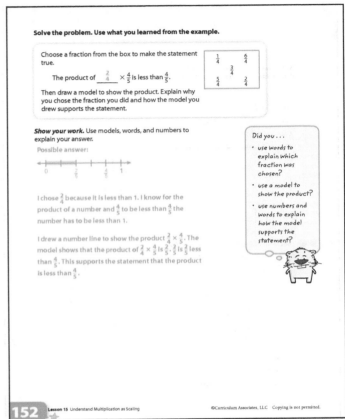

I chose $\frac{2}{4}$ because it is less than 1. I know for the product of a number and $\frac{4}{5}$ to be less than $\frac{4}{5}$ the number has to be less than 1.

I drew a number line to show the product $\frac{2}{4}$ × $\frac{4}{5}$. The model shows that the product of $\frac{2}{4}$ × $\frac{4}{5}$ is $\frac{2}{5}$. $\frac{2}{5}$ is less than $\frac{4}{5}$. This supports the statement that the product is less than $\frac{4}{5}$.

Did you . . .
- use words to explain which fraction was chosen?
- use a model to show the product?
- use numbers and words to explain how the model supports the statement?

©Curriculum Associates, LLC   Copying is not permitted.

| Key | |
|---|---|
| B | Basic |
| M | Medium |
| C | Challenge |

©Curriculum Associates, LLC   Copying is not permitted.

Lesson 16     *Use after Ready Instruction page 137*

## Multiply Fractions in Word Problems     Name: _____

### Multiply Fractions with Models

**Study the example problem showing three ways to model multiplying fractions. Then solve problems 1–6.**

> **Example**
>
> What is $\frac{2}{3} \times \frac{3}{5}$?
>
> You can find $\frac{2}{3} \times \frac{3}{5}$ using different models.
>
> **A number line**
>
> 0 ——————— $\frac{3}{5}$ ——————— 1
>
> **An area model**
>
> **An equation**
>
> $\frac{2}{3} \times \frac{3}{5} = \frac{2 \times 3}{3 \times 5} = \frac{6}{15}$

**M  1** Look at the example showing models of $\frac{2}{3} \times \frac{3}{5}$. How are the models alike? How are the models different?

Answers will vary. Possible answer: All three models show the parts of the problem—the factors and product. The area model pictures the different quantities, the number line represents them with pictures and numbers, and the equation represents them with just numbers. For the number line and area model you need to interpret the product and write numbers to represent what's shown, while the equation shows it already as a number value.

**B  2** Write the product for $\frac{2}{3} \times \frac{3}{5}$ shown by each model in the example.

number line ___$\frac{2}{5}$___     area model ___$\frac{6}{15}$___     equation ___$\frac{6}{15}$___

---

**Solve.**

**B  3** Write the missing numbers that show that $\frac{2}{5}$ and $\frac{6}{15}$ are equivalent fractions.

$\frac{2 \times \boxed{3}}{5 \times \boxed{3}} = \frac{6}{15}$

**M  4** Explain how the numbers you wrote in problem 3 show that $\frac{2}{5}$ and $\frac{6}{15}$ are equivalent.

Answers will vary. Possible answer: Since you can multiply both the numerator and denominator of $\frac{2}{5}$ by the same number, 3, to get $\frac{6}{15}$, it means that $\frac{2}{5}$ and $\frac{6}{15}$ are equivalent, because it is the same as multiplying $\frac{2}{5}$ by 1 ($\frac{3}{3} = 1$).

**M  5** What is $\frac{2}{3} \times \frac{3}{8}$?
**Show your work.**

Students might use number lines, area models, equations, or some other method to multiply $\frac{2}{3} \times \frac{3}{8}$.

Solution: ___$\frac{6}{24}$ or $\frac{2}{8}$ or $\frac{1}{4}$___

**C  6** Check your answer to problem 5 by modeling $\frac{2}{3} \times \frac{3}{8}$ a different way.
**Show your work.**

Students might use number lines, area models, equations, or some other method to multiply $\frac{2}{3} \times \frac{3}{8}$. It should be a different method than that used in problem 5.

Solution: ___$\frac{6}{24}$ or $\frac{2}{8}$ or $\frac{1}{4}$___

---

Lesson 16 · *Use after Ready Instruction page 137*     Name: _____

### Solve Word Problems with Fractions

**Study the example problem showing one way to solve a word problem with fractions. Then solve problems 1–5.**

> **Example**
>
> Vicky's favorite beach towel is green and white and has a fish design. The green part covers $\frac{5}{8}$ of the towel. A fish design is drawn on $\frac{3}{5}$ of that. What part of the towel has a fish design on it?
>
> You can draw a picture.
>
> Show a towel with $\frac{5}{8}$ shaded green.     Draw fish on $\frac{3}{5}$ of the green part.
>
> 3 of the 8 parts of the towel have fish drawn on them, so $\frac{3}{8}$ of the towel has a fish design on it.

**B  1** You can also write an equation to solve the example problem. Write the numbers to complete the equation showing what part of the towel has the fish design.

$\frac{3}{5}$ of $\frac{5}{8}$ means $\frac{3}{5} \times \frac{5}{8}$.

$\frac{3}{5} \times \frac{\boxed{5}}{\boxed{8}} = \frac{3 \times 5}{5 \times 8} = \frac{15}{40}$

**M  2** Is your answer to problem 1 the same as the answer, $\frac{3}{8}$, shown in the example problem? Explain.

Answers will vary. Possible answer: Yes; $\frac{15}{40}$ is equivalent to $\frac{3}{8}$ because $\frac{3}{8} \times \frac{5}{5} = \frac{15}{40}$.

---

**Solve.**

**M  3** Suppose the green part of Vicky's towel covers $\frac{4}{5}$ of the towel and the fish design is drawn on $\frac{3}{4}$ of that. Draw a picture to find the part of the towel that has the fish design on it. Then write the answer.

Solution: ___$\frac{3}{5}$ of the towel has the fish design.___

**M  4** Write an equation to show the answer to problem 3.

Solution: ___$\frac{3}{4} \times \frac{4}{5} = \frac{3 \times 4}{4 \times 5} = \frac{12}{20}$___

**C  5** At noon Ada and Kent had $\frac{3}{8}$ gallon of lemonade left at their lemonade stand. The next customer bought $\frac{1}{3}$ of the remaining lemonade. How much lemonade did the customer buy?
**Show your work.**

Students might use pictures, equations, or some other method to find $\frac{1}{3}$ of $\frac{3}{8}$.

Solution: ___$\frac{3}{24}$ or $\frac{1}{8}$ gallon___

Lesson 16 · Use after Ready Instruction page 139

Name: _____

## Multiply Mixed Numbers in Word Problems

**Study the example problem showing one way to solve a word problem with a mixed number. Then solve problems 1–4.**

### Example

Mr. Urrego is painting his deck to get it ready for the summer. He's painted an area that is $3\frac{1}{5}$-meters long and $\frac{2}{3}$-meter wide. How many square meters of deck are painted?

You can use an area model.

The larger sections of the area model are $\frac{1}{3} \times 1 = \frac{1}{3}$ square meter.

The smaller sections of the area model are $\frac{1}{3} \times \frac{1}{5} = \frac{1}{15}$ square meter.

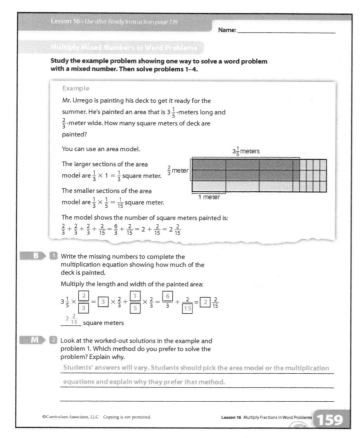

The model shows the number of square meters painted is:

$\frac{2}{3} + \frac{2}{3} + \frac{2}{3} + \frac{2}{15} = \frac{6}{3} + \frac{2}{15} = 2 + \frac{2}{15} = 2\frac{2}{15}$

**B** **1** Write the missing numbers to complete the multiplication equation showing how much of the deck is painted.

Multiply the length and width of the painted area:

$3\frac{1}{5} \times \boxed{\frac{2}{3}} = \boxed{3} \times \frac{2}{3} + \boxed{\frac{1}{5}} \times \frac{2}{3} = \frac{6}{3} + \boxed{\frac{2}{15}} = \boxed{2}\,\frac{2}{15}$

$2\frac{2}{15}$ square meters

**M** **2** Look at the worked-out solutions in the example and problem 1. Which method do you prefer to solve the problem? Explain why.

Students' answers will vary. Students should pick the area model or the multiplication

equations and explain why they prefer that method.

©Curriculum Associates, LLC   Copying is not permitted.
Lesson 16 Multiply Fractions in Word Problems **159**

---

**Solve.**

**B** **3** To multiply a mixed number you can also write it first as a fraction and then multiply. Write the missing numbers to show this way of multiplying to find how much of the deck is painted.

Here's the equation you've already used to solve the problem.

$3\frac{1}{5} \times \boxed{\frac{2}{3}} = \boxed{3} \times \frac{2}{3} + \boxed{\frac{1}{5}} \times \frac{2}{3} = \frac{6}{3} + \frac{2}{15} = \boxed{2}\,\frac{2}{15}$

$2\frac{2}{15}$ square meters

Now here is a new way to multiply.

Write $3\frac{1}{5}$ as a fraction.     Multiply using $\frac{16}{5}$ as a factor.

$3\frac{1}{5} = \boxed{3} + \boxed{\frac{1}{5}}$     $\frac{16}{5} \times \frac{2}{3} = \boxed{\frac{16 \times 2}{5 \times 3}}$

$= \frac{15}{5} + \frac{1}{5}$     $= \boxed{\frac{32}{15}}$

$= \boxed{\frac{16}{5}}$     $= 2\,\boxed{\frac{2}{15}}$

$2\frac{2}{15}$ square meters

**C** **4** The multipurpose room at the Cortez School is being set up for the annual book sale. Graphic novels will be displayed in an area $1\frac{1}{4}$-yards long and $\frac{3}{4}$-yard wide. Will the graphic novels be displayed in an area greater than or less than 1 square yard?

**Show your work.**

Students may use area models, equations, or some other method to find that $1\frac{1}{4} \times \frac{3}{4} = \frac{15}{16}$ square yard.

Solution: _less than 1 square yard_

**160** Lesson 16 Multiply Fractions in Word Problems
©Curriculum Associates, LLC   Copying is not permitted.

---

Lesson 16 · Use after Ready Instruction page 141

Name: _____

## Multiply Fractions in Word Problems

**Solve the problems.**

**B** **1** Tell whether each equation showing a mixed number written as a fraction is *True* or *False*.

a. $1\frac{3}{4} = \frac{7}{4}$   ☒ True  ☐ False

b. $4\frac{2}{5} = \frac{22}{5}$   ☒ True  ☐ False

c. $3\frac{2}{3} = \frac{11}{2}$   ☐ True  ☒ False

d. $2\frac{7}{10} = \frac{27}{10}$   ☒ True  ☐ False

*How do you know what the denominator is when you write a mixed number as a fraction?*

**M** **2** Camilla's class played soccer for $\frac{2}{3}$ hour. She played for $\frac{3}{5}$ of the game. How much time did Camilla play?

A $\frac{5}{15}$ hour     C $\frac{5}{8}$ hour

Ⓑ $\frac{6}{15}$ hour     D $\frac{6}{8}$ hour

Will chose **A** as the correct answer. How did he get that answer?

Answers will vary. Possible answer: Will

multiplied the denominators but added the

numerators. He should have multiplied both the

numerators and denominators.

*What equation can I write to solve this problem?*

**C** **3** How many minutes are in $\frac{2}{3}$ hour? How many minutes are in $\frac{3}{5}$ of that time?

*How many minutes are in an hour?*

Solution: _40 minutes; 24 minutes_

©Curriculum Associates, LLC   Copying is not permitted.
Lesson 16 Multiply Fractions in Word Problems **161**

---

**Solve.**

**M** **4** Caleb has $2\frac{1}{5}$ yards of rope. He uses $\frac{3}{4}$ of the rope to make a dog leash. Which expression can be used to represent $\frac{3}{4}$ of $2\frac{1}{5}$? Circle the letter for all that apply.

A $\frac{3}{4} \times 2 \times \frac{1}{5}$     Ⓒ $\frac{3}{4} \times 2 + \frac{3}{4} \times \frac{1}{5}$

Ⓑ $\frac{3}{4} \times \frac{11}{5}$     D $\frac{3}{4} \times \frac{3}{4} + \frac{1}{5}$

*What are other ways to write the mixed number $2\frac{1}{5}$?*

**M** **5** Dante and 2 classmates are making a poster to advertise a Bike-to-School Day event. It is $1\frac{1}{2}$-yards long and $\frac{3}{4}$-yard wide. How large a writing area does that give them?

**Show your work.**

Students may use area models, equations, or some other method to find $\frac{3}{4} \times 1\frac{1}{2}$.

*What model can I use to help understand this problem?*

Solution: _$\frac{9}{8}$ or $1\frac{1}{8}$ square yards_

**C** **6** Manny hiked $6\frac{2}{5}$ miles along a mountain trail. He stopped to climb a lookout tower $\frac{1}{4}$ of the way along his hike. How many miles did Manny hike before he stopped to climb the lookout tower?

**Show your work.**

Students may use area models, equations, or some other method to find $\frac{1}{4}$ of $6\frac{2}{5}$ miles.

*Did Manny hike more or less than 1 mile before stopping to climb the tower?*

Solution: _$1\frac{12}{20}$ or $1\frac{3}{5}$ miles_

**162** Lesson 16 Multiply Fractions in Word Problems
©Curriculum Associates, LLC   Copying is not permitted.

©Curriculum Associates, LLC   Copying is not permitted.

Lesson 17    *Use after Ready Instruction page 145*

**Understand**
**Division with Unit Fractions**                    Name: _____

How do you find a fraction of a fraction?

**Study the example problem showing two ways to find a fraction of a fraction. Then solve problems 1–5.**

Example

The Padis family had $\frac{1}{2}$ pan of lasagna left from dinner. They ate $\frac{2}{3}$ of the leftovers the next day for lunch. What fraction of the whole pan of lasagna did they eat for lunch?

You need to find $\frac{2}{3}$ of $\frac{1}{2}$. $\frac{2}{3}$ of $\frac{1}{2}$ means $\frac{2}{3} \times \frac{1}{2}$.

You can draw a picture.          You can write an equation.

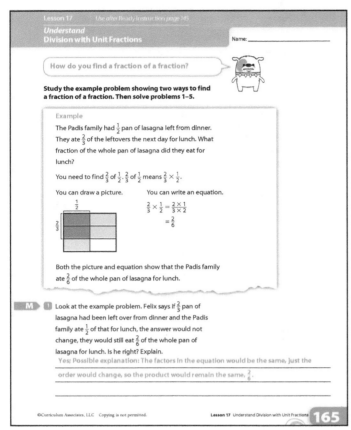

$$\frac{2}{3} \times \frac{1}{2} = \frac{2 \times 1}{3 \times 2}$$
$$= \frac{2}{6}$$

Both the picture and equation show that the Padis family ate $\frac{2}{6}$ of the whole pan of lasagna for lunch.

**M** 1 Look at the example problem. Felix says if $\frac{2}{3}$ pan of lasagna had been left over from dinner and the Padis family ate $\frac{1}{2}$ of that for lunch, the answer would not change, they would still eat $\frac{2}{6}$ of the whole pan of lasagna for lunch. Is he right? Explain.

Yes; Possible explanation: The factors in the equation would be the same, just the order would change, so the product would remain the same, $\frac{2}{6}$.

---

**Solve.**

**B** 2 Look at the area model. Which of the following products is represented by the model? Circle the letter for all that apply.

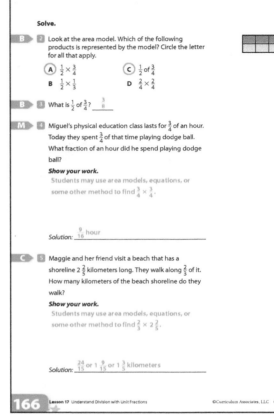

(A) $\frac{1}{2} \times \frac{3}{4}$          (C) $\frac{1}{2}$ of $\frac{3}{4}$

B  $\frac{1}{2} \times \frac{1}{3}$          D  $\frac{2}{4} \times \frac{2}{4}$

**B** 3 What is $\frac{1}{2}$ of $\frac{3}{4}$? $\frac{3}{8}$

**M** 4 Miguel's physical education class lasts for $\frac{3}{4}$ of an hour. Today they spent $\frac{3}{4}$ of that time playing dodge ball. What fraction of an hour did he spend playing dodge ball?
*Show your work.*

Students may use area models, equations, or some other method to find $\frac{3}{4} \times \frac{3}{4}$.

*Solution:* $\frac{9}{16}$ hour _____

**C** 5 Maggie and her friend visit a beach that has a shoreline $2\frac{2}{5}$ kilometers long. They walk along $\frac{2}{3}$ of it. How many kilometers of the beach shoreline do they walk?
*Show your work.*

Students may use area models, equations, or some other method to find $\frac{2}{3} \times 2\frac{2}{5}$.

*Solution:* $\frac{24}{15}$ or $1\frac{9}{15}$ or $1\frac{3}{5}$ kilometers

---

Lesson 17 • *Use after Ready Instruction page 147*
                                                Name: _____

**Use Unit Fractions in Division**

**Study the example problem showing dividing a whole number by a unit fraction. Then solve problems 1–6.**

Example

Teams of students in Mr. Reed's classroom are presenting Social Studies projects. Each team has $\frac{1}{5}$ hour for their presentation. How many projects are presented in 2 hours?

The 2 large rectangles represent the 2 hours.

Each presentation is $\frac{1}{5}$ hour so each rectangle is divided into 5 equal sections.

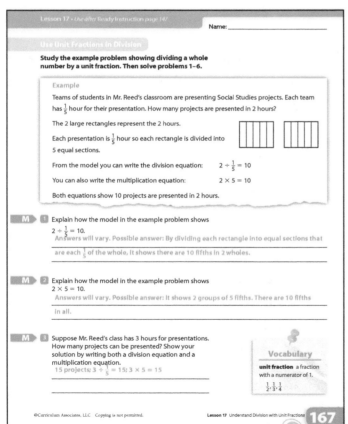

From the model you can write the division equation:     $2 \div \frac{1}{5} = 10$

You can also write the multiplication equation:     $2 \times 5 = 10$

Both equations show 10 projects are presented in 2 hours.

**M** 1 Explain how the model in the example problem shows $2 \div \frac{1}{5} = 10$.
Answers will vary. Possible answer: By dividing each rectangle into equal sections that are each $\frac{1}{5}$ of the whole, it shows there are 10 fifths in 2 wholes.

**M** 2 Explain how the model in the example problem shows $2 \times 5 = 10$.
Answers will vary. Possible answer: It shows 2 groups of 5 fifths. There are 10 fifths in all.

**M** 3 Suppose Mr. Reed's class has 3 hours for presentations. How many projects can be presented? Show your solution by writing both a division equation and a multiplication equation.
15 projects; $3 \div \frac{1}{5} = 15$; $3 \times 5 = 15$

**Vocabulary**

**unit fraction** a fraction with a numerator of 1.
$\frac{1}{2}, \frac{1}{3}, \frac{1}{4}$

---

**Solve.**

**M** 4 Mr. Reed put 3 students on each team. The teams divide the $\frac{1}{5}$ hour presentation time so that each student talks an equal amount of time. Complete the steps to find what fraction of the presentation time each student talks.

a. Use the rectangle at the right. Shade $\frac{1}{5}$ of the rectangle to show $\frac{1}{5}$ hour, the time of one presentation.

b. Divide the rectangle into 3 equal parts to represent the 3 students.

c. Shade $\frac{1}{3}$ of the rectangle to represent 1 student.

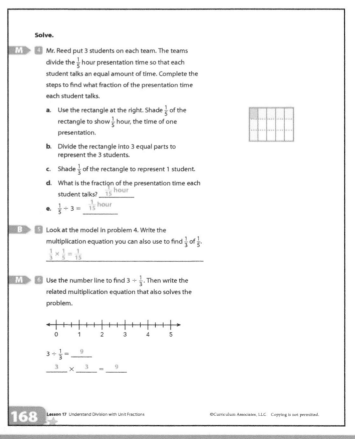

d. What is the fraction of the presentation time each student talks? $\frac{1}{15}$ hour

e. $\frac{1}{5} \div 3 = \frac{1}{15}$ hour

**B** 5 Look at the model in problem 4. Write the multiplication equation you can also use to find $\frac{1}{3}$ of $\frac{1}{5}$.
$\frac{1}{3} \times \frac{1}{5} = \frac{1}{15}$

**M** 6 Use the number line to find $3 \div \frac{1}{3}$. Then write the related multiplication equation that also solves the problem.

$$3 \div \frac{1}{3} = 9$$

$$\underline{3} \times \underline{3} = 9$$

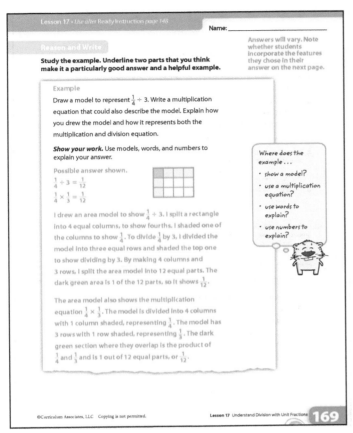

Lesson 17 · *Use after* Ready Instruction *page 148*

Name: _____

**Reason and Write**

Answers will vary. Note whether students incorporate the features they chose in their answer on the next page.

**Study the example. Underline two parts that you think make it a particularly good answer and a helpful example.**

Example

Draw a model to represent $\frac{1}{4} \div 3$. Write a multiplication equation that could also describe the model. Explain how you drew the model and how it represents both the multiplication and division equation.

***Show your work.*** Use models, words, and numbers to explain your answer.

Possible answer shown.

$\frac{1}{4} \div 3 = \frac{1}{12}$

$\frac{1}{4} \times \frac{1}{3} = \frac{1}{12}$

I drew an area model to show $\frac{1}{4} \div 3$. I split a rectangle into 4 equal columns, to show fourths. I shaded one of the columns to show $\frac{1}{4}$. To divide $\frac{1}{4}$ by 3, I divided the model into three equal rows and shaded the top one to show dividing by 3. By making 4 columns and 3 rows, I split the area model into 12 equal parts. The dark green area is 1 of the 12 parts, so it shows $\frac{1}{12}$.

The area model also shows the multiplication equation $\frac{1}{4} \times \frac{1}{3}$. The model is divided into 4 columns with 1 column shaded, representing $\frac{1}{4}$. The model has 3 rows with 1 row shaded, representing $\frac{1}{3}$. The dark green section where they overlap is the product of $\frac{1}{4}$ and $\frac{1}{3}$ and is 1 out of 12 equal parts, or $\frac{1}{12}$.

Where does the example . . .
- show a model?
- use a multiplication equation?
- use words to explain?
- use numbers to explain?

**Solve the problem. Use what you learned from the example.**

Draw a model to represent $6 \div \frac{1}{3}$. Write a multiplication equation that could also describe the model. Explain how you drew the model and how it represents both the multiplication and division equation.

***Show your work.*** Use models, words, and numbers to explain your answer.

Possible answer shown.

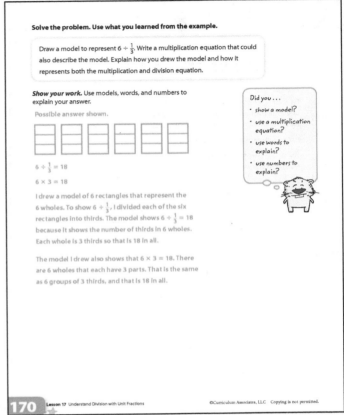

$6 \div \frac{1}{3} = 18$

$6 \times 3 = 18$

I drew a model of 6 rectangles that represent the 6 wholes. To show $6 \div \frac{1}{3}$, I divided each of the six rectangles into thirds. The model shows $6 \div \frac{1}{3} = 18$ because it shows the number of thirds in 6 wholes. Each whole is 3 thirds so that is 18 in all.

The model I drew also shows that $6 \times 3 = 18$. There are 6 wholes that each have 3 parts. That is the same as 6 groups of 3 thirds, and that is 18 in all.

Did you . . .
- show a model?
- use a multiplication equation?
- use words to explain?
- use numbers to explain?

| Key | |
|---|---|
| B | Basic |
| M | Medium |
| C | Challenge |

## Divide Unit Fractions in Word Problems

Name: _____

### Divide with Unit Fractions

**Study the example showing a word problem about dividing unit fractions by a whole number. Then solve problems 1–5.**

> **Example**
>
> Eva and her two brothers, Bo and Sam, have $\frac{1}{2}$ hour to play on the computer and want to share the time equally. What fraction of an hour will they each have on the computer?
>
> Eva, Bo, and Sam will each get $\frac{1}{3}$ of the $\frac{1}{2}$ hour.
>
> You can represent this with a division expression or a multiplication expression:
>
> $\frac{1}{2} \div 3$          $\frac{1}{3} \times \frac{1}{2}$
>
> You can solve by drawing a picture, or by multiplying fractions:
>
> $\frac{1}{3} \times \frac{1}{2} = \frac{1}{6}$
>
> Eva, Bo, and Sam will each have $\frac{1}{6}$ hour on the computer.

The circle represents 1 hour. The green shading is the $\frac{1}{2}$ hour they have to play. And the dark shading is the $\frac{1}{3}$ of $\frac{1}{2}$ hour for each child.

**M  1** You divide to find either the number of groups or the quantity in each group. Which of those are you trying to find in the example problem? Explain.

The quantity in each group; Possible explanation: You want to know how much time Eva, Bo, and Sam will each have. You know the number of groups, or parts, is 3.

**B  2** Suppose only Eva and Bo share the $\frac{1}{2}$-hour computer time. Write the multiplication equation that you can use to solve $\frac{1}{2}$ of $\frac{1}{2}$.  $\frac{1}{2} \times \frac{1}{2} = \frac{1}{4}$

---

**Solve.**

**M  3** Fifth-grade students are selling popcorn at a school festival. Pairs of students work in $\frac{1}{3}$-hour shifts. Complete the steps to find how many shifts there are in 3 hours.

   **a.** To solve $3 \div \frac{1}{3}$ you need to find the number of thirds in 3 hours. The circle represents 1 hour. Divide it to show the number of thirds in 1 hour.

   **b.** How many thirds are in 3 hours? ___9___

   **c.** Complete the division and multiplication equations for this problem.

   $3 \times 3 = $ ___9___          $3 \div \frac{1}{3} = $ ___9___

   **d.** How many $\frac{1}{3}$-hour shifts are in 3 hours?

   ___9 shifts___

**M  4** In problem 3 did you divide to find the number of groups or the quantity in each group? Explain.

The number of groups; Possible explanation: You want to know the number of groups, or shifts. You know the quantity of each shift. It is $\frac{1}{3}$ hour.

**C  5** Each lap around the track at Emma's high school is $\frac{1}{4}$ mile. How many laps will Emma need to jog if she wants to jog 3 miles?

Show how you can use multiplication to find $3 \div \frac{1}{4}$.
Possible answer:

Solution: ___$3 \times 4 = 12$; 12 laps___

---

Name: _____

### Divide a fraction by a Whole Number

**Study the example problem showing one way to solve a word problem involving dividing a fraction by a whole number. Then solve problems 1–5.**

> **Example**
>
> Felicia makes $\frac{1}{2}$ gallon of fruit punch. She pours an equal amount into 8 glasses. What fraction of a gallon of fruit punch is in each glass?
>
> Find $\frac{1}{2} \div 8$.
>
> The model shows a rectangle divided into halves, then divided into 8 equal parts. There are a total of 16 parts, and one part is the amount of fruit punch in 1 glass.
>
> $\frac{1}{2} \div 8 = \frac{1}{16}$.
>
> The amount in 1 glass is $\frac{1}{16}$ gallon.

glass 1
glass 2
glass 3
glass 4
glass 5
glass 6
glass 7
glass 8

**B  1** What multiplication equation could you write to solve the example problem?
$\frac{1}{2} \times \frac{1}{8} = \frac{1}{16}$

**M  2** Suppose Felicia had made $\frac{1}{4}$ gallon of punch and poured an equal amount into 8 glasses. Would the amount in each glass be more or less than $\frac{1}{16}$ gallon? Explain how the model in the example problem would change to show this.

Less than; Possible explanation: The model would be divided into fourths instead of halves so all the sections would be smaller.

---

**Solve.**

**M  3** Donal buys a $\frac{1}{4}$-pound package of cheese. There are 8 slices of cheese in the package. Each slice has the same weight. What fraction of a pound is each slice?
**Show your work.**

Students may use area models, equations, or some other method to find $\frac{1}{4} \div 8$.

Solution: ___$\frac{1}{32}$ pound___

**M  4** Student volunteers are getting ready to hand out programs at a talent show. Leah and Tomas are each given $\frac{1}{2}$ of a stack of programs to hand out. Leah divides her $\frac{1}{2}$ equally among herself and 2 friends. What fraction of the original stack of programs do Leah and her 2 friends each have?
**Show your work.**

Students may use area models, equations, or some other method to find $\frac{1}{2} \div 3$.

Solution: ___$\frac{1}{6}$ of the original stack___

**M  5** Look at problem 4. If Tomas divides his stack of programs between himself and his 3 friends, what fraction of the original stack will each of his friends have?
**Show your work.**

Possible work:
$\frac{1}{2} \div 4 = \frac{1}{2} \times \frac{1}{4} = \frac{1}{8}$

Solution: ___$\frac{1}{8}$ of the original stack___

Name: _____

### Divide a Whole Number by a Fraction

Study the example showing one way to solve a word problem involving dividing a whole number by a fraction. Then solve problems 1–6.

**Example**

Darius walks dogs at an animal shelter. He walks each dog for $\frac{1}{5}$ hour. How many dog walks can he do in 2 hours?

Find $2 \div \frac{1}{5}$.

The number line shows two hours. Each hour is divided into fifths.

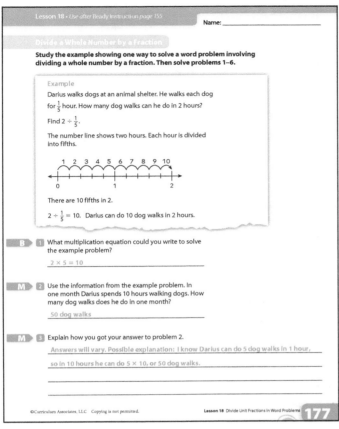

There are 10 fifths in 2.

$2 \div \frac{1}{5} = 10$. Darius can do 10 dog walks in 2 hours.

**B** 1 What multiplication equation could you write to solve the example problem?

$2 \times 5 = 10$

**M** 2 Use the information from the example problem. In one month Darius spends 10 hours walking dogs. How many dog walks does he do in one month?

50 dog walks

**M** 3 Explain how you got your answer to problem 2.

Answers will vary. Possible explanation: I know Darius can do 5 dog walks in 1 hour, so in 10 hours he can do 5 × 10, or 50 dog walks.

---

**Solve.**

**M** 4 Mrs. Wing is preparing to tape up posters made by her students on the wall. She cuts tape into $\frac{1}{4}$-foot pieces. How many $\frac{1}{4}$-foot pieces can she cut from 5 feet of tape?

**Show your work.**

Students may use area models, equations, or some other method to find $5 \div \frac{1}{4}$.

Solution: _____ $20\frac{1}{4}$-foot pieces of tape

**M** 5 Taylor is helping decorate tables with flowers for a graduation celebration. She has 7 dozen tulips. She will put $\frac{1}{2}$ dozen tulips in each vase. How many vases does she need?

**Show your work.**

Students may use area models, equations, or some other method to find $7 \div \frac{1}{2}$.

Solution: 14 vases

**C** 6 Look at how you solved problem 5. Show how to solve problem 5 a different way.

**Show your work.**

Students may use area models, equations, or some other method to find $7 \div \frac{1}{2}$. It should be different than the way shown in problem 5.

Solution: 14 vases

---

Name: _____

### Divide Unit Fractions in Word Problems

**Solve the problems.**

**B** 1 Ms. Kaimal prints out address labels on 3 sheets of paper. Each sheet is entirely covered in labels. Each label takes up $\frac{1}{12}$ of a sheet. How many labels did she print?

(A) 36 labels          C  15 labels

B  24 labels          D  12 labels

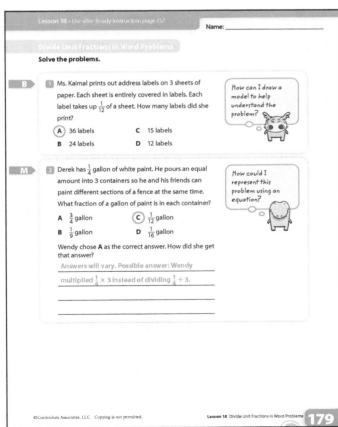

*How can I draw a model to help understand the problem?*

**M** 2 Derek has $\frac{1}{4}$ gallon of white paint. He pours an equal amount into 3 containers so he and his friends can paint different sections of a fence at the same time. What fraction of a gallon of paint is in each container?

A  $\frac{3}{4}$ gallon          (C) $\frac{1}{12}$ gallon

B  $\frac{1}{9}$ gallon          D  $\frac{1}{16}$ gallon

*How could I represent this problem using an equation?*

Wendy chose **A** as the correct answer. How did she get that answer?

Answers will vary. Possible answer: Wendy multiplied $\frac{1}{4} \times 3$ instead of dividing $\frac{1}{4} \div 3$.

---

**Solve.**

**M** 3 Jameson is following a 3-kilometer exercise route. After every $\frac{1}{5}$ kilometer there is a sign describing an exercise to do, including at the end of the route. Which expression can be used to find the number of exercise signs along the route? Circle the letter for all that apply.

(A) $3 \div \frac{1}{5}$          (C) $3 \times 5$

B  $\frac{1}{5} \div 3$          D  $1 \times 3$

*How is this problem like other problems that I've seen?*

**M** 4 Olivia has $\frac{1}{2}$ pound of raisins. She plans to eat them for snacks over the next 6 days. If she eats the same amount each day, what fraction of a pound of raisins will she eat each day?

**Show your work.**

Students may use area models, equations, or some other method to find $\frac{1}{2} \div 6$.

*How can you use multiplication to solve this problem?*

Solution: $\frac{1}{12}$ pound

**M** 5 Complete each sentence by writing either *greater than* or *less than* in the blank.

a. When you divide a unit fraction by a whole number, the quotient is ___ less than ___ the unit fraction.

b. When you divide a whole number by a unit fraction, the quotient is ___ greater than ___ the whole number.

*Think of an example problem with a fraction and whole number to help you answer this question.*

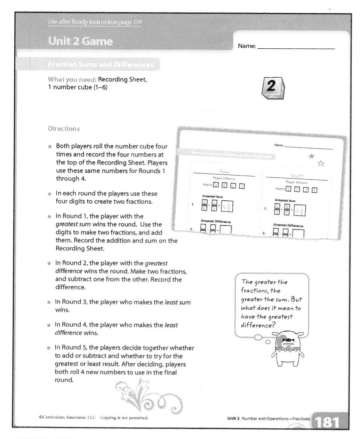

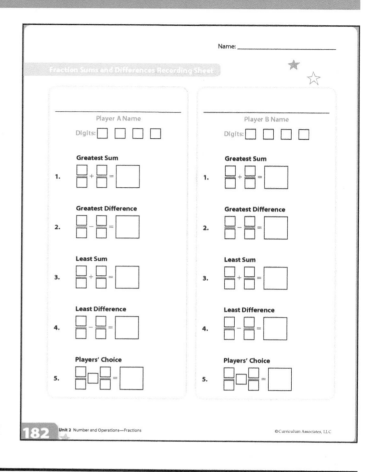

## STEP BY STEP

| **CCSS Focus** - 5.NF.A.1    *Embedded SMPs* - 3, 6, 7, 8 <br> **Objective:** Add and subtract fractions. | **Materials** For each pair: Recording Sheet (TR 3), 1 number cube (1–6) |
| --- | --- |

- Both players roll the number cube four times and record the four numbers at the top of the Recording Sheet. Players use these same numbers for the whole game.

- In each round the players use these four digits to create two fractions.

- In Round 1, the player with the *greatest sum* wins the round. Use the digits to make two fractions, and add them. Record the addition and sum on the Recording Sheet.

- In Round 2, the player with the *greatest difference* wins the round. Make two fractions, and subtract one from the other. Record the difference.

- In Round 3, the player who makes the *least sum* wins.

- In Round 4, the player who makes the *least difference* wins.

- In Round 5, the players decide together whether to add or subtract and whether to try for the greatest or least result.

- Model one complete round for students before they play. Discuss strategies for making fractions that result in greater or lesser sums and differences. Ask students, *What happens if you put a greater number in the numerator? In the denominator?* Elicit thinking about what makes a greater or lesser difference.

- After playing, have students discuss their strategies, explain how their strategies worked, and explore each other's ideas.

**Vary the Game** Multiply in each round, seeking the least or greatest products.

**Extra Support** Use only 2 or 4 in the denominators. Choose numerators from the 4 numbers rolled.

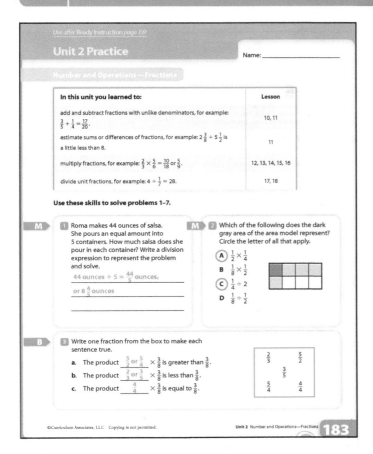

## Unit 2 Practice

Name: _____

Number and Operations—Fractions

| In this unit you learned to: | Lesson |
|---|---|
| add and subtract fractions with unlike denominators, for example: $\frac{3}{5} + \frac{1}{4} = \frac{17}{20}$. | 10, 11 |
| estimate sums or differences of fractions, for example: $2\frac{3}{8} + 5\frac{1}{2}$ is a little less than 8. | 11 |
| multiply fractions, for example: $\frac{2}{3} \times \frac{5}{6} = \frac{10}{18}$ or $\frac{5}{9}$. | 12, 13, 14, 15, 16 |
| divide unit fractions, for example: $4 \div \frac{1}{7} = 28$. | 17, 18 |

**Use these skills to solve problems 1–7.**

**M** 1 Roma makes 44 ounces of salsa. She pours an equal amount into 5 containers. How much salsa does she pour in each container? Write a division expression to represent the problem and solve.

44 ounces ÷ 5 = $\frac{44}{5}$ ounces,

or $8\frac{4}{5}$ ounces

**M** 2 Which of the following does the dark gray area of the area model represent? Circle the letter of all that apply.

(A) $\frac{1}{2} \times \frac{1}{4}$

B $\frac{1}{8} \times \frac{1}{2}$

(C) $\frac{1}{4} \div 2$

D $\frac{1}{8} \div \frac{1}{2}$

**B** 3 Write one fraction from the box to make each sentence true.

a. The product $\frac{5}{2}$ or $\frac{5}{4}$ $\times \frac{3}{8}$ is greater than $\frac{3}{8}$.

b. The product $\frac{2}{3}$ or $\frac{3}{5}$ $\times \frac{3}{8}$ is less than $\frac{3}{8}$.

c. The product $\frac{4}{4}$ $\times \frac{3}{8}$ is equal to $\frac{3}{8}$.

| $\frac{2}{3}$ | | $\frac{5}{2}$ |
|---|---|---|
| | $\frac{3}{5}$ | |
| $\frac{5}{4}$ | | $\frac{4}{4}$ |

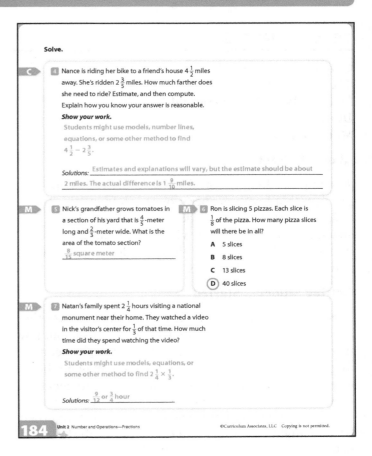

**Solve.**

**C** 4 Nance is riding her bike to a friend's house $4\frac{1}{2}$ miles away. She's ridden $2\frac{3}{5}$ miles. How much farther does she need to ride? Estimate, and then compute. Explain how you know your answer is reasonable.

***Show your work.***

Students might use models, number lines, equations, or some other method to find

$4\frac{1}{2} - 2\frac{3}{5}$.

Solutions: Estimates and explanations will vary, but the estimate should be about

2 miles. The actual difference is $1\frac{9}{10}$ miles.

**M** 5 Nick's grandfather grows tomatoes in a section of his yard that is $\frac{4}{5}$-meter long and $\frac{2}{3}$-meter wide. What is the area of the tomato section?

$\frac{8}{15}$ square meter

**M** 6 Ron is slicing 5 pizzas. Each slice is $\frac{1}{8}$ of the pizza. How many pizza slices will there be in all?

A  5 slices

B  8 slices

C  13 slices

(D) 40 slices

**M** 7 Natan's family spent $2\frac{1}{4}$ hours visiting a national monument near their home. They watched a video in the visitor's center for $\frac{1}{3}$ of that time. How much time did they spend watching the video?

***Show your work.***

Students might use models, equations, or some other method to find $2\frac{1}{4} \times \frac{1}{3}$.

Solutions: $\frac{9}{12}$ or $\frac{3}{4}$ hour

©Curriculum Associates, LLC   Copying is not permitted.

## TEACHER NOTES

**Common Core Standards:** 5.NF.A.1, 5.NF.B.4, 5.NF.B.6, 5.NF.B.7
**Standards for Mathematical Practice:** 1, 2, 3, 4, 6, 7, 8
**DOK:** 3
**Materials:** None

### About the Task

To complete this task, students solve a multi-step problem that involves operations with fractions. The task requires them to decide how many batches of snack mix they will make with given quantities of ingredients. They will use visual models and equations and explain their decisions.

### Getting Students Started

Read the problem aloud with students and go over the checklist. Talk about how to make decisions about how much of each recipe to make. For example, someone might not like certain ingredients, there may not be enough of an ingredient, etc. Discuss ways to decide how many batches to make. If students suggest making one batch and subtracting each time, suggest that their friends might be hungry and that making all the batches at once is more efficient. **(SMP 1, 2)**

### Completing the Task

Students may take different approaches to completing the first part of the task. Some may decide on a number of batches and then see if they have enough ingredients. Others may first see how many batches of one recipe they can make. Encourage students to take a systematic approach, so that they don't have to spend a lot of time guessing. Encourage them to use visual models to clarify their thinking. **(SMP 1, 4)**

To answer part 2, students must find how much of each ingredient they used for all batches. They may have already found this information in part 1 and just need to add the to find the total for all batches of each recipe. When students are finished, have them explain their process to the class and discuss the different approaches that students used. **(SMP 3, 7)**

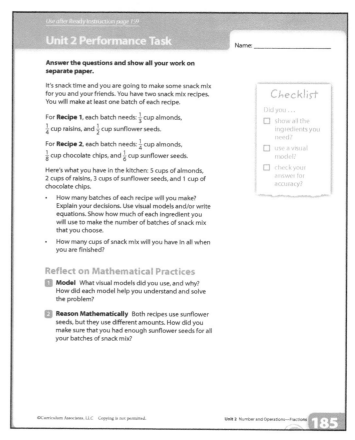

### Extension

If some students have more time to spend on this problem, you can have them solve this extension:

There's not much left in the kitchen for making snack mixes! Write a shopping list to buy more snack mix ingredients. Tell how much of each ingredient to buy, and why.

## SAMPLE RESPONSES AND RUBRIC

**4-Point Solution**

Students' solutions may also include visual models like the ones on the student book page or like other models that appear in the unit.

1. My friends and I like chocolate so I want to make a lot of recipe 2. If I use all the chocolate chips, I can make 1 cup $\div \frac{1}{8}$ cup = 8 batches. Next, I'll find what's needed for 8 batches of recipe 1 and what's left. Almonds: $8 \times \frac{1}{4} = 2$ cups; $5 - 2 = 3$ cups left. Sunflower seeds: $8 \times \frac{1}{6} = 1\frac{1}{3}$ cups; $3 - 1\frac{1}{3} = 1\frac{2}{3}$ cups left.

   Only a few of my friends like raisins so, I'll find what I need to make 2 batches of recipe 1. Almonds: $\frac{1}{3} \times 2 = \frac{2}{3}$ cup; Raisins: $\frac{1}{4} \times 2 = \frac{2}{4}$ or $\frac{1}{2}$ cup; Sunflower seeds: $\frac{1}{2} \times 2 = 1$ cup. I have more than enough ingredients to make 2 batches of recipe 2.

2. In 2 batches of recipe 1, there are $\frac{2}{3}$ cup almonds, $\frac{1}{2}$ cup raisins, and 1 cup sunflower seeds. That's $\frac{4}{6} + \frac{3}{6} + 1 = \frac{7}{6} + 1$, or $2\frac{1}{6}$ cups. In 8 batches of recipe 2, there are 2 cups almonds + $1\frac{1}{3}$ cups sunflower seeds + 1 cup of chocolate chips = $4\frac{1}{3}$ cups. In both mixes together there are $2\frac{1}{6} + 4\frac{1}{3} = 6\frac{1}{2}$ cups of snack mix.

## REFLECT ON MATHEMATICAL PRACTICES

1. Students may use any reasonable fraction model as long as they can explain their choices and the model correctly displays the fractional parts. **(SMP 4)**

2. Students may use any reasonable method for determining if there are enough sunflower seeds for their batches. They might try different combinations until they find one that works. **(SMP 2)**

## SCORING RUBRIC

**4 points**    The student has completed all parts of the problem and shows understanding of the problem. All equations and visual models are accurate. The explanation is clear and complete. The student shows the total number of cups in all batches.

**3 points**    The student has completed all parts of the problem, with one or two errors. Most of the equations and visual models are accurate. The explanation is clear and complete. The student shows how many cups were made.

**2 points**    The student has attempted all parts of the problem, with a number of errors. There are some equations and some visual models but they are not all correct. The explanation is unclear or incomplete.

**1 point**    The student has not completed all parts of the problem. There are several errors, including incorrect equations and inaccurate visual models. The explanation is unclear and incomplete.

## SOLUTION TO THE EXTENSION

**Possible Solution**

I only used $\frac{1}{2}$ cup raisins. We don't need more. I used all of the chocolate chips. I will buy 2 cups. We have $2\frac{2}{3}$ cups almonds and $\frac{1}{3}$ cups seeds left. I will buy 2 cups of each.

©Curriculum Associates, LLC    Copying is not permitted.

Lesson 19    *Use after Ready Instruction page 165*

## Evaluate and Write Expressions

Name: _____

### Solve Multiplication Word Problems

**Study the example problem showing multiplication as a way to compare two numbers. Then solve problems 1–5.**

**Example**

Isak has 7 baseball cards. He has 3 times as many basketball cards as baseball cards. How many basketball cards does he have?

You can use a bar model to help you understand the relationship between the numbers.

| baseball cards | 7 |
|---|---|

| basketball cards | 7 | 7 | 7 |
|---|---|---|---|

? 

You can describe the relationship two ways.

Use words:    What is 3 times as many as 7?

Use an equation:    $? = 3 \times 7$

Solve: $21 = 3 \times 7$    Isak has 21 basketball cards.

**M  1**  Draw and label a bar model to show the number that is 7 times as many as 3. Then complete the equation.

| 3 |
|---|

| 3 | 3 | 3 | 3 | 3 | 3 | 3 |
|---|---|---|---|---|---|---|

21

__21__ = 7 × 3

**B  2**  How does 21 compare to 7? How does 21 compare to 3? Write the numbers to describe the relationships.

21 is __3__ times as many as 7.

21 is __7__ times as many as 3.

©Curriculum Associates, LLC   Copying is not permitted.

Lesson 19 Evaluate and Write Expressions **195**

---

**Solve.**

**M  3**  Lauren babysat over the summer. In June she had $20 dollars. At the end of August she had 12 times that amount. How much money did Lauren have at the end of August?

*Show your work.*

Possible student work:

$12 \times 20 = 240$

*Solution:* __$240__

**M  4**  Kyle swam 4 laps in the pool on Monday. He swam 6 times as many laps on Tuesday. Choose *True* or *False* for each statement.

a.  The expression 6 × 4 represents the number of laps Kyle swam on Tuesday.    ☒ True  ☐ False

b.  The words *6 times as many as 4* represents the number of laps Kyle swam on Tuesday.    ☒ True  ☐ False

c.  The number of laps Kyle swam on Tuesday can be found by solving the equation ? = 6 × 4.    ☒ True  ☐ False

d.  Kyle swam 10 laps on Tuesday.    ☐ True  ☒ False

**C  5**  Mrs. Altman's class recycled 72 water bottles in March. The number of juice cans they recycled was $\frac{1}{4}$ times as many. What is the total number of water bottles and juice cans they recycled in March?

*Show your work.*

Possible student work:

$\frac{1}{4} \times 72 = \frac{72}{4} = 18$     $18 + 72 = 90$

*Solution:* __90 bottles and cans__

**196** Lesson 19 Evaluate and Write Expressions

©Curriculum Associates, LLC   Copying is not permitted.

---

Lesson 19 • *Use after Ready Instruction page 167*

Name: _____

### Evaluate Expressions

**Study the example problem showing two ways to think about an expression that has parentheses. Then solve problems 1–6.**

**Example**

Ms. Nakos works 4 hours on Mondays and 8 hours on Tuesdays in the school library. During one week in May she worked $\frac{1}{4}$ of her regular hours. Evaluate the expression $\frac{1}{4} \times (4 + 8)$ to find the number of hours she worked that week.

To understand the problem you can:

Use a picture.

$\frac{1}{4}$ of (4 + 8)

Monday Hours + Tuesday Hours

| M | T T |
|---|---|
| M | T T |
| M | T T |
| M | T T |

Use words.

$\frac{1}{4}$    ×    (4 + 8)

↑ One fourth    ↑ of    ↑ the sum of the number of Monday and Tuesday hours

$\frac{1}{4} \times (4 + 8) = \frac{1}{4} \times 12 = \frac{12}{4} = 3$

Ms. Nakos worked 3 hours that week.

**C  1**  Look at the expression in the example. There are parentheses around 4 + 8 to show it is to be evaluated first. Are the parentheses necessary? Explain.

Yes. Possible explanation: If you multiplied $\frac{1}{4}$ × 4 first, then added 8, you would get 9

as the answer instead of 3. You need to find $\frac{1}{4}$ of the total number of hours, not just the

4 hours she works on Monday.

**B  2**  The expression $\frac{1}{2} \times (4 + 8)$ represents the number of hours Ms. Nakos works the last week of school. Evaluate the expression to find the number of hours she works that week.

6 hours

**Vocabulary**

**evaluate** to find the value of an expression.

3 × 5 is 15.

©Curriculum Associates, LLC   Copying is not permitted.

Lesson 19 Evaluate and Write Expressions **197**

---

**Solve.**

**M  3**  Each day, Theo walks his dog 15 minutes in the morning and 25 minutes in the afternoon. Evaluate the expression 7 × (15 + 25) to find how many minutes Theo walks his dog each week.

*Show your work.*

Possible student work:

$7 \times (15 + 25) = 7 \times 40$

$= 280$

*Solution:* __280 minutes__

**M  4**  Lin, Mac, and Starr spend $6 on supplies to set up a lemonade stand. They sell $21 worth of lemonade. They are going to share the money equally. Evaluate the expression (21 − 6) ÷ 3 to find how much money each one will make.

*Show your work.*

Possible student work:

$(21 - 6) \div 3 = 15 \div 3$

$= 5$

*Solution:* __$5__

**B  5**  Which of the following shows another way to write the expression (21 − 6) ÷ 3?

A  $\frac{21 - 6}{3}$     C  $\frac{21}{3} - 6$

B  $\frac{3}{21 - 6}$     D  $21 - \frac{6}{3}$

**M  6**  Describe what happens if you divide a difference by 3.

Answers will vary. Possible answer: The value is one-third that of the original

difference.

**198** Lesson 19 Evaluate and Write Expressions

©Curriculum Associates, LLC   Copying is not permitted.

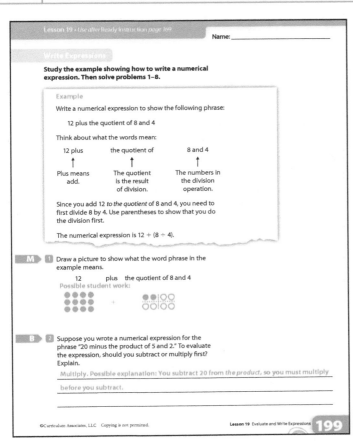

Lesson 19 • Use after Ready Instruction page 169

Name: _____

**Write Expressions**

Study the example showing how to write a numerical expression. Then solve problems 1–8.

**Example**

Write a numerical expression to show the following phrase:

12 plus the quotient of 8 and 4

Think about what the words mean:

12 plus　　the quotient of　　8 and 4

Plus means add.　The quotient is the result of division.　The numbers in the division operation.

Since you add 12 *to the quotient* of 8 and 4, you need to first divide 8 by 4. Use parentheses to show that you do the division first.

The numerical expression is $12 + (8 ÷ 4)$.

**1** Draw a picture to show what the word phrase in the example means.

12　　plus　　the quotient of 8 and 4

Possible student work:

**2** Suppose you wrote a numerical expression for the phrase "20 minus the product of 5 and 2." To evaluate the expression, should you subtract or multiply first? Explain.

Multiply. Possible explanation: You subtract 20 from *the product*, so you must multiply before you subtract.

---

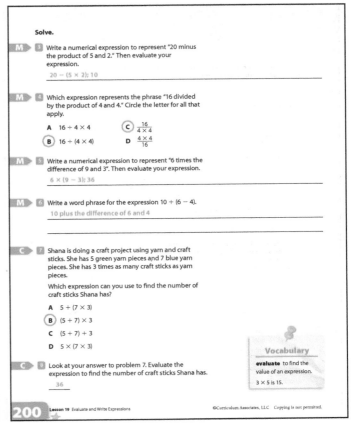

**Solve.**

**3** Write a numerical expression to represent "20 minus the product of 5 and 2." Then evaluate your expression.

$20 - (5 × 2)$; 10

**4** Which expression represents the phrase "16 divided by the product of 4 and 4." Circle the letter for all that apply.

A　$16 ÷ 4 × 4$　　C　$\frac{16}{4 × 4}$

B　$16 ÷ (4 × 4)$　　D　$\frac{4 × 4}{16}$

**5** Write a numerical expression to represent "6 times the difference of 9 and 3". Then evaluate your expression.

$6 × (9 - 3)$; 36

**6** Write a word phrase for the expression $10 + (6 - 4)$.

10 plus the difference of 6 and 4

**7** Shana is doing a craft project using yarn and craft sticks. She has 5 green yarn pieces and 7 blue yarn pieces. She has 3 times as many craft sticks as yarn pieces.

Which expression can you use to find the number of craft sticks Shana has?

A　$5 + (7 × 3)$

B　$(5 + 7) × 3$

C　$(5 + 7) + 3$

D　$5 × (7 × 3)$

**8** Look at your answer to problem 7. Evaluate the expression to find the number of craft sticks Shana has.

36

**Vocabulary**

**evaluate** to find the value of an expression.

$3 × 5$ is 15.

©Curriculum Associates, LLC　Copying is not permitted.

---

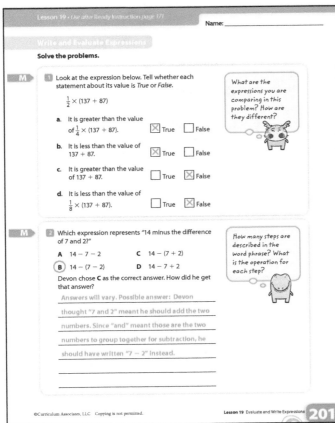

Lesson 19 • Use after Ready Instruction page 171

Name: _____

**Write and Evaluate Expressions**

Solve the problems.

**1** Look at the expression below. Tell whether each statement about its value is *True* or *False*.

$\frac{1}{2} × (137 + 87)$

a. It is greater than the value of $\frac{1}{4} × (137 + 87)$.　☒ True　☐ False

b. It is less than the value of $137 + 87$.　☒ True　☐ False

c. It is greater than the value of $137 + 87$.　☐ True　☒ False

d. It is less than the value of $\frac{1}{8} × (137 + 87)$.　☐ True　☒ False

*What are the expressions you are comparing in this problem? How are they different?*

**2** Which expression represents "14 minus the difference of 7 and 2?"

A　$14 - 7 - 2$　　C　$14 - (7 + 2)$

B　$14 - (7 - 2)$　　D　$14 - 7 + 2$

Devon chose **C** as the correct answer. How did he get that answer?

Answers will vary. Possible answer: Devon thought "7 and 2" meant he should add the two numbers. Since "and" meant those are the two numbers to group together for subtraction, he should have written "7 – 2" instead.

*How many steps are described in the word phrase? What is the operation for each step?*

---

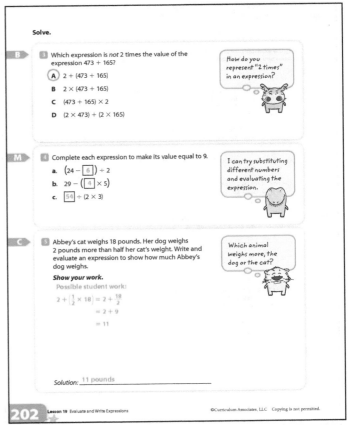

**Solve.**

**3** Which expression is *not* 2 times the value of the expression $473 + 165$?

A　$2 + (473 + 165)$

B　$2 × (473 + 165)$

C　$(473 + 165) × 2$

D　$(2 × 473) + (2 × 165)$

*How do you represent "2 times" in an expression?*

**4** Complete each expression to make its value equal to 9.

a.　$(24 - \boxed{6}) ÷ 2$

b.　$29 - (\boxed{4} × 5)$

c.　$\boxed{54} ÷ (2 × 3)$

*I can try substituting different numbers and evaluating the expression.*

**5** Abbey's cat weighs 18 pounds. Her dog weighs 2 pounds more than half her cat's weight. Write and evaluate an expression to show how much Abbey's dog weighs.

*Which animal weighs more, the dog or the cat?*

**Show your work.**

Possible student work:

$2 + \left(\frac{1}{2} × 18\right) = 2 + \frac{18}{2}$
$= 2 + 9$
$= 11$

Solution: 11 pounds

©Curriculum Associates, LLC　Copying is not permitted.

Lesson 20          *Use after Ready Instruction page 175*

## Analyze Patterns and Relationships          Name: _____

### Find Number Patterns

**Study the example of using a number line to describe and extend a number pattern. Then solve problems 1–6.**

**Example**

Elaine wrote the pattern below.

3, 6, 9, 12, 15

What is the rule for the pattern? What would be the next number in the pattern?

A number line can help you find a pattern.

```
        +3    +3    +3    +3
   ◄──┬───┬───┬───┬───┬───┬───►
      0   3   6   9   12  15  18
```

The rule for the pattern is "add 3." The next number would be 15 + 3, or 18.

**M** ▸ **1** Harry looks at the example and says you multiply 3 by 2 to get 6, so the rule is "multiply by 2." Can you use this rule to describe the pattern in the example problem? Explain.

No. Possible explanation: The rule of a pattern must work for all the numbers in the

pattern. The number after 6 is 9. If you multiply 6 by 2 you get 12, not 9.

_____

**M** ▸ **2** What other pattern(s) do you see in the set of numbers in the example?

Answers will vary. Possible answers: The numbers follow a pattern of odd, even, odd,

even.

---

**Solve.**

**M** ▸ **3** Use the same rule as in the example, "add 3," but start at 1. Write the next 3 numbers in the pattern. Use the number line to show the pattern.

1, __4__, __7__, __10__

```
        +3    +3    +3
   ◄──┬──┬──┬──┬──┬──┬──┬──┬──┬──┬──┬──►
      0  2  4  6  8  10 12 14 16 18 20
```

**M** ▸ **4** Tell whether each statement is *True* or *False* for the following pattern.

1, 5, 9, 13, 17, 21

a. The rule is "multiply by 5."  ☐ True  ☒ False

b. The rule is "add 4."  ☒ True  ☐ False

c. If the pattern continues, the next number will be an even number.  ☐ True  ☒ False

d. If the pattern continues, the next number will be an odd number.  ☒ True  ☐ False

**M** ▸ **5** The rule for a pattern is "multiply by 10." Write the next 3 numbers in the pattern.

7, __70__, __700__, __7,000__

**C** ▸ **6** Look at the pattern below.

45, 39, 33, 27, 21, 15

a. What is the rule for the pattern?

Subtract 6.

b. If the pattern continues, what would be the next number?

__9__

---

Lesson 20 • *Use after Ready Instruction page 177*

Name: _____

### Compare Two Numerical Patterns

**Study the example problem showing one way to identify relationships between two numerical patterns. Then solve problems 1–6.**

**Example**

The school store sells laces and decals in the school colors. Laces cost $1, and decals cost $5. Write ordered pairs to compare the cost of laces to decals for selling 0, 1, 2, 3, 4, and 5 of each item.

Use a table to show the two numerical patterns. Then write the corresponding terms as ordered pairs.

The cost of laces pattern follows the rule "add 1."
0, 1, 2, 3, 4, 5

The cost of decals pattern follows the rule "add 5."
0, 5, 10, 15, 20, 25

| Cost of Laces (Add 1) | Cost of Decals (Add 5) | Ordered Pairs |
|---|---|---|
| 0 | 0 | (0, 0) |
| 1 | 5 | (1, 5) |
| 2 | 10 | (2, 10) |
| 3 | 15 | (3, 15) |
| 4 | 20 | (4, 20) |
| 5 | 25 | (5, 25) |

**B** ▸ **1** Look at the example. What is the cost for 6 decals? Explain how you got your answer.

$30. Student explanations may indicate that they continued the pattern of "add 5," or

multiplied 6 by 5.

**M** ▸ **2** Look at the example. How are the terms in the cost of decals pattern related to the corresponding terms in the cost of laces pattern?

Answers will vary. Possible answer: The terms in the decals pattern are always 5 times

the corresponding terms in the laces pattern.

---

**Solve.**

**C** ▸ **3** Suppose school bookmarks cost $3 each. Complete the table to show how the terms in this pattern compare to the corresponding terms in the pattern for the cost of laces.

| Cost of Laces | Cost of Bookmarks | Ordered Pairs |
|---|---|---|
| 0 | 0 | (0, 0) |
| 1 | 3 | (1, 3) |
| 2 | 6 | (2, 6) |
| 3 | 9 | (3, 9) |
| 4 | 12 | (4, 12) |
| 5 | 15 | (5, 15) |

**M** ▸ **4** Look at problem 3. How do the corresponding terms of the two patterns compare?

Answers will vary. Possible answer: The terms in the second pattern are always 3 times

the corresponding terms in the first pattern.

**M** ▸ **5** Look at problem 3. What is the rule for finding the cost of bookmarks?

Add 3.

**M** ▸ **6** Look at problem 3. If the table was continued, which ordered pair could be in it? Circle the letter for all that apply.

A (8, 21)          C (12, 36)

**B** (10, 30)          D (15, 60)

**Vocabulary**

**corresponding terms** the numbers that are in the same place in two or more related patterns.

**ordered pair** a pair of numbers that locate a point on a coordinate plane.

---

Lesson 20 · Use after Ready Instruction page 179

Name: _____

**Graph Ordered Pairs**

**Study the example comparing two patterns on a graph. Then solve problems 1–8.**

**Example**

Luke compared a numeric pattern with the rule "add 2" to a pattern with the rule "add 6."

He started at 0 and wrote the first three numbers of each pattern.
add 2: 0, 2, 4
add 6: 0, 6, 12

He wrote three ordered pairs:
(0, 0)    (2, 6)    (4, 12)

Then he plotted the ordered pairs on a graph.

The first number in each ordered pair shows the location on the *x*-axis.

The second number in each ordered pair shows the location on the *y*-axis.

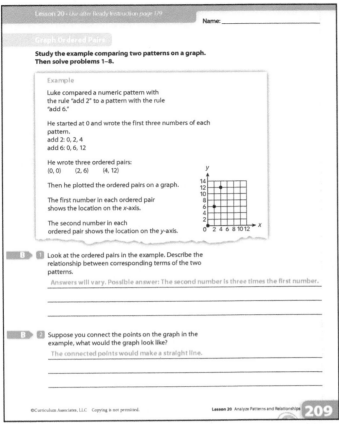

**B** 1 Look at the ordered pairs in the example. Describe the relationship between corresponding terms of the two patterns.

Answers will vary. Possible answer: The second number is three times the first number.

**B** 2 Suppose you connect the points on the graph in the example, what would the graph look like?

The connected points would make a straight line.

©Curriculum Associates, LLC   Copying is not permitted.          Lesson 20 Analyze Patterns and Relationships **209**

---

**Solve.**

At a bake sale, cookies are sold in packages of 4 and fruit bars are sold in packages of 2.

**M** 3 Complete the table comparing the number of cookies and fruit bars sold for 0, 1, 2, and 3 packages.

| Number of Cookies (x) | Number of Fruit Bars (y) | Ordered Pairs (x, y) |
|---|---|---|
| 0 | 0 | (0, 0) |
| 4 | 2 | (4, 2) |
| 8 | 4 | (8, 4) |
| 12 | 6 | (12, 6) |

**M** 4 What is the rule for the number of cookies pattern?

Add 4.

**M** 5 What is the rule for the number of fruit bars pattern?

Add 2.

**M** 6 Plot the ordered pairs on the coordinate plane to the right.

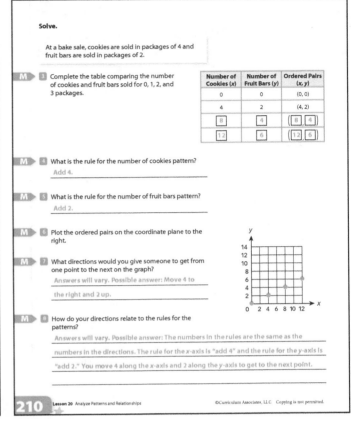

**M** 7 What directions would you give someone to get from one point to the next on the graph?

Answers will vary. Possible answer: Move 4 to the right and 2 up.

**M** 8 How do your directions relate to the rules for the patterns?

Answers will vary. Possible answer: The numbers in the rules are the same as the numbers in the directions. The rule for the x-axis is "add 4" and the rule for the y-axis is "add 2." You move 4 along the x-axis and 2 along the y-axis to get to the next point.

**210** Lesson 20 Analyze Patterns and Relationships          ©Curriculum Associates, LLC   Copying is not permitted.

---

Lesson 20 · Use after Ready Instruction page 181

Name: _____

**Analyze Patterns and Relationships**

**Solve the problems.**

**M** 1 How do the corresponding terms compare in a pattern that has the rule "add 3" and a pattern that has the rule "add 9"? Start each pattern at 0.

*How do I generate the patterns?*

**Show your work.**

Add 3: 0, 3, 6, 9, 12, . . .

Add 9: 0, 9, 18, 27, 36, . . . .

Solution: ___ Answers will vary. Possible answer: The terms in the pattern for "add 9" are three times the corresponding terms in the pattern for "add 3."

**M** 2 Peg is counting nickels and dimes and comparing the values for 0, 1, 2, and 3 coins in a table. What ordered pair will Peg write next? Circle the letter of the correct answer.

*How many coins does the next row of the table represent?*

| Value of Nickels (x) | Value of Dimes (y) | Ordered Pairs (x, y) |
|---|---|---|
| 0 | 0 | (0, 0) |
| 5 | 10 | (5, 10) |
| 10 | 20 | (10, 20) |

**A** (20, 40)          **C** (15, 40)

**B** (20, 30)          **(D)** (15, 30)

Leroy chose **A** as the correct answer. How did he get that answer?

Answers will vary. Possible answer: Leroy thought the rule for both the nickel and dime patterns was "multiply by 2" instead of "add 5" and "add 10."

©Curriculum Associates, LLC   Copying is not permitted.          Lesson 20 Analyze Patterns and Relationships **211**

---

**Solve.**

**B** 3 Complete the table for the rules "add 6" and "add 2."

*How do you know which number to write first in an ordered pair?*

| Add 6 | Add 2 | Ordered Pairs (x, y) |
|---|---|---|
| 0 | 0 | (0, 0) |
| 6 | 2 | (6, 2) |
| 12 | 4 | (12, 4) |
| 18 | 6 | (18, 6) |

**C** 4 Plot the ordered pairs from problem 3 on the coordinate plane below.

How do the corresponding terms in the patterns compare?

*Do you move along the x-axis or y-axis first when you plot ordered pairs on a graph?*

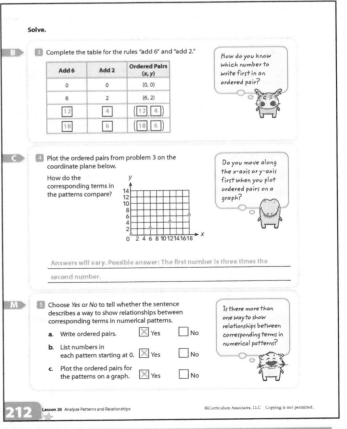

Answers will vary. Possible answer: The first number is three times the second number.

**M** 5 Choose *Yes* or *No* to tell whether the sentence describes a way to show relationships between corresponding terms in numerical patterns.

*Is there more than one way to show relationships between corresponding terms in numerical patterns?*

a.  Write ordered pairs.        ☒ Yes    ☐ No

b.  List numbers in each pattern starting at 0.    ☒ Yes    ☐ No

c.  Plot the ordered pairs for the patterns on a graph.    ☒ Yes    ☐ No

**212** Lesson 20 Analyze Patterns and Relationships          ©Curriculum Associates, LLC   Copying is not permitted.

---

©Curriculum Associates, LLC   Copying is not permitted.

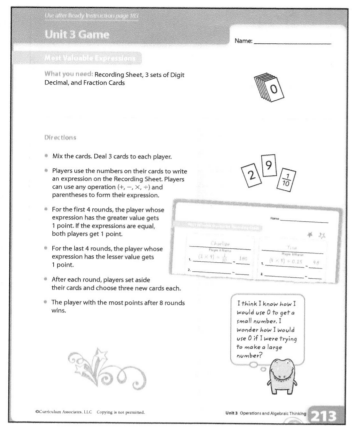

## STEP BY STEP

| | |
|---|---|
| **CCSS Focus** - 5.OA.A.1 *Embedded SMPs* - 2, 3, 7, 8 <br> **Objective:** Write and evaluate expressions containing parentheses, using whole numbers, fractions, and decimals. | **Materials** For each pair: Recording Sheet (TR 4), 3 sets of Digit, Decimal, and Fraction Cards (TR 5) |

- The goal of this game is to write expressions with the greater or lesser value.

- Mix the cards. Deal 3 cards to each player.

- Players use the numbers on their cards to write an expression on the Recording Sheet.

- Each player will evaluate their expression to determine its value.

- For the first 4 rounds, the player whose expression has the greater value gets 1 point. If the expressions are equal, both players get 1 point.

- For the last 4 rounds, the player whose expression has the lesser value gets 1 point.

- After each round, players set aside their cards and choose three new cards each.

- The player with the most points after 8 rounds wins.

- Read the directions aloud. Model one turn for students before they play. Afterwards, discuss strategies for maximizing the value of these expressions. Ask, *How do the grouping symbols affect the value of your expression?*

**Vary the Game** Use 4 numbers for each round and require 2 sets of parentheses and 2 different operations. Play 6 rounds.

**Extra Support** Play the same game, using only the whole-number cards.

©Curriculum Associates, LLC   Copying is not permitted.

*Use after Ready Instruction page 183*

## Unit 3 Practice

Name: _____

**Operations and Algebraic Thinking**

| In this unit you learned to: | Lesson |
|---|---|
| evaluate expressions, for example: 48 ÷ (6 + 10) = 3. | 19 |
| write expressions, for example: "subtract 5 from 12, then multiply by 4" can be written as (12 − 5) × 4. | 19 |
| find the relationship between two sequences, for example: sequence 1: 0, 2, 4, 6, 8, . . . sequence 2: 0, 8, 16, 24, 32, . . . Each term in sequence 2 is 4 times the corresponding term in sequence 1. | 20 |
| create ordered pairs for two sequences and graph the relationship on the coordinate plane, for example: ordered pairs for sequence 1 and 2 above are (0, 0), (2, 8), (4, 16), (6, 24), (8, 32). | 20 |

**Use these skills to solve problems 1–5.**

**M** ▶ 1 Replace ☐ with a number from the box to write the expression described.

| 6 | 10 | 8 |
|---|---|---|
| 14 | 9 | 7 |

$12 \times (☐ - 5)$

a. The expression with the greatest value.

$12 \times (\boxed{14} - 5)$

b. The expression with the least value.

$12 \times (\boxed{6} - 5)$

**M** ▶ 2 Write numerical expressions for "the quotient of 18 and 6, plus 3" and "18 divided by the sum of 6 and 3." Compare the expressions using <, >, or =.

$\underline{(18 \div 6) + 3}$  Ⓖ  $\underline{18 \div (6 + 3)}$

**Solve.**

**M** ▶ 3 Begin at 0 and use the rules "add 3" and "add 1" to complete the table. Then plot the ordered pairs on the graph.

| Add 3 (x) | Add 1 (y) | Ordered Pairs (x, y) |
|---|---|---|
| 0 | 0 | (0, 0) |
| 3 | 1 | (3, 1) |
| 6 | 2 | (6, 2) |
| 9 | 3 | (9, 3) |

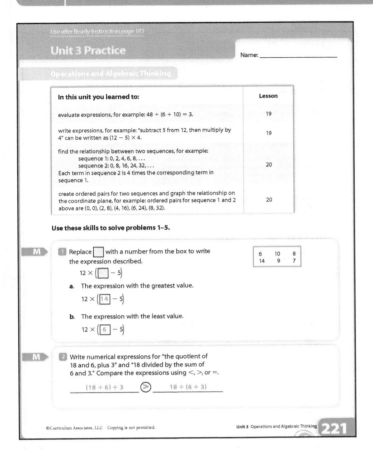

**M** ▶ 4 Look at the ordered pairs in problem 3. How do the values of the x-coordinates compare to the values of the y-coordinates?

Ⓐ They are 3 times as great.

B They are $\frac{1}{3}$ as great.

C They are 4 times as great.

D They are $\frac{1}{4}$ as great.

**C** ▶ 5 If you were to connect the points on the graph in problem 3, what would the graph look like?

Answers will vary. Possible answer: The connected points would make a straight

line.

## TEACHER NOTES

**Common Core Standards:** 5.OA.B.3
**Standards for Mathematical Practice:** 1, 2, 4, 7, 8
**DOK:** 3
**Materials:** graph paper

### About the Task

In this task, students make decisions in order to keep a cost within a given range. Then they investigate numeric sequences based on the rules that come from the choices they made. They form ordered pairs and use the resulting graph or chart to find an additional value.

### Getting Students Started

Read the problem aloud with students and go over the checklist. Have students discuss various strategies for deciding which flowers to use. Remind students to keep the acceptable price range in mind as they work. **(SMP 1)**

### Completing the Task

Some students will recognize immediately that the number of flowers in one vase is the number that is added each time, i.e., the rule for that type of flower. Others will need the concrete experience of completing the chart in order to discern the rule. Check that students keep the first and second terms of each ordered pair in the correct order.

Some students may struggle with creating their own graph. Ask, *How do you know what the greatest number should be on the x-axis? On the y-axis?* Guide them to see that the labels need to accommodate at least the quantities on their chart. **(SMP 2, 4)**

Some students may be tempted to find the number of flowers for 9 tables without using the table or the graph. Challenge them to stick with the rule—or the graph—so that they can see how the relationship between the two quantities is maintained. **(SMP 7)**

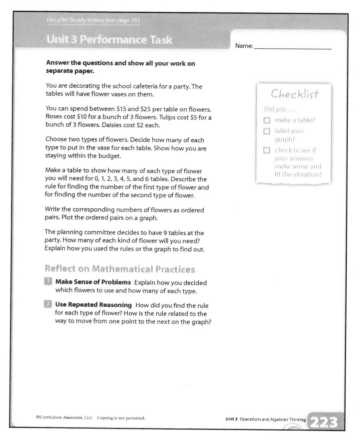

### Extension

If some students have more time to spend on this problem, you can have them solve this extension:

What is the relationship between the number of the second type of flower in 1 vase and the number of the first type of flower in the same vase? Is this relationship the same or different for the flowers in all vases? Explain how you know.

©Curriculum Associates, LLC   Copying is not permitted.

## SAMPLE RESPONSES AND RUBRIC

### 4-Point Solution

I tried different combinations of flowers and found the prices. I decided to use 3 roses and 5 daisies in each vase. That's $10 for roses and $10 for daisies, which equals $20. $20 is between $15 and $25.

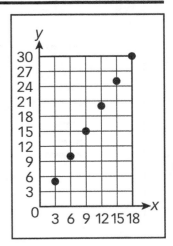

To find the number of roses for different number of tables, keep adding 3. For daisies, keep adding 5. The rule for roses is +3 and for daisies +5.

I used the rules to find how many flowers I need for 9 tables. If I add 3 nine times, that's 3 × 9, which is 27 roses. If I add 5 nine times that's 9 × 5, which is 45 daisies.

| Roses (x) | Daisies (y) | Ordered Pairs (x, y) |
|---|---|---|
| 0 | 0 | (0, 0) |
| 3 | 5 | (3, 5) |
| 6 | 10 | (6, 10) |
| 9 | 15 | (9, 15) |
| 12 | 20 | (12, 20) |
| 15 | 25 | (15, 25) |
| 18 | 30 | (18, 30) |

## REFLECT ON MATHEMATICAL PRACTICES

1.  Look for responses that describe multiplying the cost per flower and the proposed quantity. Some students may write an expression for each flower's cost. **(SMP 2)**

2.  Students should recognize that the first flower is seen in equal jumps along the x-axis and the second flower's rule is seen in equal jumps along the y-axis. **(SMP 4, 8)**

## SCORING RUBRIC

**4 points**   The student has correctly completed all parts of the problem. The cost of the two kinds of flowers falls between $15 and $25. The rule for each and the graph and chart are correct. The student correctly uses precise language to explain how to find the number of flowers for 9 tables.

**3 points**   There are one or two errors in the solution. For example, the rule for the number of one type of flower may not be correct of the graph or chart may contain an error. The explanation for finding the number of flowers for 9 tables is accurate although maybe not as precise as it could be.

**2 points**   The student has attempted all parts of the problem with a number of errors. The cost of the flowers may not fit the given range. The graph and/or chart are incomplete or incorrect. The explanation of the flowers for 9 tables may be inaccurate or lack detail.

**1 point**    The student has not completed all parts of the problem. The graph and/or chart is missing. The cost of the flowers is incorrect or incomplete. The explanation of the flowers for 9 tables is inaccurate.

## SOLUTION TO THE EXTENSION

### Possible Solution

If one vase has 5 of the second type of flower (y) and 3 of the first type of flower (x), the number of the second type of flower is $\frac{y}{x}$, or $\frac{5}{3}$ times the number of the first. The relationship is the same for all vases because the same rules were used to create all the numbers.

©Curriculum Associates, LLC   Copying is not permitted.

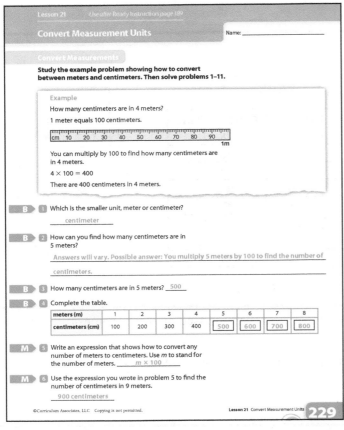

Lesson 21 *Use after Ready Instruction page 189*

**Convert Measurement Units**

Name: _____

**Convert Measurements**

Study the example problem showing how to convert between meters and centimeters. Then solve problems 1–11.

**Example**

How many centimeters are in 4 meters?

1 meter equals 100 centimeters.

| cm 10 20 30 40 50 60 70 80 90 |
| 1m |

You can multiply by 100 to find how many centimeters are in 4 meters.

$4 \times 100 = 400$

There are 400 centimeters in 4 meters.

**B** **1** Which is the smaller unit, meter or centimeter?

_____centimeter_____

**B** **2** How can you find how many centimeters are in 5 meters?

Answers will vary. Possible answer: You multiply 5 meters by 100 to find the number of

centimeters.

**B** **3** How many centimeters are in 5 meters? __500__

**B** **4** Complete the table.

| meters (m) | 1 | 2 | 3 | 4 | 5 | 6 | 7 | 8 |
|---|---|---|---|---|---|---|---|---|
| centimeters (cm) | 100 | 200 | 300 | 400 | 500 | 600 | 700 | 800 |

**M** **5** Write an expression that shows how to convert any number of meters to centimeters. Use *m* to stand for the number of meters. ___$m \times 100$___

**M** **6** Use the expression you wrote in problem 5 to find the number of centimeters in 9 meters.

___900 centimeters___

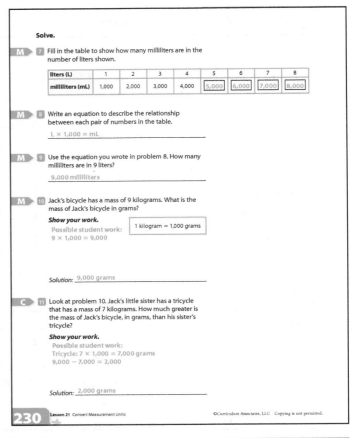

**Solve.**

**M** **7** Fill in the table to show how many milliliters are in the number of liters shown.

| liters (L) | 1 | 2 | 3 | 4 | 5 | 6 | 7 | 8 |
|---|---|---|---|---|---|---|---|---|
| milliliters (mL) | 1,000 | 2,000 | 3,000 | 4,000 | 5,000 | 6,000 | 7,000 | 8,000 |

**M** **8** Write an equation to describe the relationship between each pair of numbers in the table.

___$L \times 1,000 = mL$___

**M** **9** Use the equation you wrote in problem 8. How many milliliters are in 9 liters?

___9,000 milliliters___

**M** **10** Jack's bicycle has a mass of 9 kilograms. What is the mass of Jack's bicycle in grams?

**Show your work.**

Possible student work:    | 1 kilogram = 1,000 grams |

$9 \times 1,000 = 9,000$

Solution: __9,000 grams__

**C** **11** Look at problem 10. Jack's little sister has a tricycle that has a mass of 7 kilograms. How much greater is the mass of Jack's bicycle, in grams, than his sister's tricycle?

**Show your work.**

Possible student work:

Tricycle: $7 \times 1,000 = 7,000$ grams

$9,000 - 7,000 = 2,000$

Solution: __2,000 grams__

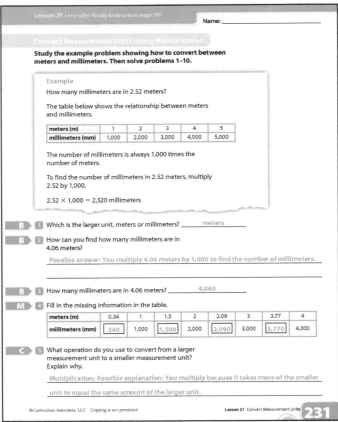

Lesson 21 • *Use after Ready Instruction page 191*

Name: _____

**Convert Measurement Units Using Multiplication**

Study the example problem showing how to convert between meters and millimeters. Then solve problems 1–10.

**Example**

How many millimeters are in 2.52 meters?

The table below shows the relationship between meters and millimeters.

| meters (m) | 1 | 2 | 3 | 4 | 5 |
|---|---|---|---|---|---|
| millimeters (mm) | 1,000 | 2,000 | 3,000 | 4,000 | 5,000 |

The number of millimeters is always 1,000 times the number of meters.

To find the number of millimeters in 2.52 meters, multiply 2.52 by 1,000.

$2.52 \times 1,000 = 2,520$ millimeters

**B** **1** Which is the larger unit, meters or millimeters? ___meters___

**B** **2** How can you find how many millimeters are in 4.06 meters?

Possible answer: You multiply 4.06 meters by 1,000 to find the number of millimeters.

**B** **3** How many millimeters are in 4.06 meters? ___4,060___

**M** **4** Fill in the missing information in the table.

| meters (m) | 0.34 | 1 | 1.5 | 2 | 2.09 | 3 | 3.77 | 4 |
|---|---|---|---|---|---|---|---|---|
| millimeters (mm) | 340 | 1,000 | 1,500 | 2,000 | 2,090 | 3,000 | 3,770 | 4,000 |

**C** **5** What operation do you use to convert from a larger measurement unit to a smaller measurement unit? Explain why.

Multiplication; Possible explanation: You multiply because it takes more of the smaller

unit to equal the same amount of the larger unit.

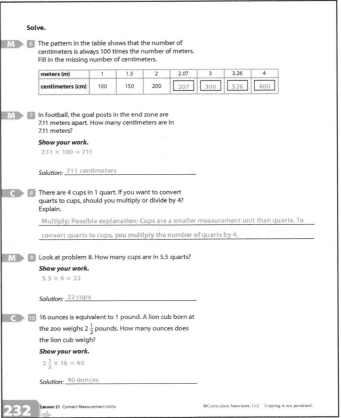

**Solve.**

**M** **6** The pattern in the table shows that the number of centimeters is always 100 times the number of meters. Fill in the missing number of centimeters.

| meters (m) | 1 | 1.5 | 2 | 2.07 | 3 | 3.26 | 4 |
|---|---|---|---|---|---|---|---|
| centimeters (cm) | 100 | 150 | 200 | 207 | 300 | 326 | 400 |

**M** **7** In football, the goal posts in the end zone are 7.11 meters apart. How many centimeters are in 7.11 meters?

**Show your work.**

$7.11 \times 100 = 711$

Solution: __711 centimeters__

**C** **8** There are 4 cups in 1 quart. If you want to convert quarts to cups, should you multiply or divide by 4? Explain.

Multiply; Possible explanation: Cups are a smaller measurement unit than quarts. To

convert quarts to cups, you multiply the number of quarts by 4.

**M** **9** Look at problem 8. How many cups are in 5.5 quarts?

**Show your work.**

$5.5 \times 4 = 22$

Solution: __22 cups__

**C** **10** 16 ounces is equivalent to 1 pound. A lion cub born at the zoo weighs $2\frac{1}{2}$ pounds. How many ounces does the lion cub weigh?

**Show your work.**

$2\frac{1}{2} \times 16 = 40$

Solution: __40 ounces__

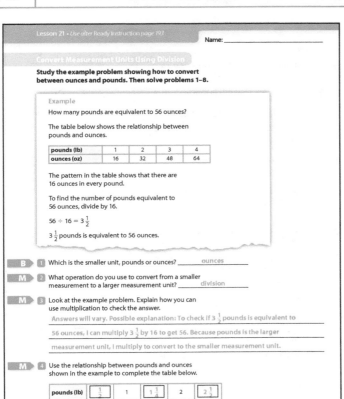

Lesson 21 • Use after Ready Instruction page 191

Name: _____

### Convert Measurement Units Using Division

**Study the example problem showing how to convert between ounces and pounds. Then solve problems 1–8.**

> **Example**
>
> How many pounds are equivalent to 56 ounces?
>
> The table below shows the relationship between pounds and ounces.
>
> | pounds (lb) | 1 | 2 | 3 | 4 |
> |---|---|---|---|---|
> | ounces (oz) | 16 | 32 | 48 | 64 |
>
> The pattern in the table shows that there are 16 ounces in every pound.
>
> To find the number of pounds equivalent to 56 ounces, divide by 16.
>
> $56 \div 16 = 3\frac{1}{2}$
>
> $3\frac{1}{2}$ pounds is equivalent to 56 ounces.

**B** 1 Which is the smaller unit, pounds or ounces? _____ounces_____

**M** 2 What operation do you use to convert from a smaller measurement to a larger measurement unit? _____division_____

**M** 3 Look at the example problem. Explain how you can use multiplication to check the answer.

Answers will vary. Possible explanation: To check if $3\frac{1}{2}$ pounds is equivalent to

56 ounces, I can multiply $3\frac{1}{2}$ by 16 to get 56. Because pounds is the larger

measurement unit, I multiply to convert to the smaller measurement unit.

**M** 4 Use the relationship between pounds and ounces shown in the example to complete the table below.

| pounds (lb) | $\frac{1}{2}$ | 1 | $1\frac{1}{2}$ | 2 | $2\frac{1}{2}$ |
|---|---|---|---|---|---|
| ounces (oz) | 8 | 16 | 20 | 32 | 40 |

©Curriculum Associates, LLC   Copying is not permitted.

Lesson 21  Convert Measurement Units **233**

---

**234**  Lesson 21  Convert Measurement Units

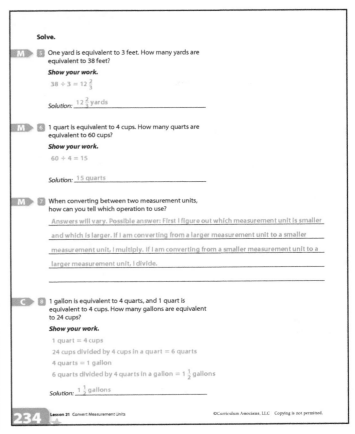

**Solve.**

**M** 5 One yard is equivalent to 3 feet. How many yards are equivalent to 38 feet?

**Show your work.**

$38 \div 3 = 12\frac{2}{3}$

Solution: $12\frac{2}{3}$ yards _____

**M** 6 1 quart is equivalent to 4 cups. How many quarts are equivalent to 60 cups?

**Show your work.**

$60 \div 4 = 15$

Solution: 15 quarts _____

**M** 7 When converting between two measurement units, how can you tell which operation to use?

Answers will vary. Possible answer: First I figure out which measurement unit is smaller

and which is larger. If I am converting from a larger measurement unit to a smaller

measurement unit, I multiply. If I am converting from a smaller measurement unit to a

larger measurement unit, I divide.

**C** 8 1 gallon is equivalent to 4 quarts, and 1 quart is equivalent to 4 cups. How many gallons are equivalent to 24 cups?

**Show your work.**

1 quart = 4 cups

24 cups divided by 4 cups in a quart = 6 quarts

4 quarts = 1 gallon

6 quarts divided by 4 quarts in a gallon = $1\frac{1}{2}$ gallons

Solution: $1\frac{1}{2}$ gallons

©Curriculum Associates, LLC   Copying is not permitted.

---

Lesson 21 • Use after Ready Instruction page 195

Name: _____

### Convert Measurement Units

**Solve the problems.**

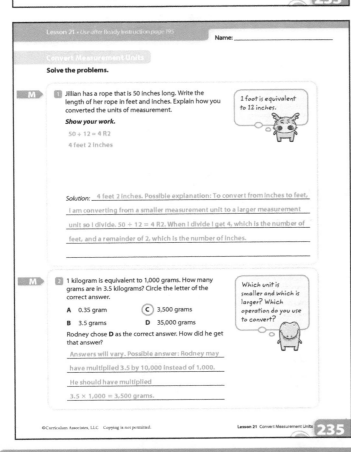

**M** 1 Jillian has a rope that is 50 inches long. Write the length of her rope in feet and inches. Explain how you converted the units of measurement.

*1 foot is equivalent to 12 inches.*

**Show your work.**

$50 \div 12 = 4$ R2

4 feet 2 inches

Solution: 4 feet 2 inches. Possible explanation: To convert from inches to feet,

I am converting from a smaller measurement unit to a larger measurement

unit so I divide. $50 \div 12 = 4$ R2. When I divide I get 4, which is the number of

feet, and a remainder of 2, which is the number of inches.

**M** 2 1 kilogram is equivalent to 1,000 grams. How many grams are in 3.5 kilograms? Circle the letter of the correct answer.

*Which unit is smaller and which is larger? Which operation do you use to convert?*

**A** 0.35 gram

**(C)** 3,500 grams

**B** 3.5 grams

**D** 35,000 grams

Rodney chose **D** as the correct answer. How did he get that answer?

Answers will vary. Possible answer: Rodney may

have multiplied 3.5 by 10,000 instead of 1,000.

He should have multiplied

$3.5 \times 1,000 = 3,500$ grams.

©Curriculum Associates, LLC   Copying is not permitted.

Lesson 21  Convert Measurement Units **235**

---

**236**  Lesson 21  Convert Measurement Units

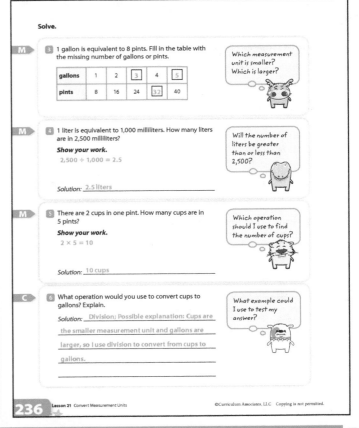

**Solve.**

**M** 3 1 gallon is equivalent to 8 pints. Fill in the table with the missing number of gallons or pints.

| gallons | 1 | 2 | 3 | 4 | 5 |
|---|---|---|---|---|---|
| pints | 8 | 16 | 24 | 32 | 40 |

*Which measurement unit is smaller? Which is larger?*

**M** 4 1 liter is equivalent to 1,000 milliliters. How many liters are in 2,500 milliliters?

**Show your work.**

$2,500 \div 1,000 = 2.5$

Solution: 2.5 liters

*Will the number of liters be greater than or less than 2,500?*

**M** 5 There are 2 cups in one pint. How many cups are in 5 pints?

**Show your work.**

$2 \times 5 = 10$

Solution: 10 cups

*Which operation should I use to find the number of cups?*

**C** 6 What operation would you use to convert cups to gallons? Explain.

Solution: Division; Possible explanation: Cups are

the smaller measurement unit and gallons are

larger, so I use division to convert from cups to

gallons.

*What example could I use to test my answer?*

©Curriculum Associates, LLC   Copying is not permitted.

---

Lesson 22    Use after Ready Instruction page 199

## Solve Word Problems Involving Conversions

Name: _____

### Convert Measurement Units

**Study the example problem showing how to convert between feet and yards. Then solve problems 1–13.**

**Example**

How many feet are in $7\frac{1}{3}$ yards?

1 yard is equivalent to 3 feet.

| 1 yard (yd) | |
|---|---|

| 3 feet (ft) | | |
|---|---|---|

To find how many feet are in $7\frac{1}{3}$ yards, multiply the number of yards by 3.

$7 \times 3 = 21$     $\frac{1}{3} \times 3 = 1$     $21 + 1 = 22$

There are 22 feet in $7\frac{1}{3}$ yards.

**B** **1** Which is the smaller unit of measurement, foot or yard? _foot_

**B** **2** How many feet are in 5 yards? Explain how you calculated your answer.

15 feet; Possible explanation: I multiplied 5 yards by 3, to find the number of feet, 15 feet.

**B** **3** Complete the table.

| yards (yd) | 1 | 2 | 3 | 4 | 5 | 6 | 7 | 8 |
|---|---|---|---|---|---|---|---|---|
| feet (ft) | 3 | 6 | 9 | 12 | 15 | 18 | 21 | 24 |

**M** **4** How many yards are equivalent to 30 feet? Explain how you calculated your answer.

10 yards; Possible explanation: I divided 30 feet by 3 to find the number of yards, $30 \div 3 = 10$ yards.

---

**Solve.**

**B** **5** Which is the larger unit of measurement, meter or centimeter? _meter_

1 meter = 100 centimeters.

**B** **6** Look at problem 5. How did you know which unit of measurement was larger?

Possible answer: There are 100 centimeters in every meter, so I know that meters are larger than centimeters.

**M** **7** How many centimeters are in $x$ meters?

_$100x$_

**M** **8** Use your expression from problem 7. How many centimeters are in 2.7 meters?

_270 centimeters_

**M** **9** Write an expression to show how many meters are equivalent to $x$ centimeters. _$x \div 100$_

**M** **10** Use your expression from problem 9. How many meters are equivalent to 400 centimeters?

_4 meters_

**M** **11** Complete the table.

| centimeters (cm) | 100 | 150 | 200 | 270 | 300 | 320 | 400 | 480 |
|---|---|---|---|---|---|---|---|---|
| meters (m) | 1 | 1.5 | 2 | 2.7 | 3 | 3.2 | 4 | 4.8 |

**C** **12** How many meters are equivalent to 175 centimeters?

_1.75 meters_

**C** **13** How many centimeters are in 2.37 meters?

_237 centimeters_

---

Lesson 22 · Use after Ready Instruction page 201

Name: _____

### Convert Units Using Equations

**Study the example problem showing how to solve a word problem by converting units. Then solve problems 1–5.**

**Example**

Michael is planning a party for 30 people. He plans that each guest will drink 1 cup of juice. He has $2\frac{1}{2}$ gallons of juice. Does he have enough juice for the party?

Michael multiplies $2\frac{1}{2}$ by 16 to find the number of cups of juice he has.

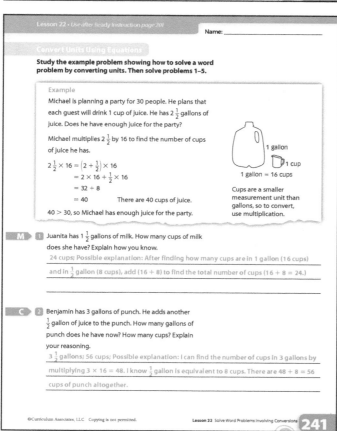

$2\frac{1}{2} \times 16 = \left(2 + \frac{1}{2}\right) \times 16$

$\qquad = 2 \times 16 + \frac{1}{2} \times 16$

$\qquad = 32 + 8$

$\qquad = 40$     There are 40 cups of juice.

$40 > 30$, so Michael has enough juice for the party.

1 gallon

1 cup

1 gallon = 16 cups

Cups are a smaller measurement unit than gallons, so to convert, use multiplication.

**M** **1** Juanita has $1\frac{1}{2}$ gallons of milk. How many cups of milk does she have? Explain how you know.

24 cups; Possible explanation: After finding how many cups are in 1 gallon (16 cups) and in $\frac{1}{2}$ gallon (8 cups), add (16 + 8) to find the total number of cups (16 + 8 = 24.)

**C** **2** Benjamin has 3 gallons of punch. He adds another $\frac{1}{2}$ gallon of juice to the punch. How many gallons of punch does he have now? How many cups? Explain your reasoning.

$3\frac{1}{2}$ gallons; 56 cups; Possible explanation: I can find the number of cups in 3 gallons by multiplying $3 \times 16 = 48$. I know $\frac{1}{2}$ gallon is equivalent to 8 cups. There are 48 + 8 = 56 cups of punch altogether.

---

**Solve.**

| **Units of Capacity** |
|---|
| 1 quart = 4 cups |

**M** **3** Ms. Monet, the art teacher at Giverny School, has 3 quarts of liquid glue and 24 empty glue bottles that each hold 1 cup. Does she have enough glue to fill all of the bottles? Explain.

No; Possible explanation: There are 4 cups in every quart, so there are $4 \times 3 = 12$ cups in 3 quarts. Ms. Monet can fill 12 glue bottles. So she does not have enough glue to fill all of the 24 bottles.

**M** **4** Ms. Monet gave 1 cup of red paint to each of her 20 students. How many quarts of red paint did she give out?

**Show your work.**

$20 \div 4 = 5$

Solution: _5 quarts_

**C** **5** Ms. Monet is combining 15 cups of green paint with 15 cups of white paint. She is pouring the paint mixture into empty quart bottles. How many quart bottles does she need? Explain.

**Show your work.**

$15 + 15 = 30$
$30 \div 4 = 7$ R2

Solution: _8 bottles; Possible explanation: She has 30 cups of paint. $30 \div 4 = 7$ R2. Since she has 2 extra cups, she will need 1 more quart bottle, even though it will only fill up halfway. So she will need 8 quart bottles altogether.

©Curriculum Associates, LLC   Copying is not permitted.

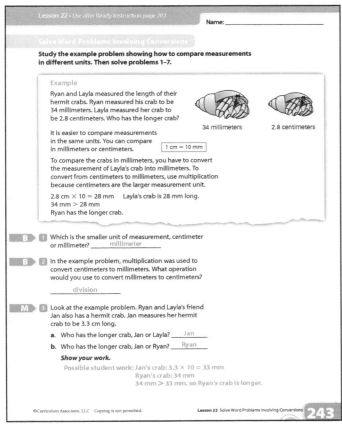

Lesson 22 · Use after Ready Instruction page 203

Name: _____

**Solve Word Problems Involving Conversions**

Study the example problem showing how to compare measurements in different units. Then solve problems 1–7.

**Example**

Ryan and Layla measured the length of their hermit crabs. Ryan measured his crab to be 34 millimeters long. Layla measured her crab to be 2.8 centimeters. Who has the longer crab?

34 millimeters     2.8 centimeters

It is easier to compare measurements in the same units. You can compare in millimeters or centimeters.

1 cm = 10 mm

To compare the crabs in millimeters, you have to convert the measurement of Layla's crab into millimeters. To convert from centimeters to millimeters, use multiplication because centimeters are the larger measurement unit.

2.8 cm × 10 = 28 mm     Layla's crab is 28 mm long.
34 mm > 28 mm
Ryan has the longer crab.

**B** 1 Which is the smaller unit of measurement, centimeter or millimeter? __millimeter__

**B** 2 In the example problem, multiplication was used to convert centimeters to millimeters. What operation would you use to convert millimeters to centimeters?
__division__

**M** 3 Look at the example problem. Ryan and Layla's friend Jan also has a hermit crab. Jan measures her hermit crab to be 3.3 cm long.

a. Who has the longer crab, Jan or Layla? __Jan__

b. Who has the longer crab, Jan or Ryan? __Ryan__

**Show your work.**

Possible student work: Jan's crab: 3.3 × 10 = 33 mm
Ryan's crab: 34 mm
34 mm > 33 mm, so Ryan's crab is longer.

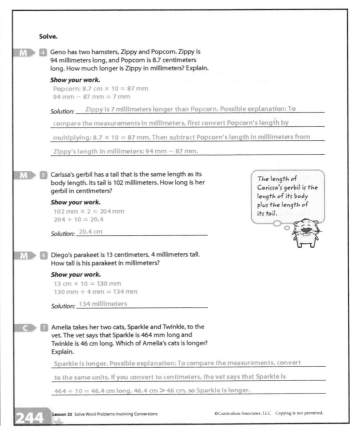

**Solve.**

**M** 4 Geno has two hamsters, Zippy and Popcorn. Zippy is 94 millimeters long, and Popcorn is 8.7 centimeters long. How much longer is Zippy in millimeters? Explain.

**Show your work.**
Popcorn: 8.7 cm × 10 = 87 mm
94 mm − 87 mm = 7 mm

Solution: __Zippy is 7 millimeters longer than Popcorn. Possible explanation: To__
compare the measurements in millimeters, first convert Popcorn's length by
multiplying: 8.7 × 10 = 87 mm. Then subtract Popcorn's length in millimeters from
Zippy's length in millimeters: 94 mm − 87 mm.

**M** 5 Carissa's gerbil has a tail that is the same length as its body length. Its tail is 102 millimeters. How long is her gerbil in centimeters?

The length of Carissa's gerbil is the length of its body plus the length of its tail.

**Show your work.**
102 mm × 2 = 204 mm
204 ÷ 10 = 20.4

Solution: __20.4 cm__

**M** 6 Diego's parakeet is 13 centimeters, 4 millimeters tall. How tall is his parakeet in millimeters?

**Show your work.**
13 cm × 10 = 130 mm
130 mm + 4 mm = 134 mm

Solution: __134 millimeters__

**C** 7 Amelia takes her two cats, Sparkle and Twinkle, to the vet. The vet says that Sparkle is 464 mm long and Twinkle is 46 cm long. Which of Amelia's cats is longer? Explain.

Sparkle is longer. Possible explanation: To compare the measurements, convert
to the same units. If you convert to centimeters, the vet says that Sparkle is
464 ÷ 10 = 46.4 cm long. 46.4 cm > 46 cm, so Sparkle is longer.

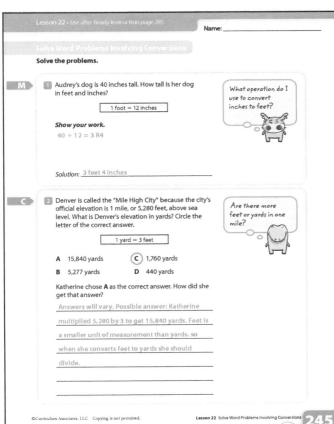

Lesson 22 · Use after Ready Instruction page 205

Name: _____

**Solve Word Problems Involving Conversions**

Solve the problems.

**M** 1 Audrey's dog is 40 inches tall. How tall is her dog in feet and inches?

What operation do I use to convert inches to feet?

1 foot = 12 inches

**Show your work.**
40 ÷ 12 = 3 R4

Solution: __3 feet 4 inches__

**C** 2 Denver is called the "Mile High City" because the city's official elevation is 1 mile, or 5,280 feet, above sea level. What is Denver's elevation in yards? Circle the letter of the correct answer.

Are there more feet or yards in one mile?

1 yard = 3 feet

A  15,840 yards          **C**  1,760 yards

B  5,277 yards          D  440 yards

Katherine chose A as the correct answer. How did she get that answer?

Answers will vary. Possible answer: Katherine
multiplied 5,280 by 3 to get 15,840 yards. Feet is
a smaller unit of measurement than yards, so
when she converts feet to yards she should
divide.

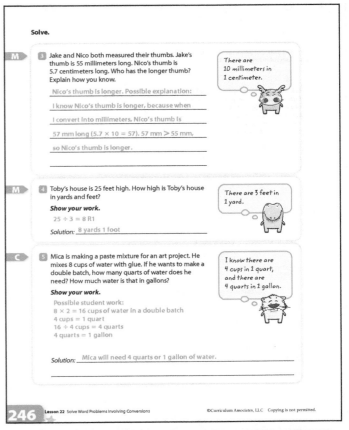

**Solve.**

**M** 3 Jake and Nico both measured their thumbs. Jake's thumb is 55 millimeters long. Nico's thumb is 5.7 centimeters long. Who has the longer thumb? Explain how you know.

There are 10 millimeters in 1 centimeter.

Nico's thumb is longer. Possible explanation:
I know Nico's thumb is longer, because when
I convert into millimeters, Nico's thumb is
57 mm long (5.7 × 10 = 57). 57 mm > 55 mm,
so Nico's thumb is longer.

**M** 4 Toby's house is 25 feet high. How high is Toby's house in yards and feet?

There are 3 feet in 1 yard.

**Show your work.**
25 ÷ 3 = 8 R1

Solution: __8 yards 1 foot__

**C** 5 Mica is making a paste mixture for an art project. He mixes 8 cups of water with glue. If he wants to make a double batch, how many quarts of water does he need? How much water is that in gallons?

I know there are 4 cups in 1 quart, and there are 4 quarts in 1 gallon.

**Show your work.**
Possible student work:
8 × 2 = 16 cups of water in a double batch
4 cups = 1 quart
16 ÷ 4 cups = 4 quarts
4 quarts = 1 gallon

Solution: __Mica will need 4 quarts or 1 gallon of water.__

### Page 249

Lesson 23   Use after Ready Instruction page 209

**Make Line Plots and Interpret Data**

Name: _____

**Read a Line Plot**

Study the example problem showing how to solve a problem by reading a line plot. Then solve problems 1–7.

**Example**

Mason sold pumpkin seeds at the farmer's market on Saturday. The line plot shows the different weights of bags that he sold. What is the total weight of pumpkin seeds sold on Saturday?

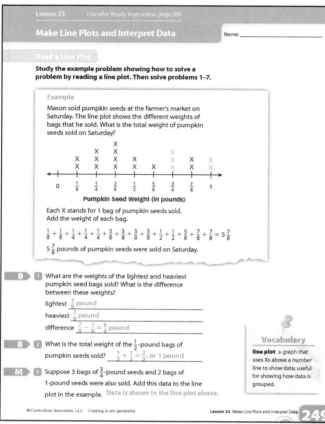

**Pumpkin Seed Weight (in pounds)**

Each X stands for 1 bag of pumpkin seeds sold. Add the weight of each bag.

$$\frac{1}{8}+\frac{1}{8}+\frac{1}{4}+\frac{1}{4}+\frac{3}{8}+\frac{3}{8}+\frac{3}{8}+\frac{1}{2}+\frac{1}{2}+\frac{5}{8}+\frac{7}{8}+\frac{7}{8}=5\frac{7}{8}$$

$5\frac{7}{8}$ pounds of pumpkin seeds were sold on Saturday.

**B  1** What are the weights of the lightest and heaviest pumpkin seed bags sold? What is the difference between these weights?

lightest $\frac{1}{8}$ pound

heaviest $\frac{7}{8}$ pound

difference $\frac{7}{8}-\frac{1}{8}=\frac{6}{8}$ pound

**B  2** What is the total weight of the $\frac{1}{2}$-pound bags of pumpkin seeds sold?   $\frac{1}{2}+\frac{1}{2}=\frac{2}{2}$, or 1 pound

**M  3** Suppose 3 bags of $\frac{3}{4}$-pound seeds and 2 bags of 1-pound seeds were also sold. Add this data to the line plot in the example.   Data is shown in the line plot above.

**Vocabulary**

**line plot** a graph that uses Xs above a number line to show data; useful for showing how data is grouped.

©Curriculum Associates, LLC   Copying is not permitted.

Lesson 23 Make Line Plots and Interpret Data **249**

### Page 250

**250** Lesson 23 Make Line Plots and Interpret Data

**Solve.**

Rodrigo recorded the weight of each acorn squash he sold at the farmer's market. The weights are shown below.

| $2\frac{1}{4}$ | $2\frac{3}{8}$ | $2\frac{3}{4}$ | $2\frac{1}{4}$ | $2\frac{3}{4}$ | $2\frac{5}{8}$ | $2\frac{1}{2}$ | $2\frac{1}{4}$ | $2\frac{3}{4}$ | $2\frac{1}{8}$ |
|---|---|---|---|---|---|---|---|---|---|
| $2\frac{1}{2}$ | $2\frac{7}{8}$ | $2\frac{1}{8}$ | $2\frac{1}{2}$ | $2\frac{1}{4}$ | $2\frac{3}{4}$ | $2\frac{1}{8}$ | $2\frac{5}{8}$ | $2\frac{3}{8}$ | $2\frac{1}{4}$ |

**M  4** Use the data in the table to complete the line plot.

**Squash Weight (pounds)**

**M  5** What is the difference between the weights of the heaviest and lightest squash sold?

$2\frac{7}{8}-2\frac{1}{8}=\frac{6}{8}$ pound

**M  6** Which weight includes the greatest number of squashes? Explain how you know.

$2\frac{1}{4}$ pounds; Possible explanation: The weight with the most Xs includes the greatest number of squashes. It is also the tallest stack of Xs.

**C  7** What is the total weight of all the squashes that weigh less than $2\frac{1}{2}$ pounds?

**Show your work.**

$2\frac{1}{8}+2\frac{1}{8}+2\frac{1}{8}+2\frac{1}{4}+2\frac{1}{4}+2\frac{1}{4}+2\frac{1}{4}+2\frac{1}{4}+2\frac{3}{8}+2\frac{3}{8}=22\frac{3}{8}$

Solution: _____$22\frac{3}{8}$ pounds_____

©Curriculum Associates, LLC   Copying is not permitted.

### Page 251

Lesson 23 • Use after Ready Instruction page 211

Name: _____

**Make a Line Plot**

Study the example problem showing how to make a line plot. Then solve problems 1–4.

**Example**

Rosa's grandfather gave her a box of old foreign coins. She measured the diameter of each coin. Then she made a table that showed the diameters and how many coins she had of each diameter. How can Rosa show this data in a line plot?

| Diameter (in inches) | Number of Coins |
|---|---|
| $\frac{3}{8}$ | 3 |
| $\frac{5}{8}$ | 8 |
| $\frac{3}{4}$ | 11 |
| $\frac{7}{8}$ | 5 |

Make one X to stand for each coin in the table. The line plot below shows the number of coins with a $\frac{3}{8}$-inch diameter.

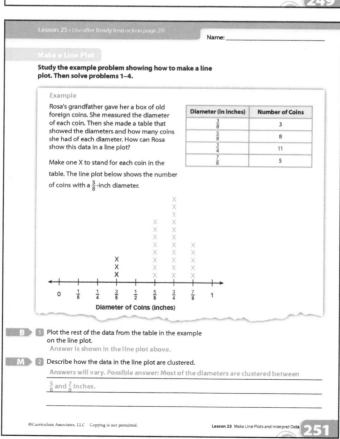

**Diameter of Coins (inches)**

**B  1** Plot the rest of the data from the table in the example on the line plot.
Answer is shown in the line plot above.

**M  2** Describe how the data in the line plot are clustered.
Answers will vary. Possible answer: Most of the diameters are clustered between $\frac{5}{8}$ and $\frac{7}{8}$ inches.

©Curriculum Associates, LLC   Copying is not permitted.

Lesson 23 Make Line Plots and Interpret Data **251**

### Page 252

**252** Lesson 23 Make Line Plots and Interpret Data

**Solve.**

Gabe has a collection of stamps. He recorded the heights of the stamps along with the number of stamps at each height.

| Height (in inches) | Number of Stamps |
|---|---|
| $\frac{1}{2}$ | 2 |
| 1 | 5 |
| $1\frac{1}{2}$ | 9 |
| 2 | 6 |
| $2\frac{1}{2}$ | 3 |
| 3 | 1 |

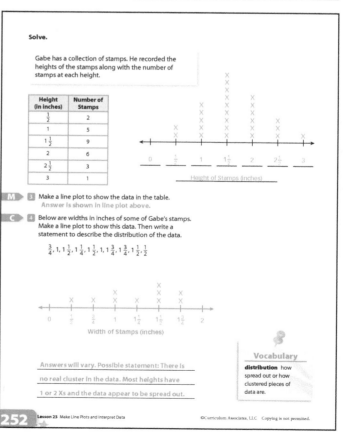

**Height of Stamps (inches)**

**M  3** Make a line plot to show the data in the table.
Answer is shown in line plot above.

**C  4** Below are widths in inches of some of Gabe's stamps. Make a line plot to show this data. Then write a statement to describe the distribution of the data.

$$\frac{3}{4}, 1, 1\frac{1}{2}, 1\frac{1}{4}, 1\frac{1}{2}, 1, 1\frac{3}{4}, 1\frac{3}{4}, 1\frac{1}{2}, \frac{1}{2}$$

**Width of Stamps (inches)**

Answers will vary. Possible statement: There is no real cluster in the data. Most heights have 1 or 2 Xs and the data appear to be spread out.

**Vocabulary**

**distribution** how spread out or how clustered pieces of data are.

©Curriculum Associates, LLC   Copying is not permitted.

©Curriculum Associates, LLC   Copying is not permitted.

## Page 253

Lesson 23 · Use after Ready Instruction page 213

Name: _____

**Solve Problems Using Data in a Line Plot**

Study the example showing how to solve a problem using data in a line plot. Then solve problems 1–7.

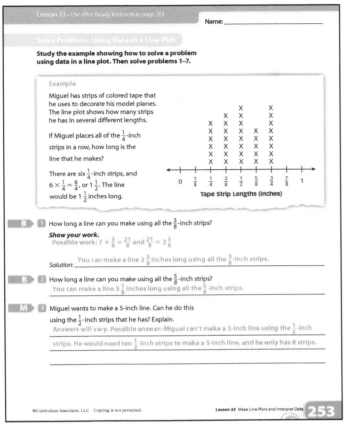

Example

Miguel has strips of colored tape that he uses to decorate his model planes. The line plot shows how many strips he has in several different lengths.

If Miguel places all of the $\frac{1}{4}$-inch strips in a row, how long is the line that he makes?

There are six $\frac{1}{4}$-inch strips, and $6 \times \frac{1}{4} = \frac{6}{4}$, or $1\frac{1}{2}$. The line would be $1\frac{1}{2}$ inches long.

**Tape Strip Lengths (inches)**

**B** 1 How long a line can you make using all the $\frac{3}{8}$-inch strips?

**Show your work.**
Possible work: $7 \times \frac{3}{8} = \frac{21}{8}$ and $\frac{21}{8} = 2\frac{5}{8}$

Solution: You can make a line $2\frac{5}{8}$ inches long using all the $\frac{3}{8}$-inch strips.

**B** 2 How long a line can you make using all the $\frac{5}{8}$-inch strips?
You can make a line $3\frac{1}{8}$ inches long using all the $\frac{5}{8}$-inch strips.

**M** 3 Miguel wants to make a 5-inch line. Can he do this using the $\frac{1}{2}$-inch strips that he has? Explain.
Answers will vary. Possible answer: Miguel can't make a 5-inch line using the $\frac{1}{2}$-inch strips. He would need ten $\frac{1}{2}$-inch strips to make a 5-inch line, and he only has 8 strips.

©Curriculum Associates, LLC   Copying is not permitted.
Lesson 23 Make Line Plots and Interpret Data **253**

## Page 254

**254** Lesson 23 Make Line Plots and Interpret Data

Use the data in the line plot to solve.

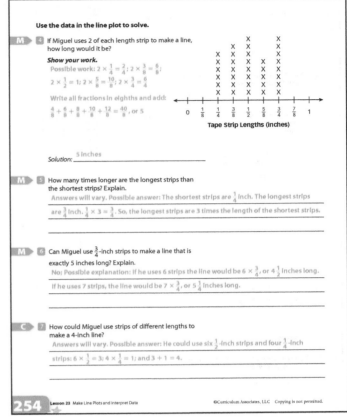

**M** 4 If Miguel uses 2 of each length strip to make a line, how long would it be?

**Show your work.**
Possible work: $2 \times \frac{1}{4} = \frac{2}{4}$; $2 \times \frac{3}{8} = \frac{6}{8}$;
$2 \times \frac{1}{2} = 1$; $2 \times \frac{5}{8} = \frac{10}{8}$; $2 \times \frac{3}{4} = \frac{6}{4}$

Write all fractions in eighths and add:
$\frac{4}{8} + \frac{6}{8} + \frac{8}{8} + \frac{10}{8} + \frac{12}{8} = \frac{40}{8}$, or 5

**Tape Strip Lengths (inches)**

Solution: _____5 inches_____

**M** 5 How many times longer are the longest strips than the shortest strips? Explain.
Answers will vary. Possible answer: The shortest strips are $\frac{1}{4}$ inch. The longest strips are $\frac{3}{4}$ inch. $\frac{1}{4} \times 3 = \frac{3}{4}$. So, the longest strips are 3 times the length of the shortest strips.

**M** 6 Can Miguel use $\frac{3}{4}$-inch strips to make a line that is exactly 5 inches long? Explain.
No; Possible explanation: If he uses 6 strips the line would be $6 \times \frac{3}{4}$, or $4\frac{1}{2}$ inches long. If he uses 7 strips, the line would be $7 \times \frac{3}{4}$, or $5\frac{1}{4}$ inches long.

**C** 7 How could Miguel use strips of different lengths to make a 4-inch line?
Answers will vary. Possible answer: He could use six $\frac{1}{2}$-inch strips and four $\frac{1}{4}$-inch strips: $6 \times \frac{1}{2} = 3$; $4 \times \frac{1}{4} = 1$; and $3 + 1 = 4$.

©Curriculum Associates, LLC   Copying is not permitted.

## Page 255

Lesson 23 · Use after Ready Instruction page 215

Name: _____

**Make Line Plots and Interpret Data**

**Solve the problems.**

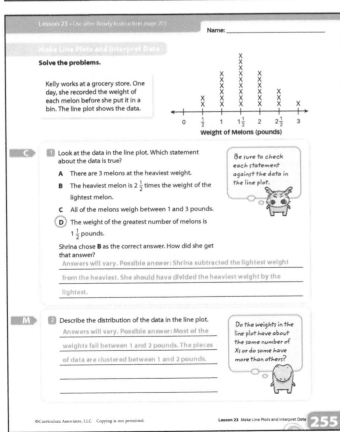

Kelly works at a grocery store. One day, she recorded the weight of each melon before she put it in a bin. The line plot shows the data.

**Weight of Melons (pounds)**

**C** 1 Look at the data in the line plot. Which statement about the data is true?

A There are 3 melons at the heaviest weight.

B The heaviest melon is $2\frac{1}{2}$ times the weight of the lightest melon.

C All of the melons weigh between 1 and 3 pounds.

**D** The weight of the greatest number of melons is $1\frac{1}{2}$ pounds.

Shrina chose **B** as the correct answer. How did she get that answer?
Answers will vary. Possible answer: Shrina subtracted the lightest weight from the heaviest. She should have divided the heaviest weight by the lightest.

> Be sure to check each statement against the data in the line plot.

**M** 2 Describe the distribution of the data in the line plot.
Answers will vary. Possible answer: Most of the weights fall between 1 and 2 pounds. The pieces of data are clustered between 1 and 2 pounds.

> Do the weights in the line plot have about the same number of Xs or do some have more than others?

©Curriculum Associates, LLC   Copying is not permitted.
Lesson 23 Make Line Plots and Interpret Data **255**

## Page 256

**256** Lesson 23 Make Line Plots and Interpret Data

**Solve.**

Dorothy has a basket of apples. She weighs them and makes a table to show how many apples she has of each weight.

| Weight (pounds) | Number of Apples |
|---|---|
| $\frac{1}{4}$ | 3 |
| $\frac{3}{8}$ | 6 |
| $\frac{1}{2}$ | 5 |
| $\frac{5}{8}$ | 4 |
| $\frac{3}{4}$ | 2 |

**M** 3 Make a line plot to show the data.

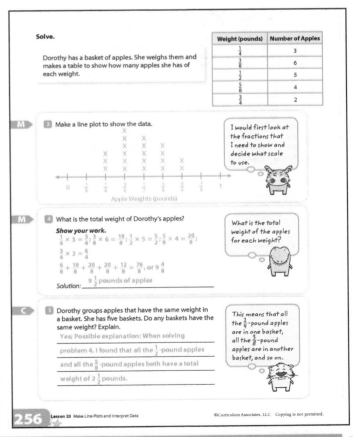

**Apple Weights (pounds)**

> I would first look at the fractions that I need to show and decide what scale to use.

**M** 4 What is the total weight of Dorothy's apples?

**Show your work.**
$\frac{1}{4} \times 3 = \frac{3}{4}$; $\frac{3}{8} \times 6 = \frac{18}{8}$; $\frac{1}{2} \times 5 = \frac{5}{2}$; $\frac{5}{8} \times 4 = \frac{20}{8}$;
$\frac{3}{4} \times 2 = \frac{6}{4}$
$\frac{6}{8} + \frac{18}{8} + \frac{20}{8} + \frac{20}{8} + \frac{12}{8} = \frac{76}{8}$, or $9\frac{4}{8}$

Solution: $9\frac{1}{2}$ pounds of apples

> What is the total weight of the apples for each weight?

**C** 5 Dorothy groups apples that have the same weight in a basket. She has five baskets. Do any baskets have the same weight? Explain.
Yes; Possible explanation: When solving problem 4, I found that all the $\frac{1}{2}$-pound apples and all the $\frac{5}{8}$-pound apples both have a total weight of $2\frac{1}{2}$ pounds.

> This means that all the $\frac{1}{4}$-pound apples are in one basket, all the $\frac{3}{8}$-pound apples are in another basket, and so on.

©Curriculum Associates, LLC   Copying is not permitted.

©Curriculum Associates, LLC   Copying is not permitted.

Lesson 24    *Use after Ready Instruction page 219*

**Understand Volume**

Name: _____

How do you measure the area of a rectangle?

**Study the example problem showing how to find the area of a rectangle. Then solve problems 1–7.**

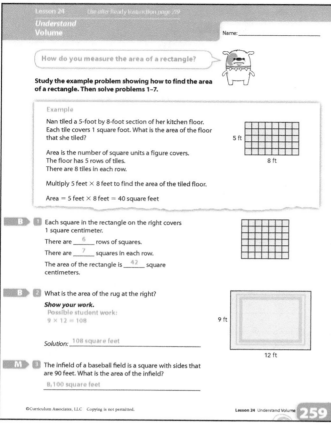

**Example**

Nan tiled a 5-foot by 8-foot section of her kitchen floor. Each tile covers 1 square foot. What is the area of the floor that she tiled?

Area is the number of square units a figure covers. The floor has 5 rows of tiles. There are 8 tiles in each row.

Multiply 5 feet × 8 feet to find the area of the tiled floor.

Area = 5 feet × 8 feet = 40 square feet

5 ft

8 ft

**B** **1** Each square in the rectangle on the right covers 1 square centimeter.

There are ___6___ rows of squares.

There are ___7___ squares in each row.

The area of the rectangle is ___42___ square centimeters.

**B** **2** What is the area of the rug at the right?

**Show your work.**
Possible student work:
9 × 12 = 108

Solution: ___108 square feet___

9 ft

12 ft

**M** **3** The infield of a baseball field is a square with sides that are 90 feet. What is the area of the infield?

8,100 square feet

---

**Solve.**

**B** **4** The diagram shows the dimensions of two desks that Hannah is thinking about buying. What is the area of each desktop?

**Show your work.**
Possible work: A: 4 × 6 = 24
          B: 3 × 7 = 21

Solution: ___area of desktop A: 24 square feet;___
___area of desktop B: 21 square feet___

4 ft   | A |
     6 ft

3 ft   | B |
     7 ft

**M** **5** The width of Andy's porch is 5 feet. Its area is 40 square feet. How long is the porch?

**Show your work.**
Possible work: 40 ÷ 5 = 8

Solution: ___The porch is 8 feet long.___

**M** **6** Look at problem 5. Andy wants to extend his porch by adding on to the length. This new section will have the same width, but he wants the porch to have a total area of 60 square feet. What should he make the length of the new section?

**Show your work.**
Possible work: 40 + 20 = 60; the new section has to have an area of 20 square feet; 5 × 4 = 20

Solution: ___He should make the new section 4 feet long.___

**C** **7** Jillian wants her rectangular garden to cover an area of 180 square feet. What are the lengths and widths of two possible rectangles she can use? Explain.

Answers will vary. Possible answer: She could use a rectangle with a length of 15 feet

and a width of 12 feet: 15 × 12 = 180. She could also use a rectangle with a length of

20 feet and a width of 9 feet: 20 × 9 = 180.

---

Lesson 24 · *Use after Ready Instruction page 221*

**Find Volume with Unit Cubes**

Name: _____

**Study the example problem showing how to use unit cubes to find the volume of a rectangular prism. Then solve problems 1–8.**

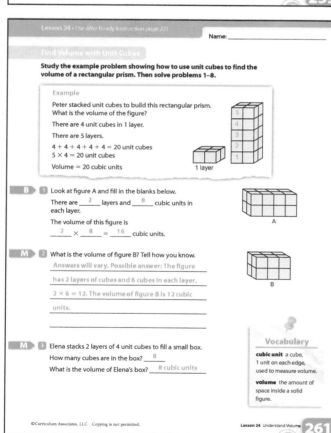

**Example**

Peter stacked unit cubes to build this rectangular prism. What is the volume of the figure?

There are 4 unit cubes in 1 layer.

There are 5 layers.

4 + 4 + 4 + 4 + 4 = 20 unit cubes

5 × 4 = 20 unit cubes

Volume = 20 cubic units

1 layer

**B** **1** Look at figure A and fill in the blanks below.

There are ___2___ layers and ___8___ cubic units in each layer.

The volume of this figure is

___2___ × ___8___ = ___16___ cubic units.

A

**M** **2** What is the volume of figure B? Tell how you know.

Answers will vary. Possible answer: The figure

has 2 layers of cubes and 6 cubes in each layer.

2 × 6 = 12. The volume of figure B is 12 cubic

units.

B

**M** **3** Elena stacks 2 layers of 4 unit cubes to fill a small box.

How many cubes are in the box? ___8___

What is the volume of Elena's box? ___8 cubic units___

**Vocabulary**

**cubic unit** a cube, 1 unit on each edge, used to measure volume.

**volume** the amount of space inside a solid figure.

---

**Solve.**

**B** **4** Look at figure C and fill in the blanks below.

There are ___2___ layers and ___10___ cubic units in each layer.

The volume of this block is

___2___ × ___10___ = ___20___ cubic units.

C

**B** **5** What is the volume of figure D? ___4 cubic units___

D

**M** **6** How many of figure D does it take to fill figure E? How does the volume of figure D relate to the volume of figure E? Explain.

Answers will vary. Possible answer: If you put 4

of figure D together you could make figure E. So,

the volume of figure E is 4 times the volume of

figure D, or 16 cubic units.

E

**M** **7** A block has a volume of 36 cubic units. It has 9 layers of cubic units. How many cubic units are in each layer?

4 cubic units

**C** **8** Draw or describe box F that has a volume of 5 cubic units. Then draw or describe a box that has 3 times the volume of box F. What is the volume of the second box?

Possible answer: Students draw or describe a box with 1 layer of 5 units or 5 layers of 1 unit. Then they draw or describe a second box that has 3 layers of 5 units or 5 layers of 3 units.

Solution: ___The volume of the second box is___
___15 cubic units.___

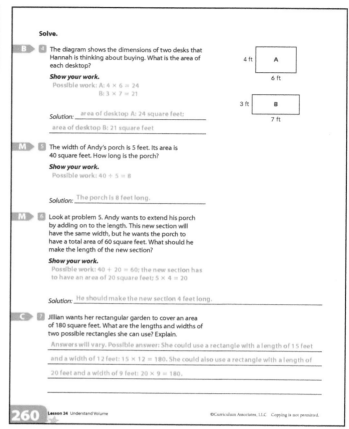

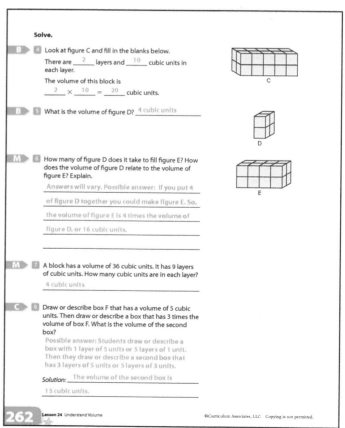

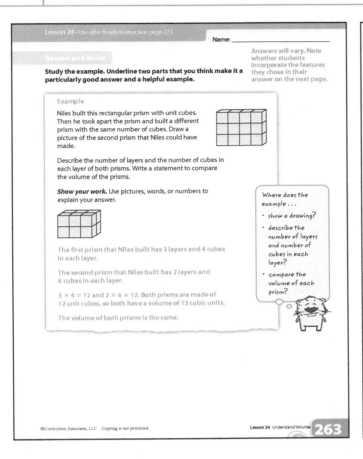

Lesson 24 · *Use after Ready Instruction page 223*

Name: _____

Answers will vary. Note whether students incorporate the features they chose in their answer on the next page.

**Reason and Write**

**Study the example. Underline two parts that you think make it a particularly good answer and a helpful example.**

**Example**

Niles built this rectangular prism with unit cubes. Then he took apart the prism and built a different prism with the same number of cubes. Draw a picture of the second prism that Niles could have made.

Describe the number of layers and the number of cubes in each layer of both prisms. Write a statement to compare the volume of the prisms.

***Show your work.*** Use pictures, words, or numbers to explain your answer.

The first prism that Niles built has 3 layers and 4 cubes in each layer.

The second prism that Niles built has 2 layers and 6 cubes in each layer.

3 × 4 = 12 and 2 × 6 = 12. Both prisms are made of 12 unit cubes, so both have a volume of 12 cubic units.

The volume of both prisms is the same.

*Where does the example . . .*

- *show a drawing?*
- *describe the number of layers and number of cubes in each layer?*
- *compare the volume of each prism?*

©Curriculum Associates, LLC   Copying is not permitted.

**Lesson 24** Understand Volume **263**

---

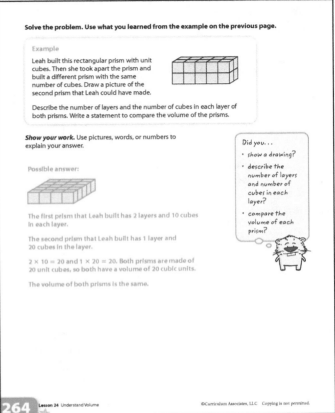

**Solve the problem. Use what you learned from the example on the previous page.**

**Example**

Leah built this rectangular prism with unit cubes. Then she took apart the prism and built a different prism with the same number of cubes. Draw a picture of the second prism that Leah could have made.

Describe the number of layers and the number of cubes in each layer of both prisms. Write a statement to compare the volume of the prisms.

***Show your work.*** Use pictures, words, or numbers to explain your answer.

Possible answer:

The first prism that Leah built has 2 layers and 10 cubes in each layer.

The second prism that Leah built has 1 layer and 20 cubes in the layer.

2 × 10 = 20 and 1 × 20 = 20. Both prisms are made of 20 unit cubes, so both have a volume of 20 cubic units.

The volume of both prisms is the same.

*Did you . . .*

- *show a drawing?*
- *describe the number of layers and number of cubes in each layer?*
- *compare the volume of each prism?*

**264** **Lesson 24** Understand Volume

©Curriculum Associates, LLC   Copying is not permitted.

| Key | |
|---|---|
| B | Basic |
| M | Medium |
| C | Challenge |

Lesson 25 · Use after Ready Instruction page 225

## Find Volume Using Unit Cubes

Name: _____

### Count Unit Cubes to Find Volume

**Study the example problem showing how to find volume by counting unit cubes. Then solve problems 1–8.**

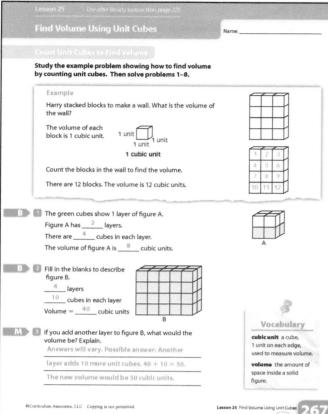

**Example**

Harry stacked blocks to make a wall. What is the volume of the wall?

The volume of each block is 1 cubic unit.

1 unit × 1 unit × 1 unit

**1 cubic unit**

Count the blocks in the wall to find the volume.

There are 12 blocks. The volume is 12 cubic units.

**B** ☐1 The green cubes show 1 layer of figure A.

Figure A has __2__ layers.

There are __4__ cubes in each layer.

The volume of figure A is __8__ cubic units.

A

**B** ☐2 Fill in the blanks to describe figure B.

__4__ layers

__10__ cubes in each layer

Volume = __40__ cubic units

B

**M** ☐3 If you add another layer to figure B, what would the volume be? Explain.

Answers will vary. Possible answer: Another

layer adds 10 more unit cubes. 40 + 10 = 50.

The new volume would be 50 cubic units.

**Vocabulary**

**cubic unit** a cube, 1 unit on each edge, used to measure volume.

**volume** the amount of space inside a solid figure.

©Curriculum Associates, LLC   Copying is not permitted.

Lesson 25 Find Volume Using Unit Cubes **267**

---

**268** Lesson 25 Find Volume Using Unit Cubes

**Solve.**

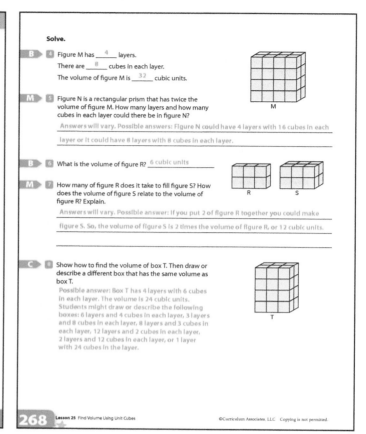

**B** ☐4 Figure M has __4__ layers.

There are __8__ cubes in each layer.

The volume of figure M is __32__ cubic units.

M

**M** ☐5 Figure N is a rectangular prism that has twice the volume of figure M. How many layers and how many cubes in each layer could there be in figure N?

Answers will vary. Possible answers: Figure N could have 4 layers with 16 cubes in each

layer or it could have 8 layers with 8 cubes in each layer.

**B** ☐6 What is the volume of figure R? __6 cubic units__

R      S

**M** ☐7 How many of figure R does it take to fill figure S? How does the volume of figure S relate to the volume of figure R? Explain.

Answers will vary. Possible answer: If you put 2 of figure R together you could make

figure S. So, the volume of figure S is 2 times the volume of figure R, or 12 cubic units.

**C** ☐8 Show how to find the volume of box T. Then draw or describe a different box that has the same volume as box T.

Possible answer: Box T has 4 layers with 6 cubes in each layer. The volume is 24 cubic units. Students might draw or describe the following boxes: 6 layers and 4 cubes in each layer, 3 layers and 8 cubes in each layer, 8 layers and 3 cubes in each layer, 12 layers and 2 cubes in each layer, 2 layers and 12 cubes in each layer, or 1 layer with 24 cubes in the layer.

T

©Curriculum Associates, LLC   Copying is not permitted.

---

Lesson 25 · Use after Ready Instruction page 227

Name: _____

### Find the Volume of a Rectangular Prism

**Study the example problem showing how to use layers to find the volume of a rectangular prism. Then solve problems 1–7.**

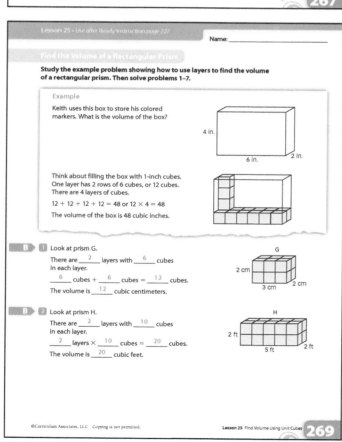

**Example**

Keith uses this box to store his colored markers. What is the volume of the box?

4 in.
6 in.   2 in.

Think about filling the box with 1-inch cubes. One layer has 2 rows of 6 cubes, or 12 cubes. There are 4 layers of cubes.

12 + 12 + 12 + 12 = 48 or 12 × 4 = 48

The volume of the box is 48 cubic inches.

**B** ☐1 Look at prism G.

There are __2__ layers with __6__ cubes in each layer.

__6__ cubes + __6__ cubes = __12__ cubes.

The volume is __12__ cubic centimeters.

G
2 cm
3 cm   2 cm

**B** ☐2 Look at prism H.

There are __2__ layers with __10__ cubes in each layer.

__2__ layers × __10__ cubes = __20__ cubes.

The volume is __20__ cubic feet.

H
2 ft
5 ft   2 ft

©Curriculum Associates, LLC   Copying is not permitted.

Lesson 25 Find Volume Using Unit Cubes **269**

---

**270** Lesson 25 Find Volume Using Unit Cubes

**Solve.**

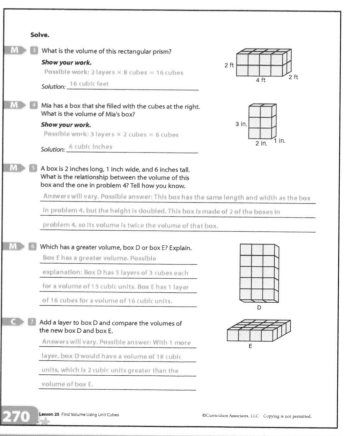

**M** ☐3 What is the volume of this rectangular prism?

**Show your work.**

Possible work: 2 layers × 8 cubes = 16 cubes

Solution: __16 cubic feet__

2 ft
4 ft   2 ft

**M** ☐4 Mia has a box that she filled with the cubes at the right. What is the volume of Mia's box?

**Show your work.**

Possible work: 3 layers × 2 cubes = 6 cubes

Solution: __6 cubic inches__

3 in.
2 in.   1 in.

**M** ☐5 A box is 2 inches long, 1 inch wide, and 6 inches tall. What is the relationship between the volume of this box and the one in problem 4? Tell how you know.

Answers will vary. Possible answer: This box has the same length and width as the box

in problem 4, but the height is doubled. This box is made of 2 of the boxes in

problem 4, so its volume is twice the volume of that box.

**M** ☐6 Which has a greater volume, box D or box E? Explain.

Box E has a greater volume. Possible

explanation: Box D has 5 layers of 3 cubes each

for a volume of 15 cubic units. Box E has 1 layer

of 16 cubes for a volume of 16 cubic units.

D

**C** ☐7 Add a layer to box D and compare the volumes of the new box D and box E.

Answers will vary. Possible answer: With 1 more

layer, box D would have a volume of 18 cubic

units, which is 2 cubic units greater than the

volume of box E.

E

©Curriculum Associates, LLC   Copying is not permitted.

©Curriculum Associates, LLC   Copying is not permitted.

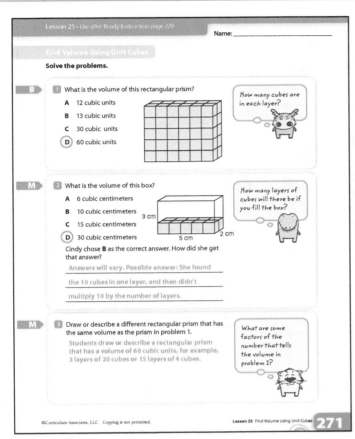

Name: _____

**Find Volume Using Unit Cubes**

**Solve the problems.**

**B**  1  What is the volume of this rectangular prism?

    A  12 cubic units

    B  13 cubic units

    C  30 cubic  units

    (D)  60 cubic units

*How many cubes are in each layer?*

**M**  2  What is the volume of this box?

    A  6 cubic centimeters

    B  10 cubic centimeters

    C  15 cubic centimeters

    (D)  30 cubic centimeters

3 cm    5 cm  2 cm

*How many layers of cubes will there be if you fill the box?*

Cindy chose **B** as the correct answer. How did she get that answer?

Answers will vary. Possible answer: She found

the 10 cubes in one layer, and then didn't

multiply 10 by the number of layers.

**M**  3  Draw or describe a different rectangular prism that has the same volume as the prism in problem 1.

Students draw or describe a rectangular prism that has a volume of 60 cubic units, for example, 3 layers of 20 cubes or 15 layers of 4 cubes.

*What are some factors of the number that tells the volume in problem 1?*

---

**Solve.**

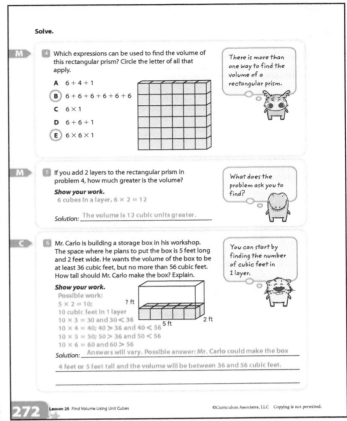

**M**  4  Which expressions can be used to find the volume of this rectangular prism? Circle the letter of all that apply.

    A  $6 + 4 + 1$

    (B)  $6 + 6 + 6 + 6 + 6 + 6$

    C  $6 \times 1$

    D  $6 + 6 + 1$

    (E)  $6 \times 6 \times 1$

*There is more than one way to find the volume of a rectangular prism.*

**M**  5  If you add 2 layers to the rectangular prism in problem 4, how much greater is the volume?

**Show your work.**

6 cubes in a layer, $6 \times 2 = 12$

Solution: _The volume is 12 cubic units greater._

*What does the problem ask you to find?*

**C**  6  Mr. Carlo is building a storage box in his workshop. The space where he plans to put the box is 5 feet long and 2 feet wide. He wants the volume of the box to be at least 36 cubic feet, but no more than 56 cubic feet. How tall should Mr. Carlo make the box? Explain.

**Show your work.**

Possible work:

$5 \times 2 = 10$;

10 cubic feet in 1 layer

$10 \times 3 = 30$ and $30 < 36$

$10 \times 4 = 40$; $40 > 36$ and $40 < 56$

$10 \times 5 = 50$; $50 > 36$ and $50 < 56$

$10 \times 6 = 60$ and $60 > 56$

? ft    5 ft  2 ft

Solution: ___Answers will vary. Possible answer: Mr. Carlo could make the box___

4 feet or 5 feet tall and the volume will be between 36 and 56 cubic feet.

*You can start by finding the number of cubic feet in 1 layer.*

| Key | |
|---|---|
| B | Basic |
| M | Medium |
| C | Challenge |

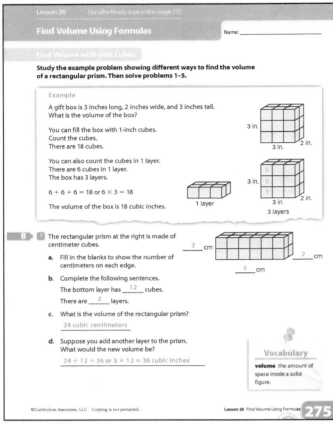

Lesson 26    *Use after Ready Instruction page 233*

## Find Volume Using Formulas

Name: _____

### Find Volume with Unit Cubes

Study the example problem showing different ways to find the volume of a rectangular prism. Then solve problems 1–5.

**Example**

A gift box is 3 inches long, 2 inches wide, and 3 inches tall. What is the volume of the box?

You can fill the box with 1-inch cubes.
Count the cubes.
There are 18 cubes.

You can also count the cubes in 1 layer.
There are 6 cubes in 1 layer.
The box has 3 layers.

$6 + 6 + 6 = 18$ or $6 \times 3 = 18$

The volume of the box is 18 cubic inches.

**B** **1** The rectangular prism at the right is made of centimeter cubes.

**a.** Fill in the blanks to show the number of centimeters on each edge.

**b.** Complete the following sentences.
The bottom layer has __12__ cubes.
There are __2__ layers.

**c.** What is the volume of the rectangular prism?
24 cubic centimeters

**d.** Suppose you add another layer to the prism. What would the new volume be?
$24 + 12 = 36$ or $3 \times 12 = 36$ cubic inches

**Vocabulary**

**volume** the amount of space inside a solid figure.

---

**Solve.**

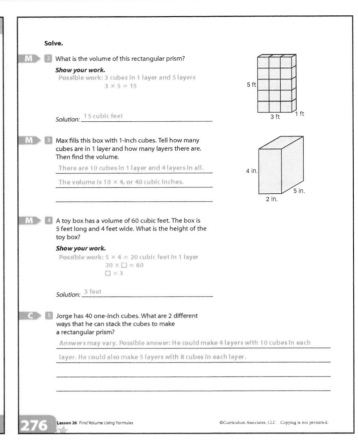

**M** **2** What is the volume of this rectangular prism?
**Show your work.**
Possible work: 3 cubes in 1 layer and 5 layers
$3 \times 5 = 15$

Solution: __15 cubic feet__

**M** **3** Max fills this box with 1-inch cubes. Tell how many cubes are in 1 layer and how many layers there are. Then find the volume.

There are 10 cubes in 1 layer and 4 layers in all.

The volume is $10 \times 4$, or 40 cubic inches.

**M** **4** A toy box has a volume of 60 cubic feet. The box is 5 feet long and 4 feet wide. What is the height of the toy box?
**Show your work.**
Possible work: $5 \times 4 = 20$ cubic feet in 1 layer
$20 \times \square = 60$
$\square = 3$

Solution: __3 feet__

**C** **5** Jorge has 40 one-inch cubes. What are 2 different ways that he can stack the cubes to make a rectangular prism?
Answers may vary. Possible answer: He could make 4 layers with 10 cubes in each

layer. He could also make 5 layers with 8 cubes in each layer.

---

Lesson 26 · *Use after Ready Instruction page 235*

Name: _____

### Use a Formula to Find the Volume of a Rectangular Prism

Study the example problem showing how to use formulas to find the volume of a rectangular prism. Then solve problems 1–7.

**Example**

Gwen puts her leftover food in a rectangular container. The container is 6 inches long, 5 inches wide, and 4 inches tall. What is the volume of the container?

Use the formula *volume = length × width × height.*

volume = $6 \times 5 \times 4$, or 120 cubic inches

Or use the formula *volume = area of the base × height.* The area of the base is the same as the length × width.

$6 \times 5 = 30$ and $30 \times 4 = 120$ cubic inches

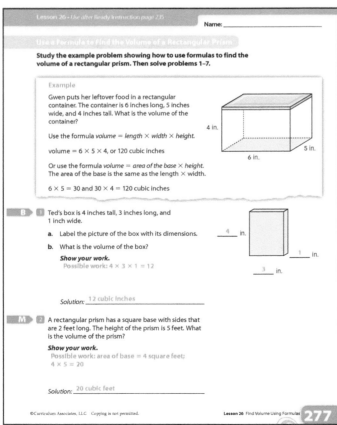

**B** **1** Ted's box is 4 inches tall, 3 inches long, and 1 inch wide.

**a.** Label the picture of the box with its dimensions.

**b.** What is the volume of the box?
**Show your work.**
Possible work: $4 \times 3 \times 1 = 12$

Solution: __12 cubic inches__

**M** **2** A rectangular prism has a square base with sides that are 2 feet long. The height of the prism is 5 feet. What is the volume of the prism?
**Show your work.**
Possible work: area of base = 4 square feet;
$4 \times 5 = 20$

Solution: __20 cubic feet__

---

**Solve.**

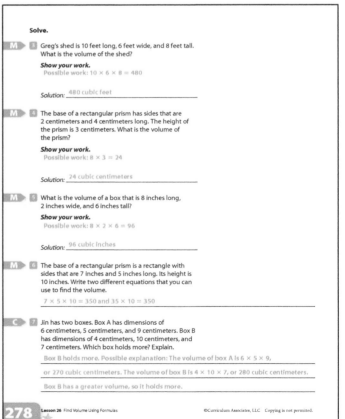

**M** **3** Greg's shed is 10 feet long, 6 feet wide, and 8 feet tall. What is the volume of the shed?
**Show your work.**
Possible work: $10 \times 6 \times 8 = 480$

Solution: __480 cubic feet__

**M** **4** The base of a rectangular prism has sides that are 2 centimeters and 4 centimeters long. The height of the prism is 3 centimeters. What is the volume of the prism?
**Show your work.**
Possible work: $8 \times 3 = 24$

Solution: __24 cubic centimeters__

**M** **5** What is the volume of a box that is 8 inches long, 2 inches wide, and 6 inches tall?
**Show your work.**
Possible work: $8 \times 2 \times 6 = 96$

Solution: __96 cubic inches__

**M** **6** The base of a rectangular prism is a rectangle with sides that are 7 inches and 5 inches long. Its height is 10 inches. Write two different equations that you can use to find the volume.
$7 \times 5 \times 10 = 350$ and $35 \times 10 = 350$

**C** **7** Jin has two boxes. Box A has dimensions of 6 centimeters, 5 centimeters, and 9 centimeters. Box B has dimensions of 4 centimeters, 10 centimeters, and 7 centimeters. Which box holds more? Explain.
Box B holds more. Possible explanation: The volume of box A is $6 \times 5 \times 9$,

or 270 cubic centimeters. The volume of box B is $4 \times 10 \times 7$, or 280 cubic centimeters.

Box B has a greater volume, so it holds more.

©Curriculum Associates, LLC   Copying is not permitted.

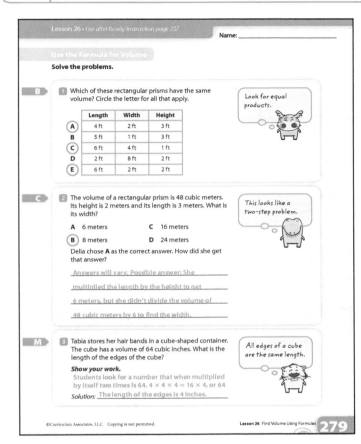

**Use the Formula for Volume**

**Solve the problems.**

**B** **1** Which of these rectangular prisms have the same volume? Circle the letter for all that apply.

*Look for equal products.*

| | Length | Width | Height |
|---|---|---|---|
| **A** | 4 ft | 2 ft | 3 ft |
| **B** | 5 ft | 1 ft | 3 ft |
| **C** | 6 ft | 4 ft | 1 ft |
| **D** | 2 ft | 8 ft | 2 ft |
| **E** | 6 ft | 2 ft | 2 ft |

**C** **2** The volume of a rectangular prism is 48 cubic meters. Its height is 2 meters and its length is 3 meters. What is its width?

*This looks like a two-step problem.*

A  6 meters          C  16 meters

B  8 meters          D  24 meters

Delia chose **A** as the correct answer. How did she get that answer?

Answers will vary. Possible answer: She

multiplied the length by the height to get

6 meters, but she didn't divide the volume of

48 cubic meters by 6 to find the width.

**M** **3** Tabia stores her hair bands in a cube-shaped container. The cube has a volume of 64 cubic inches. What is the length of the edges of the cube?

*All edges of a cube are the same length.*

**Show your work.**

Students look for a number that when multiplied by itself two times is 64. 4 × 4 × 4 = 16 × 4, or 64

Solution: The length of the edges is 4 inches.

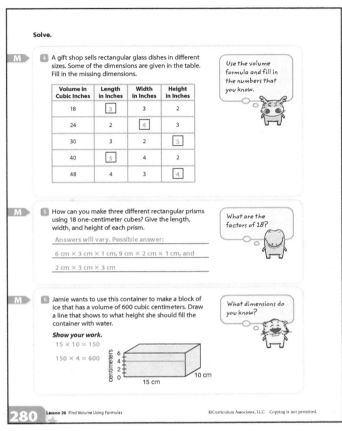

**Solve.**

**M** **4** A gift shop sells rectangular glass dishes in different sizes. Some of the dimensions are given in the table. Fill in the missing dimensions.

*Use the volume formula and fill in the numbers that you know.*

| Volume in Cubic Inches | Length in Inches | Width in Inches | Height in Inches |
|---|---|---|---|
| 18 | 3 | 3 | 2 |
| 24 | 2 | 4 | 3 |
| 30 | 3 | 2 | 5 |
| 40 | 5 | 4 | 2 |
| 48 | 4 | 3 | 4 |

**M** **5** How can you make three different rectangular prisms using 18 one-centimeter cubes? Give the length, width, and height of each prism.

*What are the factors of 18?*

Answers will vary. Possible answer:

6 cm × 3 cm × 1 cm, 9 cm × 2 cm × 1 cm, and

2 cm × 3 cm × 3 cm

**M** **6** Jamie wants to use this container to make a block of ice that has a volume of 600 cubic centimeters. Draw a line that shows to what height she should fill the container with water.

*What dimensions do you know?*

**Show your work.**

15 × 10 = 150

150 × 4 = 600

| Key | |
|---|---|
| B | Basic |
| M | Medium |
| C | Challenge |

Lesson 27    *Use after Ready Instruction page 241*

## Find Volume of Composite Figures

Name: _____

### Find Volumes of Rectangular Prisms

**Study the example problem showing how to use the dimensions of a rectangular prism to find its volume. Then solve problems 1–8.**

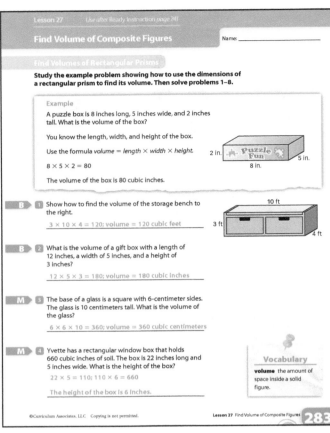

**Example**

A puzzle box is 8 inches long, 5 inches wide, and 2 inches tall. What is the volume of the box?

You know the length, width, and height of the box.

Use the formula *volume = length × width × height*.

$8 \times 5 \times 2 = 80$

The volume of the box is 80 cubic inches.

**B** ☐ 1 Show how to find the volume of the storage bench to the right.

$3 \times 10 \times 4 = 120$; volume = 120 cubic feet

**B** ☐ 2 What is the volume of a gift box with a length of 12 inches, a width of 5 inches, and a height of 3 inches?

$12 \times 5 \times 3 = 180$; volume = 180 cubic inches

**M** ☐ 3 The base of a glass is a square with 6-centimeter sides. The glass is 10 centimeters tall. What is the volume of the glass?

$6 \times 6 \times 10 = 360$; volume = 360 cubic centimeters

**M** ☐ 4 Yvette has a rectangular window box that holds 660 cubic inches of soil. The box is 22 inches long and 5 inches wide. What is the height of the box?

$22 \times 5 = 110$; $110 \times 6 = 660$

The height of the box is 6 inches.

**Vocabulary**

**volume** the amount of space inside a solid figure.

---

**Solve.**

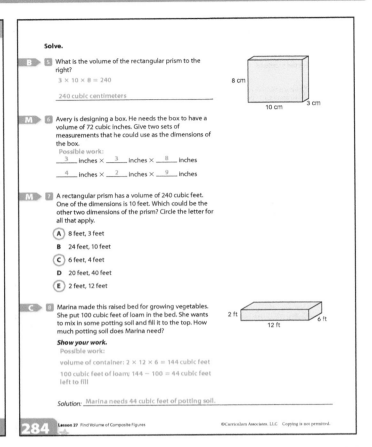

**B** ☐ 5 What is the volume of the rectangular prism to the right?

$3 \times 10 \times 8 = 240$

240 cubic centimeters

**M** ☐ 6 Avery is designing a box. He needs the box to have a volume of 72 cubic inches. Give two sets of measurements that he could use as the dimensions of the box.

Possible work:

__3__ inches × __3__ inches × __8__ inches

__4__ inches × __2__ inches × __9__ inches

**M** ☐ 7 A rectangular prism has a volume of 240 cubic feet. One of the dimensions is 10 feet. Which could be the other two dimensions of the prism? Circle the letter for all that apply.

(A) 8 feet, 3 feet

B   24 feet, 10 feet

(C) 6 feet, 4 feet

D   20 feet, 40 feet

(E) 2 feet, 12 feet

**C** ☐ 8 Marina made this raised bed for growing vegetables. She put 100 cubic feet of loam in the bed. She wants to mix in some potting soil and fill it to the top. How much potting soil does Marina need?

**Show your work.**

Possible work:

volume of container: $2 \times 12 \times 6 = 144$ cubic feet

100 cubic feet of loam; $144 - 100 = 44$ cubic feet left to fill

*Solution:* ___Marina needs 44 cubic feet of potting soil.___

---

Lesson 27 • *Use after Ready Instruction page 243*

Name: _____

### Break Apart Solid Figures to Find Volume

**Study the example problem showing how to break apart a solid figure into rectangular prisms and find its volume. Then solve problems 1–8.**

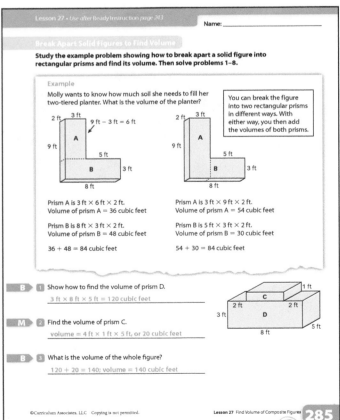

**Example**

Molly wants to know how much soil she needs to fill her two-tiered planter. What is the volume of the planter?

You can break the figure into two rectangular prisms in different ways. With either way, you then add the volumes of both prisms.

Prism A is 3 ft × 6 ft × 2 ft.
Volume of prism A = 36 cubic feet

Prism B is 8 ft × 3 ft × 2 ft.
Volume of prism B = 48 cubic feet

$36 + 48 = 84$ cubic feet

Prism A is 3 ft × 9 ft × 2 ft.
Volume of prism A = 54 cubic feet

Prism B is 5 ft × 3 ft × 2 ft.
Volume of prism B = 30 cubic feet

$54 + 30 = 84$ cubic feet

**B** ☐ 1 Show how to find the volume of prism D.

$3$ ft $\times 8$ ft $\times 5$ ft $= 120$ cubic feet

**M** ☐ 2 Find the volume of prism C.

volume = $4$ ft $\times 1$ ft $\times 5$ ft, or 20 cubic feet

**B** ☐ 3 What is the volume of the whole figure?

$120 + 20 = 140$; volume = 140 cubic feet

---

**Solve.**

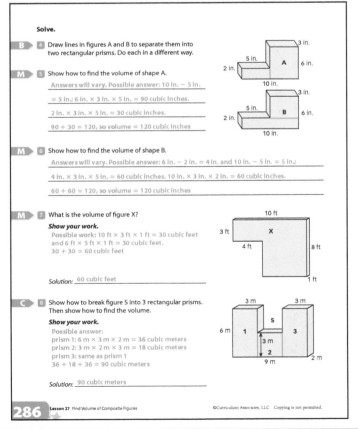

**B** ☐ 4 Draw lines in figures A and B to separate them into two rectangular prisms. Do each in a different way.

**M** ☐ 5 Show how to find the volume of shape A.

Answers will vary. Possible answer: 10 in. − 5 in.

$= 5$ in.; $6$ in. $\times 3$ in. $\times 5$ in. $= 90$ cubic inches.

$2$ in. $\times 3$ in. $\times 5$ in. $= 30$ cubic inches.

$90 + 30 = 120$, so volume = 120 cubic inches

**M** ☐ 6 Show how to find the volume of shape B.

Answers will vary. Possible answer: 6 in. − 2 in. = 4 in. and 10 in. − 5 in. = 5 in.;

$4$ in. $\times 3$ in. $\times 5$ in. $= 60$ cubic inches. $10$ in. $\times 3$ in. $\times 2$ in. $= 60$ cubic inches.

$60 + 60 = 120$, so volume = 120 cubic inches

**M** ☐ 7 What is the volume of figure X?

**Show your work.**

Possible work: 10 ft $\times 3$ ft $\times 1$ ft $= 30$ cubic feet and 6 ft $\times 5$ ft $\times 1$ ft $= 30$ cubic feet.

$30 + 30 = 60$ cubic feet

*Solution:* ___60 cubic feet___

**C** ☐ 8 Show how to break figure S into 3 rectangular prisms. Then show how to find the volume.

**Show your work.**

Possible answer:

prism 1: 6 m $\times 3$ m $\times 2$ m $= 36$ cubic meters

prism 2: 3 m $\times 2$ m $\times 3$ m $= 18$ cubic meters

prism 3: same as prism 1

$36 + 18 + 36 = 90$ cubic meters

*Solution:* ___90 cubic meters___

Lesson 27 • *Use after Ready Instruction page 245*

Name: _____

**Find Volume of Composite Figures**

**Solve the problems.**

**M** 1 Which expression can you use to find the volume of this figure? Circle the letter for all that apply.

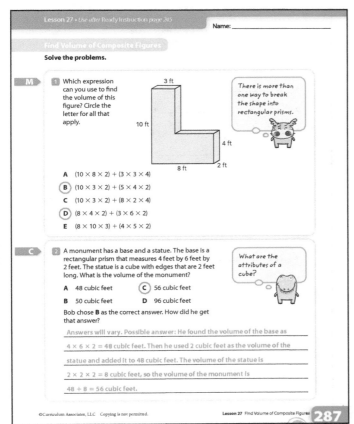

*There is more than one way to break the shape into rectangular prisms.*

A  $(10 \times 8 \times 2) + (3 \times 3 \times 4)$

**B**  $(10 \times 3 \times 2) + (5 \times 4 \times 2)$ ⊘

C  $(10 \times 3 \times 2) + (8 \times 2 \times 4)$

**D**  $(8 \times 4 \times 2) + (3 \times 6 \times 2)$ ⊘

E  $(8 \times 10 \times 3) + (4 \times 5 \times 2)$

**C** 2 A monument has a base and a statue. The base is a rectangular prism that measures 4 feet by 6 feet by 2 feet. The statue is a cube with edges that are 2 feet long. What is the volume of the monument?

*What are the attributes of a cube?*

A  48 cubic feet          **C**  56 cubic feet ⊘

B  50 cubic feet          D  96 cubic feet

Bob chose **B** as the correct answer. How did he get that answer?

Answers will vary. Possible answer: He found the volume of the base as

$4 \times 6 \times 2 = 48$ cubic feet. Then he used 2 cubic feet as the volume of the

statue and added it to 48 cubic feet. The volume of the statue is

$2 \times 2 \times 2 = 8$ cubic feet, so the volume of the monument is

$48 + 8 = 56$ cubic feet.

---

**Solve.**

**M** 3 Brody makes this wooden platform. Prism B is 10 feet long, 2 feet tall, and 4 feet deep. All dimensions of prism A are half those of prism B. What is the volume of the whole platform?

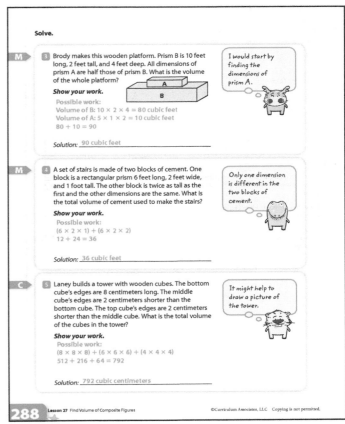

*I would start by finding the dimensions of prism A.*

**Show your work.**

Possible work:
Volume of B: $10 \times 2 \times 4 = 80$ cubic feet
Volume of A: $5 \times 1 \times 2 = 10$ cubic feet
$80 + 10 = 90$

*Solution:* __90 cubic feet__

**M** 4 A set of stairs is made of two blocks of cement. One block is a rectangular prism 6 feet long, 2 feet wide, and 1 foot tall. The other block is twice as tall as the first and the other dimensions are the same. What is the total volume of cement used to make the stairs?

*Only one dimension is different in the two blocks of cement.*

**Show your work.**

Possible work:
$(6 \times 2 \times 1) + (6 \times 2 \times 2)$
$12 + 24 = 36$

*Solution:* __36 cubic feet__

**C** 5 Laney builds a tower with wooden cubes. The bottom cube's edges are 8 centimeters long. The middle cube's edges are 2 centimeters shorter than the bottom cube. The top cube's edges are 2 centimeters shorter than the middle cube. What is the total volume of the cubes in the tower?

*It might help to draw a picture of the tower.*

**Show your work.**

Possible work:
$(8 \times 8 \times 8) + (6 \times 6 \times 6) + (4 \times 4 \times 4)$
$512 + 216 + 64 = 792$

*Solution:* __792 cubic centimeters__

| Key | |
|---|---|
| B | Basic |
| M | Medium |
| C | Challenge |

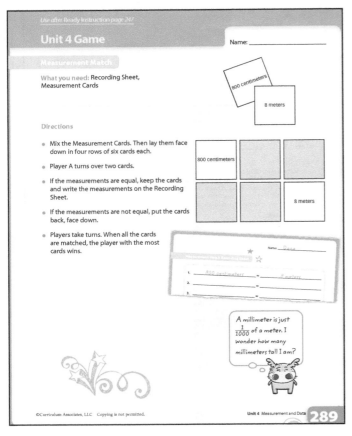

## STEP BY STEP

| | |
|---|---|
| **CCSS Focus** - 5.MD.A.1, 5.NBT.B.7   *Embedded SMPs* - 2, 6, 7<br>**Objective:** Convert between units of metric measurement: kilometers, meters, centimeters, and millimeters. | **Materials** For each pair: 2 Recording Sheets (1 for each player) (TR 6), 1 set of Measurement Cards (TR 7) |

- Mix the Game Cards. Then lay them face down in four rows of six cards each.

- Player A turns over two cards.

- If the measurements are equal, keep the cards and write the measurements on the Recording Sheet.

- If the measurements are not equal, put the cards back, face down.

- Players take turns. When all the cards are matched, the player with the most cards wins.

- Model one complete round for students before they play.

- Review the relationship between kilometers, meters, centimeters, and millimeters with students. Explain that, when they play this game, students should not look for matching units but rather for lengths that match. Ask, *How will you know if you have a match?*

**Vary the Game** Play to find any pair of cards in which one length is a power of ten times the other. Record the pair as, for example, 30 centimeters = 10 × 0.03 meter.

**Challenge** Have students make their own sets of cards. They may use metric measurements for length, capacity, or mass. Discuss with students what they feel makes the cards "harder" or "easier," and why.

*Use after Ready Instruction page 247*

## Unit 4 Practice

Name: _____

Measurement and Data

| In this unit you learned to: | Lesson |
|---|---|
| convert from one measurement to another, for example: 4 ft = 48 in. | 21, 22 |
| make a line plot of data represented as fractions of measurements. | 23 |
| find volume by counting unit cubes. | 24, 25 |
| find volume by using a formula. | 26 |
| find volumes of composite figures . | 27 |

**Use these skills to solve problems 1–5 .**

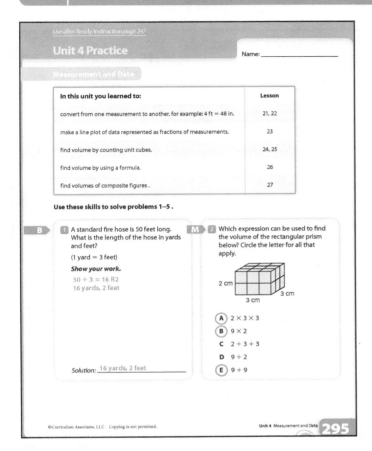

**B** 1 A standard fire hose is 50 feet long. What is the length of the hose in yards and feet?

(1 yard = 3 feet)

**Show your work.**

50 ÷ 3 = 16 R2
16 yards, 2 feet

Solution: __16 yards, 2 feet__

**M** 2 Which expression can be used to find the volume of the rectangular prism below? Circle the letter for all that apply.

2 cm
3 cm   3 cm

(A) $2 \times 3 \times 3$
(B) $9 \times 2$
C $2 + 3 + 3$
D $9 + 2$
(E) $9 + 9$

**Solve.**

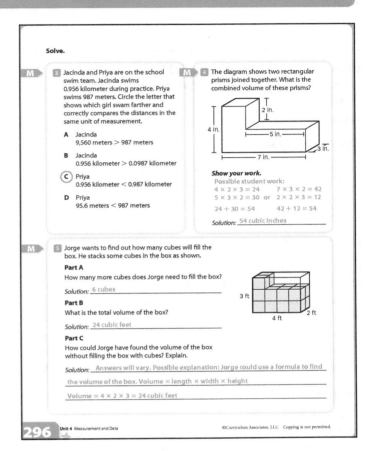

**M** 3 Jacinda and Priya are on the school swim team. Jacinda swims 0.956 kilometer during practice. Priya swims 987 meters. Circle the letter that shows which girl swam farther and correctly compares the distances in the same unit of measurement.

A Jacinda
9,560 meters > 987 meters

B Jacinda
0.956 kilometer > 0.0987 kilometer

(C) Priya
0.956 kilometer < 0.987 kilometer

D Priya
95.6 meters < 987 meters

**M** 4 The diagram shows two rectangular prisms joined together. What is the combined volume of these prisms?

2 in.
4 in.   5 in.
7 in.   3 in.

**Show your work.**
Possible student work:
4 × 2 × 3 = 24      7 × 3 × 2 = 42
5 × 3 × 2 = 30  or  2 × 2 × 3 = 12
24 + 30 = 54        42 + 12 = 54

Solution: __54 cubic inches__

**M** 5 Jorge wants to find out how many cubes will fill the box. He stacks some cubes in the box as shown.

**Part A**
How many more cubes does Jorge need to fill the box?

Solution: __6 cubes__

**Part B**
What is the total volume of the box?

Solution: __24 cubic feet__

3 ft
4 ft   2 ft

**Part C**
How could Jorge have found the volume of the box without filling the box with cubes? Explain.

Solution: __Answers will vary. Possible explanation: Jorge could use a formula to find__
the volume of the box. Volume = length × width × height
Volume = 4 × 2 × 3 = 24 cubic feet

## TEACHER NOTES

**Common Core Standards:** 5. MD.C.5b, 5.MD.C.5c
**Standards for Mathematical Practice:** 1, 2, 4, 5, 6, 7
**DOK:** 3
**Materials:** None

### About the Task

To complete this task, students solve a multi-step problem that involves determining dimensions for rectangular prisms and then finding the volume of a composite figure made of rectangular prisms.

### Getting Students Started

Read the problem aloud with students and go over the checklist. Discuss how the pool might look and have students draw rough sketches of their ideas. Talk about features different community members might prefer and why. Refer students to the table on the back of the student page. Guide students to recognize how a table like this can help them organize their work. **(SMP 1, 2)**

### Completing the Task

Some students may begin by deciding to aim for a certain volume in each section. Others may start by establishing dimensions for a section and then computing the volume. As you circulate, ask students to explain the approach they are using. Ask, *How will you know if your pool design meets the specifications?* **(SMP 6, 7)**

Students should use the formula for volume, Volume = length × width × height. If necessary, explain that *depth* means the height from the bottom of the pool to the top. After they compute the volume of each section, they must add the volumes of the sections to find the total volume of the pool. **(SMP 5, 6)**

Have students share their pool designs and descriptions. Ask them to explain how they solved the problem and talk about any snags they ran into along the way. Some students may have found that their initial designs did not fit the specifications. Ask them to describe how they changed their designs to meet the needs of the problem. **(SMP 7, 8)**

### Unit 4 Performance Task

Name: _____

**Answer the questions and show all your work on separate paper.**

There's going to be a new swimming pool at the park! The pool will be used by everyone who lives nearby. This includes people of all ages. Some just want to play in the water, others will swim laps for exercise. There will even be an area for diving.

To meet everyone's needs, the pool will have 3 sections and each section will have a different depth:
- 2 ft deep for playing,
- 4 ft deep for lap swimming, and
- 15 ft deep for diving.

Each section of the pool will be a rectangular prism, but the lengths and widths do not have to be the same.

The 4-ft deep section should be at least 80 feet long and no more than 40 feet wide.

The other sections must be 20–50 feet wide and no more than 60 feet long.

The park supervisor has decided that the total volume of the pool must be between 35,000 and 46,000 cubic feet. This will help keep costs under control.

Make a plan for the pool. Include a chart and show that your plan meets all specifications. Draw a diagram of how the sections will fit together, as seen from above. Be sure to label the dimensions. Include 2 or 3 sentences to describe the pool design to the park supervisor.

> Checklist
>
> Did you ...
> ☐ draw a diagram?
> ☐ use a formula?
> ☐ describe your plan?

#### Reflect on Mathematical Practices

1. **Make Models** What does your diagram tell you that your chart does not? Why is this important?

2. **Be Precise** Why is it important to write the units when working with measurement?

©Curriculum Associates, LLC   Copying is not permitted.     Unit 4 Measurement and Data **297**

### Extension

If some students have more time to spend on this problem, you can have them solve this extension:

The park supervisor wants to expand the width of the 4-ft section, to allow more room to play. If the total volume can now go up to 48,000 cubic feet, how much wider can you make that section in one of your pool designs?

©Curriculum Associates, LLC   Copying is not permitted.

## SAMPLE RESPONSES AND RUBRIC

### 4-Point Solution

I decided to use a U shape. For safety, the diving area is totally separate from the play area. There is plenty of room on all sides of pool for people to spread out and keep their belongings. The chart shows that the total volume of the pool is 44,800 cubic feet and this is between 35,000 and 46,000 cubic feet. The width of sections 1 and 3 (20 feet and 40 feet) are both between 20 and 50 feet. The length of these sections (50 feet) is less than 60 feet. The depths are 2 feet and 10 feet as specified. Section 2 is 4 feet deep, no more than 40 feet wide, and at least 80 feet long.

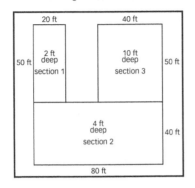

|           | length | width | depth | volume       |
|-----------|--------|-------|-------|--------------|
| Section 1 | 50 ft  | 20 ft | 2 ft  | 2,000 cu ft  |
| Section 2 | 80 ft  | 40 ft | 4 ft  | 12,800 cu ft |
| Section 3 | 50 ft  | 40 ft | 15 ft | 30,000 cu ft |
| **TOTAL** |        |       |       | 44,800 cu ft |

## REFLECT ON MATHEMATICAL PRACTICES

1. Students should recognize that the diagram shows the shape of the pool but the chart does not. Without the diagram, no one would know what the pool looks like. (**SMP 4**)

2. Students should explain that the units tell the size. (**SMP 6**)

## SCORING RUBRIC

**4 points**   The student has completed all parts of the problem correctly. The calculations and chart are accurate. The design has three sections and all dimensions are labeled correctly. The student has described the pools. The dimensions fit the problem parameters.

**3 points**   The student has completed all parts of the problem, with one or two errors. The errors may be in the calculations. The design has three sections and most dimensions are labeled correctly. The student has described the pools. The dimensions fit the problem parameters.

**2 points**   The student has attempted all parts of the problem but has a number of errors. The chart has errors. The design may be incomplete. The student may not have described the pools. Some of the dimensions fit the problem parameters.

**1 point**   The student has not completed the problem. There are several errors. The calculations and chart are mostly incorrect. The design is incomplete. There may be no description. Many of the dimensions do fit the problem parameters.

## SOLUTION TO THE EXTENSION

### Possible Solution

The total volume of my pool design is 44,800 cubic feet. I can expand the volume to 48,000 cubic feet, so I can expand the volume of the 4-foot deep section by as much as 3,200 cubic feet. If I make this section 10 feet wider, I'll be adding $10 \times 80 \times 4$, or 3,200 cubic feet to the volume, which is within the limit. I can make this section 50 feet wide.

©Curriculum Associates, LLC   Copying is not permitted.

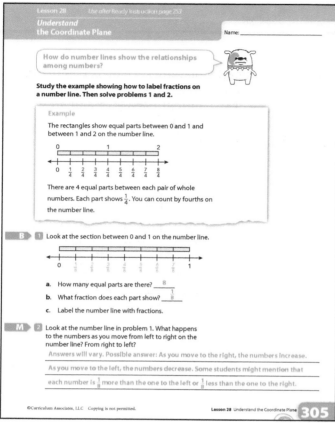

Lesson 28    *Use after Ready Instruction page 253*

**Understand**
**the Coordinate Plane**                                          Name: _____

How do number lines show the relationships among numbers?

**Study the example showing how to label fractions on a number line. Then solve problems 1 and 2.**

**Example**

The rectangles show equal parts between 0 and 1 and between 1 and 2 on the number line.

There are 4 equal parts between each pair of whole numbers. Each part shows $\frac{1}{4}$. You can count by fourths on the number line.

**B  1**  Look at the section between 0 and 1 on the number line.

**a.**  How many equal parts are there? ___8___

**b.**  What fraction does each part show? ___$\frac{1}{8}$___

**c.**  Label the number line with fractions.

**M  2**  Look at the number line in problem 1. What happens to the numbers as you move from left to right on the number line? From right to left?

Answers will vary. Possible answer: As you move to the right, the numbers increase.

As you move to the left, the numbers decrease. Some students might mention that

each number is $\frac{1}{8}$ more than the one to the left or $\frac{1}{8}$ less than the one to the right.

©Curriculum Associates, LLC   Copying is not permitted.                    **Lesson 28** Understand the Coordinate Plane  **305**

---

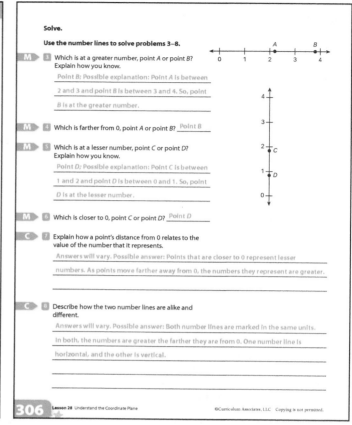

**306**   **Lesson 28** Understand the Coordinate Plane

**Solve.**

**Use the number lines to solve problems 3–8.**

**M  3**  Which is at a greater number, point A or point B? Explain how you know.

Point B; Possible explanation: Point A is between

2 and 3 and point B is between 3 and 4. So, point

B is at the greater number.

**M  4**  Which is farther from 0, point A or point B? ___Point B___

**M  5**  Which is at a lesser number, point C or point D? Explain how you know.

Point D; Possible explanation: Point C is between

1 and 2 and point D is between 0 and 1. So, point

D is at the lesser number.

**M  6**  Which is closer to 0, point C or point D? ___Point D___

**C  7**  Explain how a point's distance from 0 relates to the value of the number that it represents.

Answers will vary. Possible answer: Points that are closer to 0 represent lesser

numbers. As points move farther away from 0, the numbers they represent are greater.

**C  8**  Describe how the two number lines are alike and different.

Answers will vary. Possible answer: Both number lines are marked in the same units.

In both, the numbers are greater the farther they are from 0. One number line is

horizontal, and the other is vertical.

©Curriculum Associates, LLC   Copying is not permitted.

---

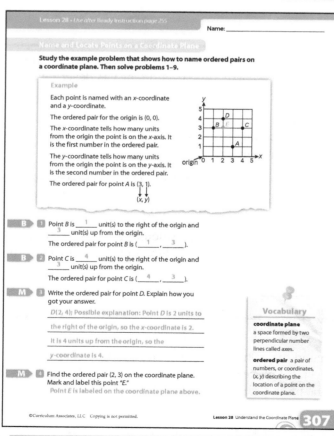

Lesson 28 · *Use after Ready Instruction page 255*

                                              Name: _____

**Name and Locate Points on a Coordinate Plane**

**Study the example problem that shows how to name ordered pairs on a coordinate plane. Then solve problems 1–9.**

**Example**

Each point is named with an *x*-coordinate and a *y*-coordinate.

The ordered pair for the origin is (0, 0).

The *x*-coordinate tells how many units from the origin the point is on the *x*-axis. It is the first number in the ordered pair.

The *y*-coordinate tells how many units from the origin the point is on the *y*-axis. It is the second number in the ordered pair.

The ordered pair for point A is (3, 1).
                                (x, y)

**B  1**  Point B is ___1___ unit(s) to the right of the origin and ___3___ unit(s) up from the origin.

The ordered pair for point B is ( ___1___ , ___3___ ).

**B  2**  Point C is ___4___ unit(s) to the right of the origin and ___3___ unit(s) up from the origin.

The ordered pair for point C is ( ___4___ , ___3___ ).

**M  3**  Write the ordered pair for point D. Explain how you got your answer.

D(2, 4); Possible explanation: Point D is 2 units to

the right of the origin, so the x-coordinate is 2.

It is 4 units up from the origin, so the

y-coordinate is 4.

**Vocabulary**

**coordinate plane** a space formed by two perpendicular number lines called axes.

**ordered pair** a pair of numbers, or coordinates, (x, y) describing the location of a point on the coordinate plane.

**M  4**  Find the ordered pair (2, 3) on the coordinate plane. Mark and label this point "E."

Point E is labeled on the coordinate plane above.

©Curriculum Associates, LLC   Copying is not permitted.                    **Lesson 28** Understand the Coordinate Plane  **307**

---

**308**   **Lesson 28** Understand the Coordinate Plane

**Solve.**

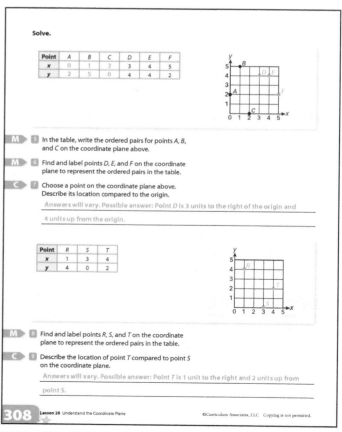

| Point | A | B | C | D | E | F |
|-------|---|---|---|---|---|---|
| x | 0 | 1 | 2 | 3 | 4 | 5 |
| y | 2 | 5 | 0 | 4 | 4 | 2 |

**M  5**  In the table, write the ordered pairs for points A, B, and C on the coordinate plane above.

**M  6**  Find and label points D, E, and F on the coordinate plane to represent the ordered pairs in the table.

**C  7**  Choose a point on the coordinate plane above. Describe its location compared to the origin.

Answers will vary. Possible answer: Point D is 3 units to the right of the origin and

4 units up from the origin.

| Point | R | S | T |
|-------|---|---|---|
| x | 1 | 3 | 4 |
| y | 4 | 0 | 2 |

**M  8**  Find and label points R, S, and T on the coordinate plane to represent the ordered pairs in the table.

**C  9**  Describe the location of point T compared to point S on the coordinate plane.

Answers will vary. Possible answer: Point T is 1 unit to the right and 2 units up from

point S.

©Curriculum Associates, LLC   Copying is not permitted.

---

                                                                    Unit 5 Geometry

©Curriculum Associates, LLC   Copying is not permitted.

Lesson 28 • *Use after Ready Instruction page 256*

Name: _____

**Reason and Write**

Answers will vary. Note whether students incorporate the features they chose in their answer on the next page.

**Study the example. Underline two parts that you think make it a particularly good answer and a helpful example.**

**Example**

Find the ordered pair (0, 4) on the coordinate plane. Label the point *P*. Use point *P* as a corner, then draw a square. Label the other corners with letters. List the coordinate pairs for all corners.

Explain how you solved the problem and how you know that you drew a square.

***Show your work.*** Use pictures, words, or numbers to explain.

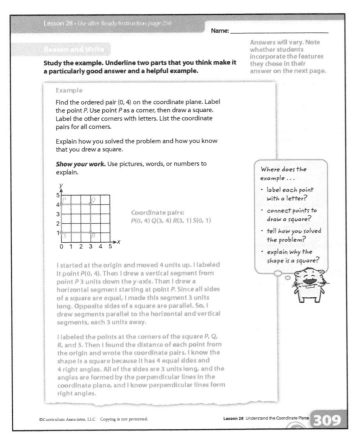

Coordinate pairs:
*P*(0, 4) *Q*(3, 4) *R*(3, 1) *S*(0, 1)

Where does the example . . .
• label each point with a letter?
• connect points to draw a square?
• tell how you solved the problem?
• explain why the shape is a square?

I started at the origin and moved 4 units up. I labeled it point *P*(0, 4). Then I drew a vertical segment from point *P* 3 units down the *y*-axis. Then I drew a horizontal segment starting at point *P*. Since all sides of a square are equal, I made this segment 3 units long. Opposite sides of a square are parallel. So, I drew segments parallel to the horizontal and vertical segments, each 3 units away.

I labeled the points at the corners of the square *P*, *Q*, *R*, and *S*. Then I found the distance of each point from the origin and wrote the coordinate pairs. I know the shape is a square because it has 4 equal sides and 4 right angles. All of the sides are 3 units long, and the angles are formed by the perpendicular lines in the coordinate plane, and I know perpendicular lines form right angles.

©Curriculum Associates, LLC   Copying is not permitted.     **Lesson 28** Understand the Coordinate Plane  **309**

**310**  Lesson 28 Understand the Coordinate Plane     ©Curriculum Associates, LLC   Copying is not permitted.

**Solve the problem. Use what you learned from the example.**

Find the ordered pair (1, 3) on the coordinate plane. Label it point *A*. Use point *A* as a corner, then draw a right triangle. Label the other corners with letters. List the coordinate pairs for all corners.

Explain how you solved the problem and how you know that you drew a right triangle.

***Show your work.*** Use models, words, and numbers to explain your answer.

Possible answer:

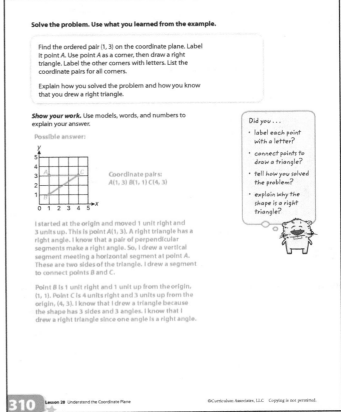

Coordinate pairs:
*A*(1, 3) *B*(1, 1) *C*(4, 3)

Did you . . .
• label each point with a letter?
• connect points to draw a triangle?
• tell how you solved the problem?
• explain why the shape is a right triangle?

I started at the origin and moved 1 unit right and 3 units up. This is point *A*(1, 3). A right triangle has a right angle. I know that a pair of perpendicular segments make a right angle. So, I drew a vertical segment meeting a horizontal segment at point *A*. These are two sides of the triangle. I drew a segment to connect points *B* and *C*.

Point *B* is 1 unit right and 1 unit up from the origin, (1, 1). Point *C* is 4 units right and 3 units up from the origin, (4, 3). I know that I drew a triangle because the shape has 3 sides and 3 angles. I know that I drew a right triangle since one angle is a right angle.

| Key | |
|---|---|
| B | Basic |
| M | Medium |
| C | Challenge |

©Curriculum Associates, LLC    Copying is not permitted.

Lesson 29   *Use after Ready Instruction page 259*

### Graph Points in the Coordinate Plane

Name: _____

**Identify Ordered Pairs**

Study the example showing how to name a point on a coordinate plane. Then solve problems 1–3.

**Example**

What is the ordered pair for point A?

The location of a point is named with an x-coordinate and a y-coordinate. The coordinates are written as an ordered pair, (x-coordinate, y-coordinate).

Start at the y-axis. Point A is 2 units to the right of the origin.

Start at the x-axis. Point A is 1 unit up from the origin.

The ordered pair for point A is (2, 1).

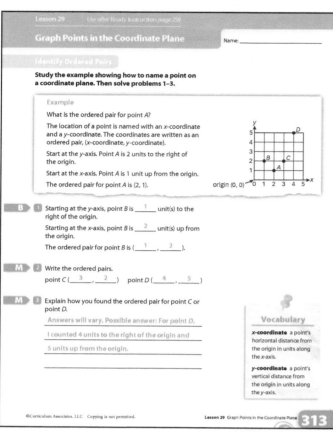

origin (0, 0)

**B** **1** Starting at the y-axis, point B is __1__ unit(s) to the right of the origin.

Starting at the x-axis, point B is __2__ unit(s) up from the origin.

The ordered pair for point B is ( __1__ , __2__ ).

**M** **2** Write the ordered pairs.

point C ( __3__ , __2__ )    point D ( __4__ , __5__ )

**M** **3** Explain how you found the ordered pair for point C or point D.

Answers will vary. Possible answer: For point D,

I counted 4 units to the right of the origin and

5 units up from the origin.

**Vocabulary**

**x-coordinate** a point's horizontal distance from the origin in units along the x-axis.

**y-coordinate** a point's vertical distance from the origin in units along the y-axis.

---

Use the coordinate plane to solve problems 4–6.

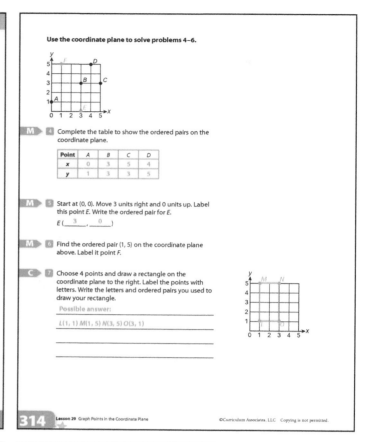

**M** **4** Complete the table to show the ordered pairs on the coordinate plane.

| Point | A | B | C | D |
|-------|---|---|---|---|
| x | 0 | 3 | 5 | 4 |
| y | 1 | 3 | 3 | 5 |

**M** **5** Start at (0, 0). Move 3 units right and 0 units up. Label this point E. Write the ordered pair for E.

E ( __3__ , __0__ )

**M** **6** Find the ordered pair (1, 5) on the coordinate plane above. Label it point F.

**C** **7** Choose 4 points and draw a rectangle on the coordinate plane to the right. Label the points with letters. Write the letters and ordered pairs you used to draw your rectangle.

Possible answer:

L(1, 1) M(1, 5) N(3, 5) O(3, 1)

_____

_____

---

Lesson 29 · *Use after Ready Instruction page 261*

Name: _____

**Show Relationships on a Coordinate Plane**

Study the example problem showing how to represent and use relationships between quantities. Then solve problems 1–7.

**Example**

Holly is playing a crane game at the arcade. With each quarter, she gets 2 tries to grab a stuffed animal with the crane. Holly wants to know how many tries she will get using different numbers of quarters.

Show the relationship between quarters and numbers of tries.

You can use equations.    You can use a table.

1 × 2 = 2 tries
2 × 2 = 4 tries
3 × 2 = 6 tries
4 × 2 = 8 tries
5 × 2 = 10 tries

| Number of Quarters | 1 | 2 | 3 | 4 | 5 |
|-------|---|---|---|---|---|
| Number of Tries | 2 | 4 | 6 | 8 | 10 |

**B** **1** Use the table in the example above. Finish plotting the ordered pairs from the table in the coordinate plane to the right.

**M** **2** What is the meaning of the ordered pair (3, 6)?

The ordered pair (3, 6) means that with

3 quarters you get 6 tries.

**C** **3** Describe a path from (1, 2) to (2, 4) and from (2, 4) to (3, 6). If you continue from point to point, what do you notice?

Answers will vary. Possible answer: Start at (1, 2). Move 1 unit right and 2 units up to

get to (2, 4). Start at (2, 4). Move 1 unit right and 2 units up to get to (3, 6). From point

to point, you move 1 unit right and 2 units up each time.

---

**Solve.**

Holly plays a different game at the arcade. It takes 2 tokens to play the game. She starts with 10 tokens.

**M** **4** Write an equation that can be used to determine how many tokens she has left after playing the game each time. Fill in the blanks.

__10__ tokens – ( __2__ tokens × number of __games__ ) = number of tokens left

**M** **5** Use the equation to complete the table.

| Number of Games Played | 1 | 2 | 3 | 4 | 5 |
|-------|---|---|---|---|---|
| Number of Tokens Left | 8 | 6 | 4 | 2 | 0 |

**M** **6** Plot the ordered pairs from the table on the coordinate plane. Choose a point on the coordinate plane and tell what it means.

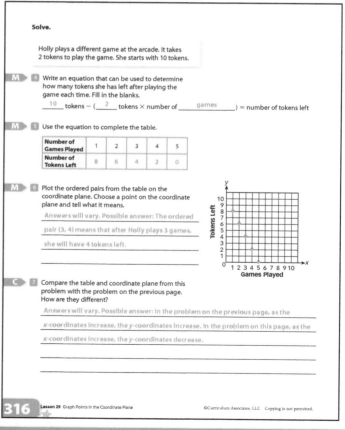

Answers will vary. Possible answer: The ordered

pair (3, 4) means that after Holly plays 3 games,

she will have 4 tokens left.

_____

**C** **7** Compare the table and coordinate plane from this problem with the problem on the previous page. How are they different?

Answers will vary. Possible answer: In the problem on the previous page, as the

x-coordinates increase, the y-coordinates increase. In the problem on this page, as the

x-coordinates increase, the y-coordinates decrease.

_____

_____

©Curriculum Associates, LLC    Copying is not permitted.

Lesson 29 • Use after Ready Instruction page 263

Name: _____

**Solve Measurement Problems on the Coordinate Plane**

Study the example that shows how to solve a measurement problem with a shape on a coordinate plane. Then solve problems 1–6.

Example

The owner plans to add a new game room to the arcade. He draws a rectangle on the coordinate plane to represent the room. What is the area of the rectangle?

From point G to point A, go up 6 units.
From point A to point M, go right 5 units.
Length of $\overline{GA}$ is 6 units and length of $\overline{AM}$ is 5 units.

Area of a rectangle = length × width
Multiply the lengths of the sides to find the area of the rectangle: 6 × 5 = 30.
Area of rectangle GAME = 30 square units

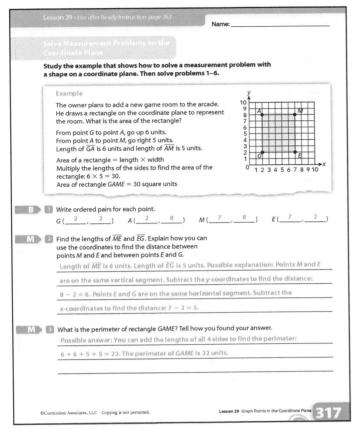

**B  1** Write ordered pairs for each point.

G ( __2__ , __2__ )   A ( __2__ , __8__ )   M ( __7__ , __8__ )   E ( __7__ , __2__ )

**M  2** Find the lengths of $\overline{ME}$ and $\overline{EG}$. Explain how you can use the coordinates to find the distance between points M and E and between points E and G.

Length of $\overline{ME}$ is 6 units. Length of $\overline{EG}$ is 5 units. Possible explanation: Points M and E

are on the same vertical segment. Subtract the y-coordinates to find the distance:

8 − 2 = 6. Points E and G are on the same horizontal segment. Subtract the

x-coordinates to find the distance: 7 − 2 = 5.

**M  3** What is the perimeter of rectangle GAME? Tell how you found your answer.

Possible answer: You can add the lengths of all 4 sides to find the perimeter:

6 + 6 + 5 + 5 = 22. The perimeter of GAME is 22 units.

---

Use the coordinate plane to solve problems 4 and 5.

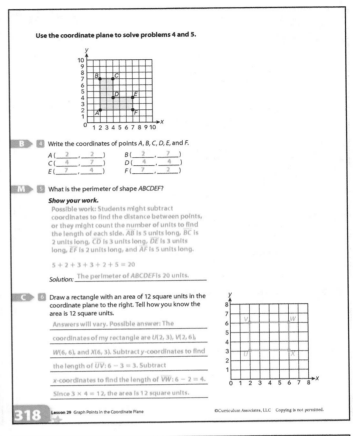

**B  4** Write the coordinates of points A, B, C, D, E, and F.

A ( __2__ , __2__ )   B ( __2__ , __7__ )
C ( __4__ , __7__ )   D ( __4__ , __4__ )
E ( __7__ , __4__ )   F ( __7__ , __2__ )

**M  5** What is the perimeter of shape ABCDEF?

*Show your work.*

Possible work: Students might subtract coordinates to find the distance between points, or they might count the number of units to find the length of each side. $\overline{AB}$ is 5 units long, $\overline{BC}$ is 2 units long, $\overline{CD}$ is 3 units long, $\overline{DE}$ is 3 units long, $\overline{EF}$ is 2 units long, and $\overline{AF}$ is 5 units long.

5 + 2 + 3 + 3 + 2 + 5 = 20

*Solution:* The perimeter of ABCDEF is 20 units.

**C  6** Draw a rectangle with an area of 12 square units in the coordinate plane to the right. Tell how you know the area is 12 square units.

Answers will vary. Possible answer: The

coordinates of my rectangle are U(2, 3), V(2, 6),

W(6, 6), and X(6, 3). Subtract y-coordinates to find

the length of $\overline{UV}$: 6 − 3 = 3. Subtract

x-coordinates to find the length of $\overline{VW}$: 6 − 2 = 4.

Since 3 × 4 = 12, the area is 12 square units.

---

Lesson 29 • Use after Ready Instruction page 261

Name: _____

**Graph Points in the Coordinate Plane**

Solve the problems.

**M  1** Look at rectangle ABCD. Tell whether each statement is True or False.

You can use 2 (l + w) to find the perimeter of a rectangle.

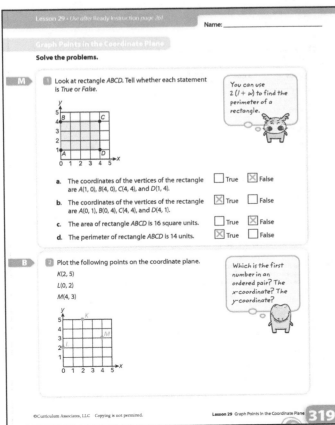

a. The coordinates of the vertices of the rectangle are A(1, 0), B(4, 0), C(4, 4), and D(1, 4).   ☐ True  ☒ False

b. The coordinates of the vertices of the rectangle are A(0, 1), B(0, 4), C(4, 4), and D(4, 1).   ☒ True  ☐ False

c. The area of rectangle ABCD is 16 square units.   ☐ True  ☒ False

d. The perimeter of rectangle ABCD is 14 units.   ☒ True  ☐ False

**B  2** Plot the following points on the coordinate plane.

K(2, 5)
L(0, 2)
M(4, 3)

Which is the first number in an ordered pair? The x-coordinate? The y-coordinate?

---

Solve.

**C  3** Use the coordinate plane to the right. Start at (0, 1). Move 2 units right and 3 units up. Which point shows this location? Circle the letter of the correct answer.

You can move right first or up first.

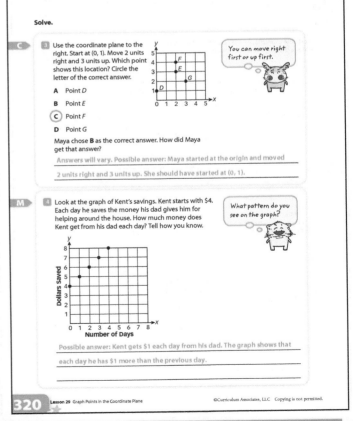

A  Point D

B  Point E

Ⓒ  Point F

D  Point G

Maya chose **B** as the correct answer. How did Maya get that answer?

Answers will vary. Possible answer: Maya started at the origin and moved

2 units right and 3 units up. She should have started at (0, 1).

**M  4** Look at the graph of Kent's savings. Kent starts with $4. Each day he saves the money his dad gives him for helping around the house. How much money does Kent get from his dad each day? Tell how you know.

What pattern do you see on the graph?

Possible answer: Kent gets $1 each day from his dad. The graph shows that

each day he has $1 more than the previous day.

Lesson 30 *Use after Ready Instruction page 209*

## Classify Two-Dimensional Figures

Name: _____

### Identify Parallel and Perpendicular Lines

**Study the example problem that shows how to sort shapes based on parallel and perpendicular sides. Then solve problems 1–6.**

**Example**

Mark each shape that appears to have at least one pair of parallel sides with the symbol ∥. Mark each shape that appears to have at least one pair of perpendicular sides with the symbol ⊥.

Parallel sides are always the same distance apart and will never cross. Perpendicular sides form a right angle (90°).

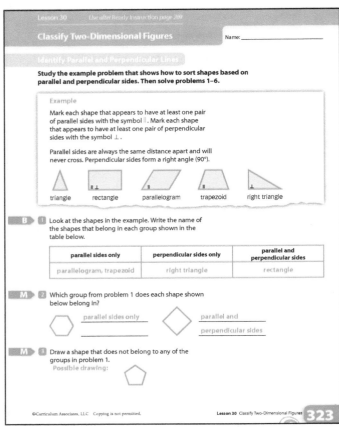

triangle   rectangle   parallelogram   trapezoid   right triangle

**B** **1** Look at the shapes in the example. Write the name of the shapes that belong in each group shown in the table below.

| parallel sides only | perpendicular sides only | parallel and perpendicular sides |
|---|---|---|
| parallelogram, trapezoid | right triangle | rectangle |

**M** **2** Which group from problem 1 does each shape shown below belong in?

⬡ _parallel sides only_

◇ _parallel and_ _perpendicular sides_

**M** **3** Draw a shape that does not belong to any of the groups in problem 1.
Possible drawing:

⬠

---

**Solve.**

A right angle is an angle that looks like a square corner and measures 90°.

An acute angle has a smaller opening than a right angle.

An obtuse angle has a wider opening than a right angle but is not a straight line.

**M** **4** Finish marking each angle in these shapes: "a" for acute, "r" for right, and "o" for obtuse.

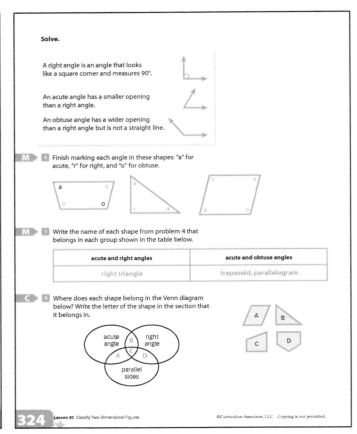

**M** **5** Write the name of each shape from problem 4 that belongs in each group shown in the table below.

| acute and right angles | acute and obtuse angles |
|---|---|
| right triangle | trapezoid, parallelogram |

**C** **6** Where does each shape belong in the Venn diagram below? Write the letter of the shape in the section that it belongs in.

---

Lesson 30 • *Use after Ready Instruction page 211*

Name: _____

### Order Shapes in a Hierarchy

**Study the example showing how to order shapes in a hierarchy. Then solve problems 1–6.**

**Example**

A hierarchy starts with the most general category and then shows how more specific groups are related. Draw a tree diagram relating the shapes in the table.

| Shape | Description |
|---|---|
| plane figure | a two-dimensional shape |
| polygon | a closed plane figure with straight sides |
| triangle | a polygon with 3 sides |
| quadrilateral | a polygon with 4 sides |
| pentagon | a polygon with 5 sides |

Polygons have all the properties that plane figures have. Polygons also have properties that plane figures don't have. Polygons appear right below plane figures in the hierarchy.

Triangles, quadrilaterals, and pentagons have all the properties that polygons have. They have other properties, too. Because triangles, quadrilaterals, and pentagons have different properties from each other, they appear side-by-side.

**Tree Diagram**

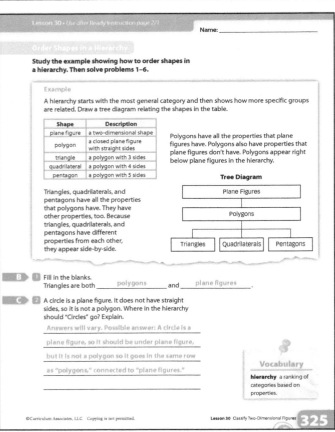

**B** **1** Fill in the blanks.
Triangles are both _____polygons_____ and __plane figures__ .

**C** **2** A circle is a plane figure. It does not have straight sides, so it is not a polygon. Where in the hierarchy should "Circles" go? Explain.
Answers will vary. Possible answer: A circle is a

plane figure, so it should be under plane figure,

but it is not a polygon so it goes in the same row

as "polygons," connected to "plane figures."

_____

**Vocabulary**

**hierarchy** a ranking of categories based on properties.

---

**Solve.**

**M** **3** Mark an X in the column if the shape always has that property.

| Shape | 4 sides | 2 pairs of parallel sides | 4 right angles |
|---|---|---|---|
| parallelogram | X | X | |
| rectangle | X | X | X |
| quadrilateral | X | | |

**M** **4** Use the table in problem 3 to make a flow chart that shows the relationship between the three shapes. Order the shapes from general to specific going from left to right.

| quadrilaterals | → | parallelograms | → | rectangles |

**M** **5** Where would you include squares in the flow chart in problem 4? Explain.
Answers will vary. Possible answer: Squares would go to the right of rectangles.

Squares have all the properties of quadrilaterals, parallelograms, and rectangles.

Squares also have another property—4 congruent sides.

**M** **6** Fill in the Venn diagram that shows the relationship between rectangles, squares, and rhombuses. Explain what the diagram shows about squares.

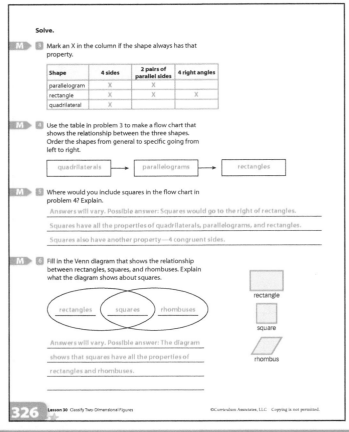

rectangles   squares   rhombuses

rectangle
square
rhombus

Answers will vary. Possible answer: The diagram

shows that squares have all the properties of

rectangles and rhombuses.

**Classify Two-Dimensional Figures**

**Solve the problems.**

**B** 1 Look at the flow chart below.

| Triangle | → | Isosceles | → | Equilateral |

Which statement is true? Circle the letter of all that apply.

(A) Equilateral triangles can be classified as isosceles triangles.

B Isosceles triangles have all the properties that equilateral triangles have.

C Isosceles triangles can be classified as equilateral triangles.

(D) Equilateral triangles have all the properties that isosceles triangles have.

*Which is the most general category? The most specific?*

**M** 2 Create a Venn diagram to show the hierarchy of triangles, quadrilaterals, isosceles triangles, and polygons.

Possible diagram:

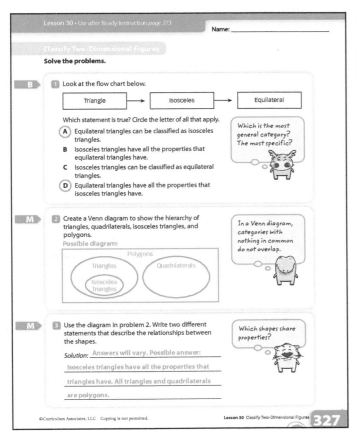

*In a Venn diagram, categories with nothing in common do not overlap.*

**M** 3 Use the diagram in problem 2. Write two different statements that describe the relationships between the shapes.

*Solution:* Answers will vary. Possible answer:

Isosceles triangles have all the properties that

triangles have. All triangles and quadrilaterals

are polygons.

*Which shapes share properties?*

**Solve.**

**M** 4 Look at the tree diagram below.

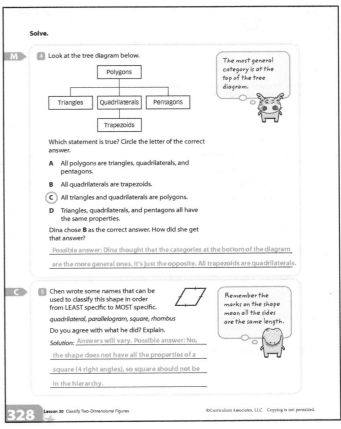

Which statement is true? Circle the letter of the correct answer.

A All polygons are triangles, quadrilaterals, and pentagons.

B All quadrilaterals are trapezoids.

(C) All triangles and quadrilaterals are polygons.

D Triangles, quadrilaterals, and pentagons all have the same properties.

Dina chose **B** as the correct answer. How did she get that answer?

Possible answer: Dina thought that the categories at the bottom of the diagram

are the more general ones. It's just the opposite. All trapezoids are quadrilaterals.

**C** 5 Chen wrote some names that can be used to classify this shape in order from LEAST specific to MOST specific.

*quadrilateral, parallelogram, square, rhombus*

Do you agree with what he did? Explain.

*Solution:* Answers will vary. Possible answer: No,

the shape does not have all the properties of a

square (4 right angles), so square should not be

in the hierarchy.

*Remember the marks on the shape mean all the sides are the same length.*

| Key | |
|---|---|
| B | Basic |
| M | Medium |
| C | Challenge |

©Curriculum Associates, LLC   Copying is not permitted.

Lesson 31    *Use after Ready Instruction page 277*

**Understand**
**Properties of Two-Dimensional Figures**          Name: _____

How do you name triangles?

**Study the example showing the different names that can be used for a triangle. Then solve problems 1–8.**

> **Example**
>
> What is the name of this triangle?
>
> You can name triangles based on their sides and angles.
>
> | Name | Description of Sides |
> |------|---------------------|
> | equilateral | 3 equal sides |
> | isosceles | at least 2 equal sides |
> | scalene | 0 equal sides |
>
> | Name | Description of Angles |
> |------|----------------------|
> | acute | 3 acute angles |
> | right | 1 right angle |
> | obtuse | 1 obtuse angle |
>
> The triangle has a right angle, so it is a right triangle.
>
> The triangle also has 2 equal sides, so it is also an isosceles triangle.
>
> The name of the triangle is a right isosceles triangle.

**B** ➊ Look at triangle A. How would you describe its sides?

Triangle A has 3 equal sides.

**B** ➋ What kinds of angles does triangle A have?

Triangle A has 3 acute angles.

**B** ➌ What are two names for triangle A?

equilateral and acute

**M** ➍ What are two names for triangle B? Explain.

Triangle B has 0 equal sides, so it's a scalene triangle. It also has 3 acute angles, so it's

an acute triangle.

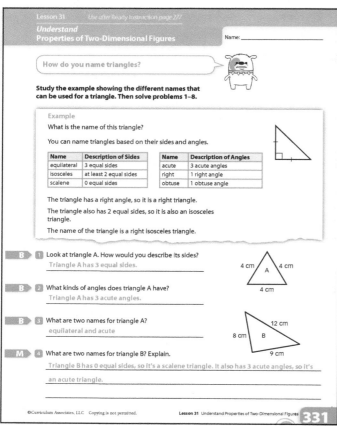

©Curriculum Associates, LLC   Copying is not permitted.    **Lesson 31** Understand Properties of Two-Dimensional Figures **331**

---

**Solve.**

**M** ➎ Can triangle C be called an acute triangle? Why or why not?

No; Possible explanation: Triangle C has 2 acute

angles. An acute triangle has 3 acute angles, so

triangle C cannot be called acute.

**C** ➏ How are these triangles alike? How are they different?

Answers will vary. Possible answer: Both

triangles have 2 equal sides, so they are isosceles

triangles. One triangle has a right angle, so it's a

right triangle. Since the other triangle has

3 acute angles, it's an acute triangle.

**M** ➐ Look at triangles D and E. Triangle D's sides are all different lengths. Triangle E has two sides of the same length. Write a letter D or E in the table below for all possible names of each triangle.

| equilateral | isosceles | scalene | acute | right | obtuse |
|-------------|-----------|---------|-------|-------|--------|
|  | E | D |  | E | D |

**C** ➑ Kelly draws a triangle F, with 3 equal sides. She writes F under equilateral and acute in the table in problem 7. Did she forget any possible names for triangle F? Explain.

Yes. Possible explanation: An isosceles triangle has to have at least two equal sides,

and triangle F has three equal sides so it can also be called isosceles.

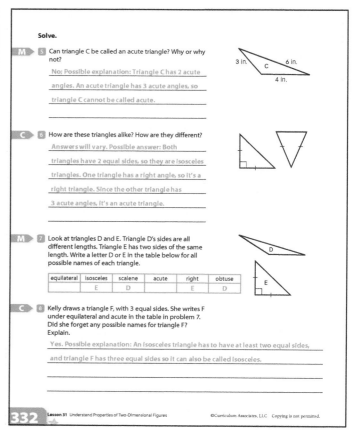

**332** **Lesson 31** Understand Properties of Two-Dimensional Figures    ©Curriculum Associates, LLC   Copying is not permitted.

---

Lesson 31 • *Use after Ready Instruction page 279*          Name: _____

**Understand Shared Properties**

**Study the example that uses a Venn diagram to show shared properties in triangles. Then solve problems 1–6.**

> **Example**
>
> The Venn diagram shows how the properties of different triangles are related.
>
> When two sections overlap, they sometimes share properties.
>
> When one section is completely inside another section, they always share properties.
>
> When two sections do not overlap at all, they never share properties.
>
> An isosceles triangle has at least 2 equal sides. An equilateral triangle has 3 equal sides. So, an equilateral triangle has all the properties of an isosceles triangle. That's why the equilateral section lies completely inside the isosceles section.

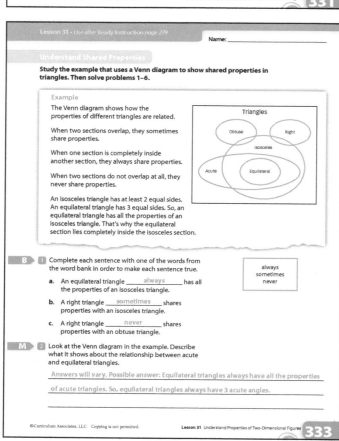

**B** ➊ Complete each sentence with one of the words from the word bank in order to make each sentence true.

always
sometimes
never

   **a.** An equilateral triangle _____always_____ has all the properties of an isosceles triangle.

   **b.** A right triangle _____sometimes_____ shares properties with an isosceles triangle.

   **c.** A right triangle _____never_____ shares properties with an obtuse triangle.

**M** ➋ Look at the Venn diagram in the example. Describe what it shows about the relationship between acute and equilateral triangles.

Answers will vary. Possible answer: Equilateral triangles always have all the properties

of acute triangles. So, equilateral triangles always have 3 acute angles.

©Curriculum Associates, LLC   Copying is not permitted.    **Lesson 31** Understand Properties of Two-Dimensional Figures **333**

---

**Solve.**

**M** ➌ Use the information in the table to fill in the tree diagram showing the hierarchy of the following quadrilaterals: parallelograms, squares, rhombuses, trapezoids, and rectangles. Remember, each category in the hierarchy has all the properties of the category above it.

| Shape | Properties |
|-------|-----------|
| parallelograms | 2 pairs of parallel sides |
| squares | 4 equal sides, 4 right angles |
| rhombuses | 4 equal sides |
| trapezoids | at least 1 pair of parallel sides |
| rectangles | 4 right angles |

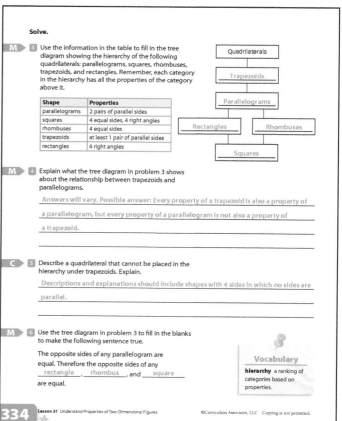

**M** ➍ Explain what the tree diagram in problem 3 shows about the relationship between trapezoids and parallelograms.

Answers will vary. Possible answer: Every property of a trapezoid is also a property of

a parallelogram, but every property of a parallelogram is not also a property of

a trapezoid.

**C** ➎ Describe a quadrilateral that cannot be placed in the hierarchy under trapezoids. Explain.

Descriptions and explanations should include shapes with 4 sides in which no sides are

parallel.

**M** ➏ Use the tree diagram in problem 3 to fill in the blanks to make the following sentence true.

The opposite sides of any parallelogram are equal. Therefore the opposite sides of any ____rectangle____, ____rhombus____, and ____square____ are equal.

**Vocabulary**

**hierarchy** a ranking of categories based on properties.

**334** **Lesson 31** Understand Properties of Two-Dimensional Figures    ©Curriculum Associates, LLC   Copying is not permitted.

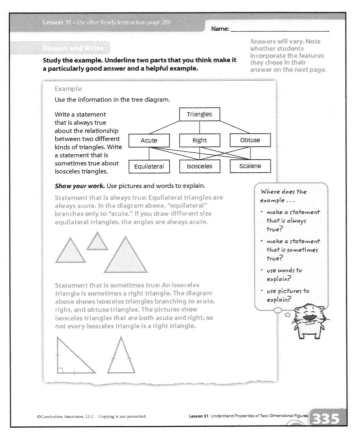

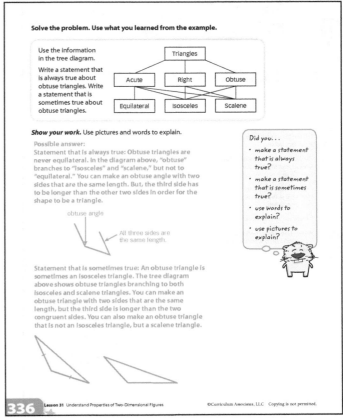

Key

B   Basic
M   Medium
C   Challenge

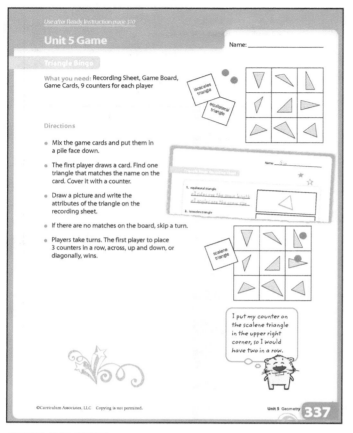

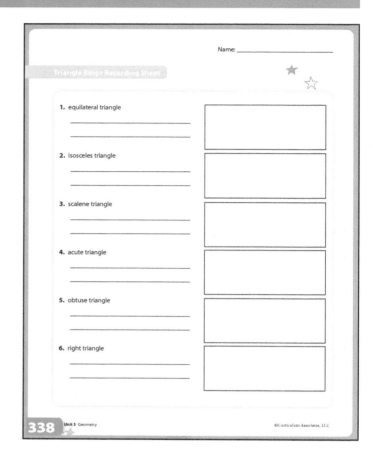

## STEP BY STEP

| **CCSS Focus** - 5.G.B.3, 5.G.B.4  *Embedded SMPs* - 3, 6, 7 <br> **Objective:** Identify/classify triangles according to their attributes. | **Materials** For each pair: Recording Sheet (TR 8), Game Board (TR 9), Game Cards (TR 10), 18 2-color counters |
| --- | --- |

- Mix the Game Cards and put them in a pile face down.

- Player A draws a Game Card. Find one triangle that matches the name on the card. Cover it with a counter.

- Draw a picture and write the attributes of the triangle on the recording sheet.

- If there are no matches on the board, the player's turn ends.

- Players take turns. The first player to place 3 counters in a row, across, up or down or diagonally, wins.

- Read the directions aloud. Model one complete round for students before they play.

- Review the classification descriptions for triangles. Elicit that equilateral, isosceles, and scalene classify triangles by their sides and that acute, right, and obtuse classify triangles by their angles.

**Vary the Game** Draw 2 cards and cover a triangle that meets both descriptions. If both cards have angle-related categories or both have side-related categories, draw another card to replace one.

**ELL Support** Provide a list of the words on the Game Cards. Then help each student write the translation of those words in their native language for reference.

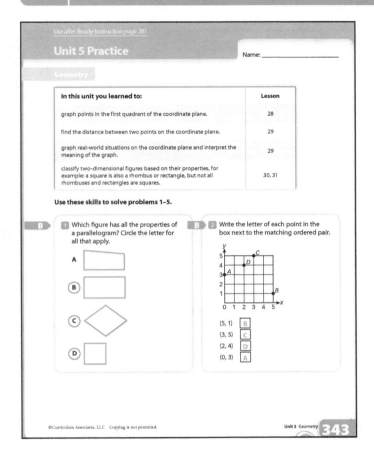

*Use after Ready Instruction page 281*

## Unit 5 Practice

Name: _____

### Geometry

| In this unit you learned to: | Lesson |
|---|---|
| graph points in the first quadrant of the coordinate plane. | 28 |
| find the distance between two points on the coordinate plane. | 29 |
| graph real-world situations on the coordinate plane and interpret the meaning of the graph. | 29 |
| classify two-dimensional figures based on their properties, for example: a square is also a rhombus or rectangle, but not all rhombuses and rectangles are squares. | 30, 31 |

**Use these skills to solve problems 1–5.**

**B** ▶ **1** Which figure has all the properties of a parallelogram? Circle the letter for all that apply.

A ▭

Ⓑ ▭

Ⓒ ◇

Ⓓ ▢

**B** ▶ **2** Write the letter of each point in the box next to the matching ordered pair.

(5, 1)  B
(3, 5)  C
(2, 4)  D
(0, 3)  A

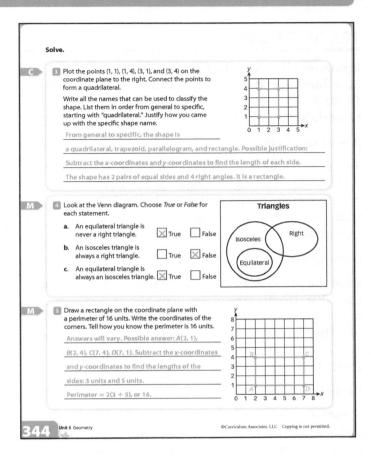

**Solve.**

**C** ▶ **3** Plot the points (1, 1), (1, 4), (3, 1), and (3, 4) on the coordinate plane to the right. Connect the points to form a quadrilateral.

Write all the names that can be used to classify the shape. List them in order from general to specific, starting with "quadrilateral." Justify how you came up with the specific shape name.

From general to specific, the shape is

a quadrilateral, trapezoid, parallelogram, and rectangle. Possible justification:

Subtract the x-coordinates and y-coordinates to find the length of each side.

The shape has 2 pairs of equal sides and 4 right angles. It is a rectangle.

**M** ▶ **4** Look at the Venn diagram. Choose *True* or *False* for each statement.

**a.** An equilateral triangle is never a right triangle. ☒ True ☐ False

**b.** An isosceles triangle is always a right triangle. ☐ True ☒ False

**c.** An equilateral triangle is always an isosceles triangle. ☒ True ☐ False

**Triangles**

Isosceles   Right   Equilateral

**M** ▶ **5** Draw a rectangle on the coordinate plane with a perimeter of 16 units. Write the coordinates of the corners. Tell how you know the perimeter is 16 units.

Answers will vary. Possible answer: A(2, 1),

B(2, 4), C(7, 4), D(7, 1). Subtract the x-coordinates

and y-coordinates to find the lengths of the

sides: 3 units and 5 units.

Perimeter = 2(3 + 5), or 16.

©Curriculum Associates, LLC   Copying is not permitted.

## TEACHER NOTES

**Common Core Standards:** 5.G.A.1, 5.G.A.2
**Standards for Mathematical Practice:** 1, 2, 3, 4, 5, 6, 7
**DOK:** 3
**Materials:** Graph paper

### About the Task

To complete this task, students solve a multi-step problem that involves drawing rectangles in the coordinate plane and finding the area of the rectangles. In addition, students reason about the shapes they create and explain their thinking.

### Getting Students Started

Read the problem aloud with students and go over the checklist. Discuss the diagram on the second page and have students explain how it relates to the problem description. Have students locate the open space on the grid where they could potentially draw their rectangles. *(SMP 1, 2)*

### Completing the Task

Some students may find it helpful to think about possible dimensions for 20 to 30 square foot rectangles before they start to draw. Others may think best by drawing. Students may need additional graph paper to help their planning. *(SMP 5)*

Students should be familiar with the area formula for rectangles. Some may struggle with finding the lengths of the various line segments they draw in the coordinate plane. Encourage students to notice patterns in the ordered pairs. For example, points on the same vertical side share *x*-coordinates and points on the same horizontal side share *y*-coordinates. Ask, *How does this help you find the length of the side?* *(SMP 7, 8)*

Have students share their garden designs and explain to classmates why they arranged the sections as they did.

---

**Unit 5 Performance Task**     Name: _____

Answer the questions and show all your work on separate paper.

Your school is getting ready to plant a garden. You are using a field on the school property that is 25 yards long and 15 yards wide. There is a shed on the field and the field is fenced in.

You need to decide where to plant three sections of the garden for tomatoes, squash, and cucumbers. Each section needs to be rectangular and between 20 and 30 square yards in area.

A math teacher had students draw a diagram of the field on a coordinate grid. It's on the back side of this page.

Here is your task:

- Draw the three sections of vegetables where you want them to go. Label each section with the vegetable name.
- On a separate piece of paper, write the ordered pairs for the vertices of the three vegetable sections on your diagram.
- Explain how you decided on the arrangement of the sections. Show how your plan meets the requirements.

**Reflect on Mathematical Practices**

1. **Repeated Reasoning** What did you notice about the corresponding *x*-coordinates and *y*-coordinates of the vertices of the rectangles?

2. **Models** How did the coordinate plane help you complete this task?

> **Checklist**
> Did you ...
> ☐ draw a diagram on the coordinate plane?
> ☐ write ordered pairs?
> ☐ show how to find the areas?

©Curriculum Associates, LLC Copying is not permitted.    Unit 5 Geometry **345**

### Extension

If some students have more time to spend on this problem, you can have them solve this extension:

Suppose that you need to put a fence around the three sections of vegetables in the garden you designed. How much fencing would you need? Explain.

©Curriculum Associates, LLC    Copying is not permitted.

## SAMPLE RESPONSES AND RUBRIC

### 4-Point Solution

Ordered pairs for squash section: (0, 0), (0, 4), (5, 4), (5, 0). Ordered pairs for cucumber section: (7, 0), (7, 4), (13, 4), (13, 0). Ordered pairs for tomato section: (15, 0) (15, 4), (22, 4), (22, 0).

I thought about the different factors I could use to get products between 20 and 30. I noticed that 20, 24 and 28 all have 4 as a factor. I decided to use 4 as the width so that all 3 sections would have the same width. This will make it easier to make paths around the different sections. I also put the three sections next to one of the fenced sides to leave lots of room for other vegetables. I decided to make my least favorite vegetable the smallest section and my favorite vegetable the largest. I used 4 × 5 for squash since 20 square yards is the smallest area I could use. I used 4 × 6 for cucumbers for an area of 24 square yards. I like tomatoes, so used 4 × 7 for an area of 28 square yards for this section. All of these areas are between 20 and 30 square yards.

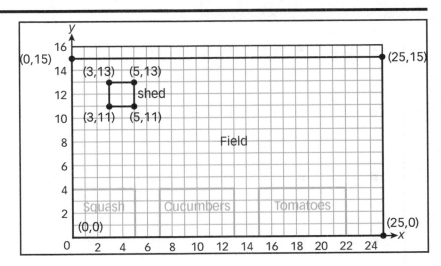

## REFLECT ON MATHEMATICAL PRACTICES

1. Students should recognize that vertical segments have the same *x*-coordinates and horizontal segments have the same *y*-coordinates **(SMP 7, 8)**

2. Students should recognize that the coordinate plane provides a visual model of the plan and the ordered pairs can be used to find the lengths of the sides of the rectangles **(SMP 4)**

## SCORING RUBRIC

**4 points**  The student has completed all parts of the problem. Diagrams and ordered pairs for vertices are accurate. Calculations for area are correct and within the given range. The student gives thorough information about planning.

**3 points**  The student has completed all parts of the problem, with one or two errors. Diagrams and areas are correct, but one may not be within the given range. The student gives adequate information about planning.

**2 points**  The student has attempted all parts of the problem, with several errors. Parts of the diagrams and some ordered pairs are inaccurate. Calculations for area have errors. The student provides little information about planning.

**1 point**  The student has not completed all parts of the problem. Diagrams, ordered pairs, and area calculations are mostly incorrect. The student provides no information about planning.

## SOLUTION TO THE EXTENSION

### Possible Solution

Squash: 5 + 4 = 9 yd; Cucumbers: 4 + 6 + 4 = 14 yd; Tomatoes: 4 + 8 + 4 = 16 yd; 9 + 14 + 16 = 39 yd

©Curriculum Associates, LLC    Copying is not permitted.

### Multi-Digit Addition—Skills Practice

Name: _____

**Add within 1,000,000.** Form A

| # | | # | | # | | # | |
|---|---|---|---|---|---|---|---|
| **1** | 4,699 + 209 = 4,908 | **2** | 733,633 + 5,678 = 739,311 | **3** | 5,050 + 5,049 = 10,099 | **4** | 35,009 + 21,991 = 57,000 |
| **5** | 123,321 + 987 = 124,308 | **6** | 806,515 + 14,372 = 820,887 | **7** | 97,342 + 728 = 98,070 | **8** | 150,225 + 145,225 = 295,450 |
| **9** | 28,403 + 26,910 = 55,313 | **10** | 5,146 + 5,915 = 11,061 | **11** | 915,412 + 15,412 = 930,824 | **12** | 42,963 + 8,825 = 51,788 |
| **13** | 188,888 + 222,222 = 411,110 | **14** | 670,780 + 9,564 = 680,344 | **15** | 16,275 + 36,334 = 52,609 | **16** | 7,741 + 2,260 = 10,001 |
| **17** | 10,864 + 864 = 11,728 | **18** | 642,002 + 80,999 = 723,001 | **19** | 22,987 + 44,789 = 67,776 | **20** | 47,247 + 8,747 = 55,994 |

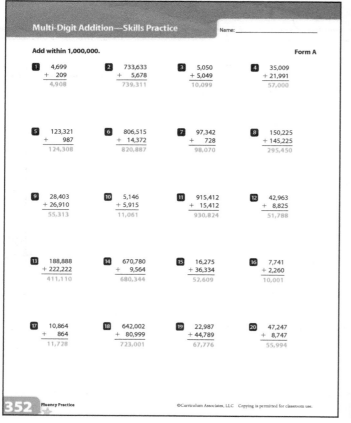

352 Fluency Practice
©Curriculum Associates, LLC  Copying is permitted for classroom use.

---

### Multi-Digit Addition—Skills Practice

Name: _____

**Add within 1,000,000.** Form B

| # | | # | | # | | # | |
|---|---|---|---|---|---|---|---|
| **1** | 3,597 + 307 = 3,904 | **2** | 644,544 + 4,567 = 649,111 | **3** | 2,020 + 8,019 = 10,039 | **4** | 42,991 + 12,009 = 55,000 |
| **5** | 234,432 + 876 = 235,308 | **6** | 705,626 + 25,261 = 730,887 | **7** | 64,751 + 429 = 65,180 | **8** | 205,336 + 204,336 = 409,672 |
| **9** | 17,210 + 15,801 = 33,011 | **10** | 8,924 + 8,157 = 17,081 | **11** | 749,241 + 49,241 = 798,482 | **12** | 53,854 + 9,945 = 63,799 |
| **13** | 133,333 + 777,777 = 911,110 | **14** | 908,847 + 1,780 = 910,627 | **15** | 28,764 + 18,145 = 46,909 | **16** | 6,632 + 3,370 = 10,002 |
| **17** | 22,552 + 552 = 23,104 | **18** | 430,999 + 70,004 = 501,003 | **19** | 33,678 + 11,876 = 45,554 | **20** | 76,356 + 7,626 = 83,982 |

©Curriculum Associates, LLC  Copying is permitted for classroom use.
Fluency Practice 353

---

### Multi-Digit Subtraction—Skills Practice

Name: _____

**Subtract within 1,000,000.** Form A

| # | | # | | # | | # | |
|---|---|---|---|---|---|---|---|
| **1** | 11,223 − 311 = 10,912 | **2** | 2,123 − 1,321 = 802 | **3** | 432,765 − 43,276 = 389,489 | **4** | 80,449 − 24,085 = 56,364 |
| **5** | 184,234 − 93,517 = 90,717 | **6** | 319,019 − 9,416 = 309,603 | **7** | 62,626 − 6,262 = 56,364 | **8** | 37,740 − 18,870 = 18,870 |
| **9** | 7,347 − 5,182 = 2,165 | **10** | 956,201 − 524,110 = 432,091 | **11** | 476,747 − 9,696 = 467,051 | **12** | 535 − 353 = 182 |
| **13** | 90,000 − 1,234 = 88,766 | **14** | 37,665 − 776 = 36,889 | **15** | 215,451 − 8,795 = 206,656 | **16** | 52,252 − 50,992 = 1,260 |
| **17** | 602,602 − 444,444 = 158,158 | **18** | 5,702 − 2,915 = 2,787 | **19** | 877,007 − 525 = 876,482 | **20** | 13,579 − 2,846 = 10,733 |

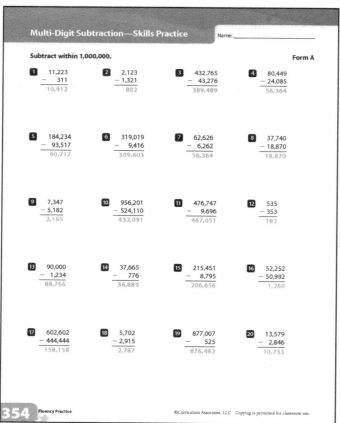

354 Fluency Practice
©Curriculum Associates, LLC  Copying is permitted for classroom use.

---

### Multi-Digit Subtraction—Skills Practice

Name: _____

**Subtract within 1,000,000.** Form B

| # | | # | | # | | # | |
|---|---|---|---|---|---|---|---|
| **1** | 13,445 − 522 = 12,923 | **2** | 8,789 − 7,987 = 802 | **3** | 654,631 − 65,432 = 589,199 | **4** | 70,338 − 13,074 = 57,264 |
| **5** | 162,478 − 81,759 = 80,719 | **6** | 518,018 − 8,515 = 509,503 | **7** | 71,717 − 7,171 = 64,546 | **8** | 51,120 − 25,560 = 25,560 |
| **9** | 6,536 − 5,372 = 1,164 | **10** | 833,021 − 312,110 = 520,911 | **11** | 596,454 − 9,393 = 587,061 | **12** | 626 − 262 = 364 |
| **13** | 70,000 − 2,345 = 67,655 | **14** | 28,776 − 887 = 27,889 | **15** | 437,673 − 9,895 = 427,778 | **16** | 32,131 − 30,881 = 1,250 |
| **17** | 501,501 − 333,333 = 168,168 | **18** | 6,803 − 4,806 = 1,997 | **19** | 966,006 − 414 = 965,592 | **20** | 14,568 − 3,725 = 10,843 |

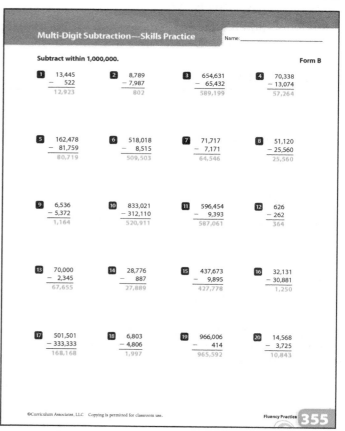

©Curriculum Associates, LLC  Copying is permitted for classroom use.
Fluency Practice 355

©Curriculum Associates, LLC  Copying is not permitted.

# Fluency Practice

## Multi-Digit Multiplication—Skills Practice

Name: _____

**Multiply.**                                                                 Form A

**1**  205
    × 33
    6,765

**2**  6,660
    ×   70
    466,200

**3**  378
    × 12
    4,536

**4**  1,221
    ×   91
    111,111

**5**  5,062
    ×   25
    126,550

**6**  829
    × 62
    51,398

**7**  116
    × 46
    5,336

**8**  7,256
    ×   56
    406,336

**9**  444
    × 99
    43,956

**10**  3,136
    ×   14
    43,904

**11**  2,222
    ×   55
    122,210

**12**  761
    × 80
    60,880

**13**  530
    × 28
    14,840

**14**  142
    × 222
    31,524

**15**  875
    × 305
    266,875

**16**  250
    × 250
    62,500

©Curriculum Associates, LLC   Copying is permitted for classroom use.

## Multi-Digit Multiplication—Skills Practice

Name: _____

**Multiply.**                                                                 Form B

**1**  305
    × 22
    6,710

**2**  7,770
    ×   60
    466,200

**3**  178
    × 32
    5,696

**4**  2,332
    ×   91
    212,212

**5**  6,052
    ×   25
    151,300

**6**  629
    × 82
    51,578

**7**  114
    × 44
    5,016

**8**  5,256
    ×   76
    399,456

**9**  555
    × 99
    54,945

**10**  1,136
    ×   34
    38,624

**11**  4,444
    ×   55
    244,420

**12**  861
    × 70
    60,270

**13**  230
    × 58
    13,340

**14**  142
    × 111
    15,762

**15**  375
    × 805
    301,875

**16**  125
    × 125
    15,625

©Curriculum Associates, LLC   Copying is permitted for classroom use.

## Multi-Digit Division—Skills Practice

Name: _____

**Divide 3- and 4-digit dividends with mental math on some steps.**          Form A

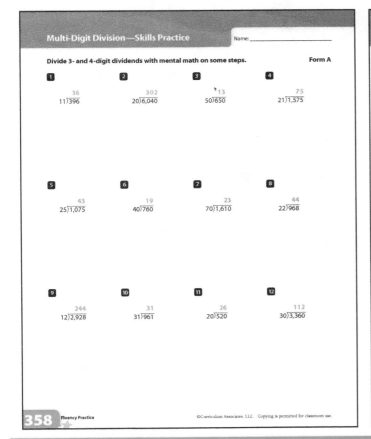

**1**
  36
11)396

**2**
   302
20)6,040

**3**
   13
50)650

**4**
   75
21)1,575

**5**
   43
25)1,075

**6**
   19
40)760

**7**
   23
70)1,610

**8**
   44
22)968

**9**
   244
12)2,928

**10**
   31
31)961

**11**
   26
20)520

**12**
   112
30)3,360

©Curriculum Associates, LLC   Copying is permitted for classroom use.

## Multi-Digit Division—Skills Practice

Name: _____

**Divide 3- and 4-digit dividends with mental math on some steps.**          Form B

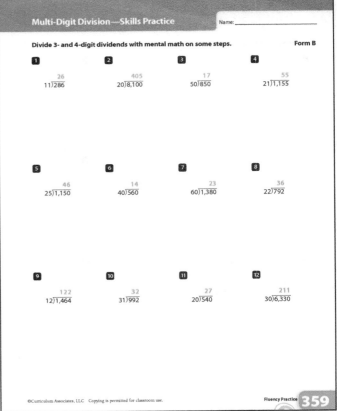

**1**
  26
11)286

**2**
   405
20)8,100

**3**
   17
50)850

**4**
   55
21)1,155

**5**
   46
25)1,150

**6**
   14
40)560

**7**
   23
60)1,380

**8**
   36
22)792

**9**
   122
12)1,464

**10**
   32
31)992

**11**
   27
20)540

**12**
   211
30)6,330

©Curriculum Associates, LLC   Copying is permitted for classroom use.

©Curriculum Associates, LLC   Copying is not permitted.

# Fluency Practice

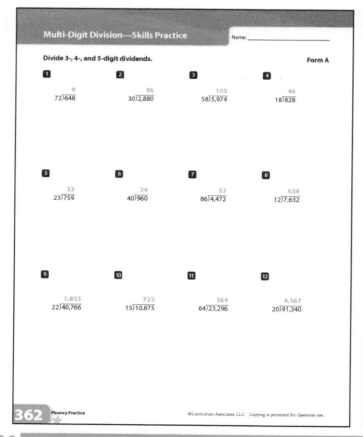

### Multi-Digit Division—Skills Practice

Name: _____

Divide 3-, 4-, and 5-digit dividends with mental math on some steps.  Form A

**1**
$$\begin{array}{r} 19 \\ 50\overline{)950} \end{array}$$

**2**
$$\begin{array}{r} 405 \\ 20\overline{)8,100} \end{array}$$

**3**
$$\begin{array}{r} 32 \\ 21\overline{)672} \end{array}$$

**4**
$$\begin{array}{r} 74 \\ 31\overline{)2,294} \end{array}$$

**5**
$$\begin{array}{r} 81 \\ 22\overline{)1,782} \end{array}$$

**6**
$$\begin{array}{r} 55 \\ 11\overline{)605} \end{array}$$

**7**
$$\begin{array}{r} 26 \\ 30\overline{)780} \end{array}$$

**8**
$$\begin{array}{r} 223 \\ 25\overline{)5,575} \end{array}$$

**9**
$$\begin{array}{r} 425 \\ 25\overline{)10,625} \end{array}$$

**10**
$$\begin{array}{r} 1,432 \\ 50\overline{)71,600} \end{array}$$

**11**
$$\begin{array}{r} 532 \\ 50\overline{)26,600} \end{array}$$

**12**
$$\begin{array}{r} 3,333 \\ 20\overline{)66,660} \end{array}$$

©Curriculum Associates, LLC   Copying is permitted for classroom use.

### Multi-Digit Division—Skills Practice

Name: _____

Divide 3-, 4-, and 5-digit dividends with mental math on some steps.  Form B

**1**
$$\begin{array}{r} 17 \\ 50\overline{)850} \end{array}$$

**2**
$$\begin{array}{r} 305 \\ 20\overline{)6,100} \end{array}$$

**3**
$$\begin{array}{r} 22 \\ 21\overline{)462} \end{array}$$

**4**
$$\begin{array}{r} 54 \\ 31\overline{)1,674} \end{array}$$

**5**
$$\begin{array}{r} 91 \\ 22\overline{)2,002} \end{array}$$

**6**
$$\begin{array}{r} 65 \\ 11\overline{)715} \end{array}$$

**7**
$$\begin{array}{r} 24 \\ 30\overline{)720} \end{array}$$

**8**
$$\begin{array}{r} 334 \\ 25\overline{)8,350} \end{array}$$

**9**
$$\begin{array}{r} 450 \\ 25\overline{)11,250} \end{array}$$

**10**
$$\begin{array}{r} 1,234 \\ 50\overline{)61,700} \end{array}$$

**11**
$$\begin{array}{r} 523 \\ 50\overline{)26,150} \end{array}$$

**12**
$$\begin{array}{r} 2,222 \\ 20\overline{)44,440} \end{array}$$

©Curriculum Associates, LLC   Copying is permitted for classroom use.

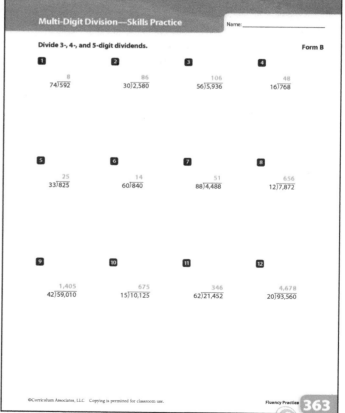

### Multi-Digit Division—Skills Practice

Name: _____

Divide 3-, 4-, and 5-digit dividends.  Form A

**1**
$$\begin{array}{r} 9 \\ 72\overline{)648} \end{array}$$

**2**
$$\begin{array}{r} 96 \\ 30\overline{)2,880} \end{array}$$

**3**
$$\begin{array}{r} 103 \\ 58\overline{)5,974} \end{array}$$

**4**
$$\begin{array}{r} 46 \\ 18\overline{)828} \end{array}$$

**5**
$$\begin{array}{r} 33 \\ 23\overline{)759} \end{array}$$

**6**
$$\begin{array}{r} 24 \\ 40\overline{)960} \end{array}$$

**7**
$$\begin{array}{r} 52 \\ 86\overline{)4,472} \end{array}$$

**8**
$$\begin{array}{r} 636 \\ 12\overline{)7,632} \end{array}$$

**9**
$$\begin{array}{r} 1,853 \\ 22\overline{)40,766} \end{array}$$

**10**
$$\begin{array}{r} 725 \\ 15\overline{)10,875} \end{array}$$

**11**
$$\begin{array}{r} 364 \\ 64\overline{)23,296} \end{array}$$

**12**
$$\begin{array}{r} 4,567 \\ 20\overline{)91,340} \end{array}$$

©Curriculum Associates, LLC   Copying is permitted for classroom use.

### Multi-Digit Division—Skills Practice

Name: _____

Divide 3-, 4-, and 5-digit dividends.  Form B

**1**
$$\begin{array}{r} 8 \\ 74\overline{)592} \end{array}$$

**2**
$$\begin{array}{r} 86 \\ 30\overline{)2,580} \end{array}$$

**3**
$$\begin{array}{r} 106 \\ 56\overline{)5,936} \end{array}$$

**4**
$$\begin{array}{r} 48 \\ 16\overline{)768} \end{array}$$

**5**
$$\begin{array}{r} 25 \\ 33\overline{)825} \end{array}$$

**6**
$$\begin{array}{r} 14 \\ 60\overline{)840} \end{array}$$

**7**
$$\begin{array}{r} 51 \\ 88\overline{)4,488} \end{array}$$

**8**
$$\begin{array}{r} 656 \\ 12\overline{)7,872} \end{array}$$

**9**
$$\begin{array}{r} 1,405 \\ 42\overline{)59,010} \end{array}$$

**10**
$$\begin{array}{r} 675 \\ 15\overline{)10,125} \end{array}$$

**11**
$$\begin{array}{r} 346 \\ 62\overline{)21,452} \end{array}$$

**12**
$$\begin{array}{r} 4,678 \\ 20\overline{)93,560} \end{array}$$

©Curriculum Associates, LLC   Copying is permitted for classroom use.

©Curriculum Associates, LLC   Copying is not permitted.

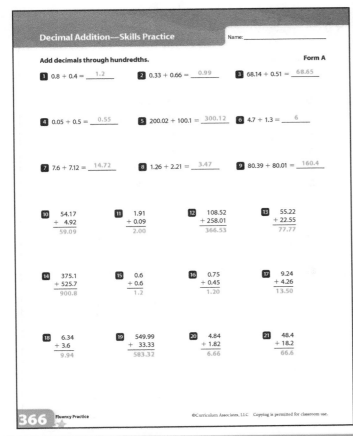

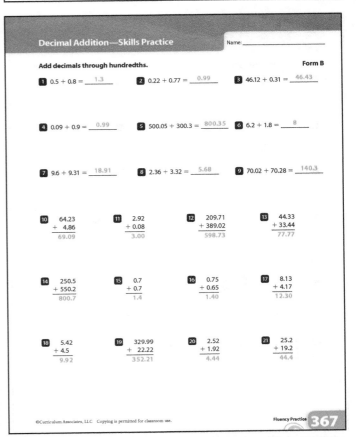

## Multi-Digit Division—Repeated Reasoning  Name:_____

**Find patterns with zeros.**

**Set A**

1. $80)\overline{800} = 10$
2. $80)\overline{8,000} = 100$
3. $80)\overline{80,000} = 1,000$
4. $40)\overline{800} = 20$
5. $40)\overline{8,000} = 200$
6. $40)\overline{80,000} = 2,000$
7. $20)\overline{800} = 40$
8. $20)\overline{8,000} = 400$
9. $20)\overline{80,000} = 4,000$

**Set B**

1. $200)\overline{8,000} = 40$
2. $400)\overline{8,000} = 20$
3. $800)\overline{8,000} = 10$
4. $20)\overline{8,000} = 400$
5. $40)\overline{8,000} = 200$
6. $80)\overline{8,000} = 100$
7. $2)\overline{8,000} = 4,000$
8. $4)\overline{8,000} = 2,000$
9. $8)\overline{8,000} = 1,000$

Describe a pattern you see in one of the sets of problems above.
Answers will vary. Students may see in Set A when the divisor is halved, the quotient is doubled; or in Set B as the number of 0s in the divisor decreases by 1, the number of 0s in the quotient increases by 1.

## Multi-Digit Division—Repeated Reasoning  Name:_____

**Find patterns in dividing by 25 or 50.**

**Set A**

1. $20)\overline{100} = 5$
2. $25)\overline{100} = 4$
3. $50)\overline{100} = 2$
4. $20)\overline{200} = 10$
5. $25)\overline{200} = 8$
6. $50)\overline{200} = 4$
7. $20)\overline{300} = 15$
8. $25)\overline{300} = 12$
9. $50)\overline{300} = 6$

**Set B**

1. $20)\overline{1,100} = 55$
2. $25)\overline{1,100} = 44$
3. $50)\overline{1,100} = 22$
4. $20)\overline{1,200} = 60$
5. $25)\overline{1,200} = 48$
6. $50)\overline{1,200} = 24$
7. $20)\overline{1,300} = 65$
8. $25)\overline{1,300} = 52$
9. $50)\overline{1,300} = 26$

Describe a pattern you see in one of the sets of problems above.
Answers will vary. Students may see when a multiple of 100 is divided by 20, the quotient is equal to 5 times the number of 100s. Or, the same pattern may be described as the quotient increases by 5 as the number of 100s increases by 1.

## Decimal Addition—Skills Practice  Name:_____

**Add decimals through hundredths.**  Form A

1. $0.8 + 0.4 = \underline{1.2}$
2. $0.33 + 0.66 = \underline{0.99}$
3. $68.14 + 0.51 = \underline{68.65}$
4. $0.05 + 0.5 = \underline{0.55}$
5. $200.02 + 100.1 = \underline{300.12}$
6. $4.7 + 1.3 = \underline{6}$
7. $7.6 + 7.12 = \underline{14.72}$
8. $1.26 + 2.21 = \underline{3.47}$
9. $80.39 + 80.01 = \underline{160.4}$

10. $54.17 + 4.92 = 59.09$
11. $1.91 + 0.09 = 2.00$
12. $108.52 + 258.01 = 366.53$
13. $55.22 + 22.55 = 77.77$

14. $375.1 + 525.7 = 900.8$
15. $0.6 + 0.6 = 1.2$
16. $0.75 + 0.45 = 1.20$
17. $9.24 + 4.26 = 13.50$

18. $6.34 + 3.6 = 9.94$
19. $549.99 + 33.33 = 583.32$
20. $4.84 + 1.82 = 6.66$
21. $48.4 + 18.2 = 66.6$

## Decimal Addition—Skills Practice  Name:_____

**Add decimals through hundredths.**  Form B

1. $0.5 + 0.8 = \underline{1.3}$
2. $0.22 + 0.77 = \underline{0.99}$
3. $46.12 + 0.31 = \underline{46.43}$
4. $0.09 + 0.9 = \underline{0.99}$
5. $500.05 + 300.3 = \underline{800.35}$
6. $6.2 + 1.8 = \underline{8}$
7. $9.6 + 9.31 = \underline{18.91}$
8. $2.36 + 3.32 = \underline{5.68}$
9. $70.02 + 70.28 = \underline{140.3}$

10. $64.23 + 4.86 = 69.09$
11. $2.92 + 0.08 = 3.00$
12. $209.71 + 389.02 = 598.73$
13. $44.33 + 33.44 = 77.77$

14. $250.5 + 550.2 = 800.7$
15. $0.7 + 0.7 = 1.4$
16. $0.75 + 0.65 = 1.40$
17. $8.13 + 4.17 = 12.30$

18. $5.42 + 4.5 = 9.92$
19. $329.99 + 22.22 = 352.21$
20. $2.52 + 1.92 = 4.44$
21. $25.2 + 19.2 = 44.4$

©Curriculum Associates, LLC  Copying is not permitted.

## Fluency Practice

### Decimal Addition—Repeated Reasoning
Name: _____

**Find place value patterns.**

Set A

**1** 0.99 + 0.01 = ___1___   **2** 2.99 + 3.01 = ___6___

**3** 0.98 + 0.02 = ___1___   **4** 2.98 + 3.02 = ___6___

**5** 0.97 + 0.03 = ___1___   **6** 2.97 + 3.03 = ___6___

**7** 10.99 + 0.01 = ___11___   **8** 20.99 + 30.01 = ___51___

**9** 10.98 + 0.02 = ___11___   **10** 20.98 + 30.02 = ___51___

**11** 10.97 + 0.03 = ___11___   **12** 20.97 + 30.03 = ___51___

Set B

**1**  0.99
   + 0.01
   ‾‾‾‾‾
   1.00

**2**  2.99
   + 3.01
   ‾‾‾‾‾
   6.00

**3**  50.99
   + 40.01
   ‾‾‾‾‾
   91.00

**4**  0.99
   + 0.02
   ‾‾‾‾‾
   1.01

**5**  2.99
   + 3.02
   ‾‾‾‾‾
   6.01

**6**  50.99
   + 40.02
   ‾‾‾‾‾
   91.01

**7**  0.99
   + 0.03
   ‾‾‾‾‾
   1.02

**8**  2.99
   + 3.03
   ‾‾‾‾‾
   6.02

**9**  50.99
   + 40.03
   ‾‾‾‾‾
   91.02

Describe a pattern you see in one of the sets of problems above.

Answers will vary. Students may see the pairings of 99 hundredths and 1 hundredth,
98 hundredths and 2 hundredths, and 97 hundredths and 3 hundredths each increase the
number of ones by 1.

©Curriculum Associates, LLC   Copying is permitted for classroom use.

---

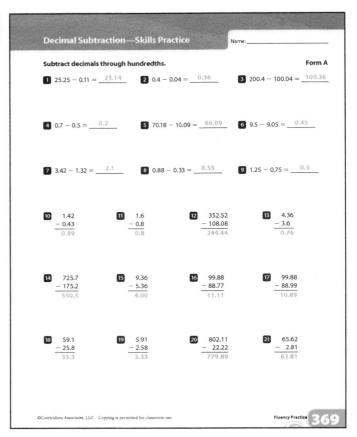

### Decimal Subtraction—Skills Practice
Name: _____

**Subtract decimals through hundredths.**   Form A

**1** 25.25 − 0.11 = ___25.14___   **2** 0.4 − 0.04 = ___0.36___   **3** 200.4 − 100.04 = ___100.36___

**4** 0.7 − 0.5 = ___0.2___   **5** 70.18 − 10.09 = ___60.09___   **6** 9.5 − 9.05 = ___0.45___

**7** 3.42 − 1.32 = ___2.1___   **8** 0.88 − 0.33 = ___0.55___   **9** 1.25 − 0.75 = ___0.5___

**10**  1.42
   − 0.43
   ‾‾‾‾‾
   0.99

**11**  1.6
   − 0.8
   ‾‾‾‾‾
   0.8

**12**  352.52
   − 108.08
   ‾‾‾‾‾
   244.44

**13**  4.36
   − 3.6
   ‾‾‾‾‾
   0.76

**14**  725.7
   − 175.2
   ‾‾‾‾‾
   550.5

**15**  9.36
   − 5.36
   ‾‾‾‾‾
   4.00

**16**  99.88
   − 88.77
   ‾‾‾‾‾
   11.11

**17**  99.88
   − 88.99
   ‾‾‾‾‾
   10.89

**18**  59.1
   − 25.8
   ‾‾‾‾‾
   33.3

**19**  5.91
   − 2.58
   ‾‾‾‾‾
   3.33

**20**  802.11
   − 22.22
   ‾‾‾‾‾
   779.89

**21**  65.62
   − 2.81
   ‾‾‾‾‾
   62.81

©Curriculum Associates, LLC   Copying is permitted for classroom use.

---

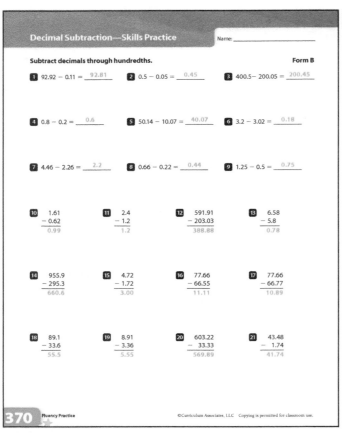

### Decimal Subtraction—Skills Practice
Name: _____

**Subtract decimals through hundredths.**   Form B

**1** 92.92 − 0.11 = ___92.81___   **2** 0.5 − 0.05 = ___0.45___   **3** 400.5 − 200.05 = ___200.45___

**4** 0.8 − 0.2 = ___0.6___   **5** 50.14 − 10.07 = ___40.07___   **6** 3.2 − 3.02 = ___0.18___

**7** 4.46 − 2.26 = ___2.2___   **8** 0.66 − 0.22 = ___0.44___   **9** 1.25 − 0.5 = ___0.75___

**10**  1.61
   − 0.62
   ‾‾‾‾‾
   0.99

**11**  2.4
   − 1.2
   ‾‾‾‾‾
   1.2

**12**  591.91
   − 203.03
   ‾‾‾‾‾
   388.88

**13**  6.58
   − 5.8
   ‾‾‾‾‾
   0.78

**14**  955.9
   − 295.3
   ‾‾‾‾‾
   660.6

**15**  4.72
   − 1.72
   ‾‾‾‾‾
   3.00

**16**  77.66
   − 66.55
   ‾‾‾‾‾
   11.11

**17**  77.66
   − 66.77
   ‾‾‾‾‾
   10.89

**18**  89.1
   − 33.6
   ‾‾‾‾‾
   55.5

**19**  8.91
   − 3.36
   ‾‾‾‾‾
   5.55

**20**  603.22
   − 33.33
   ‾‾‾‾‾
   569.89

**21**  43.48
   − 1.74
   ‾‾‾‾‾
   41.74

©Curriculum Associates, LLC   Copying is permitted for classroom use.

---

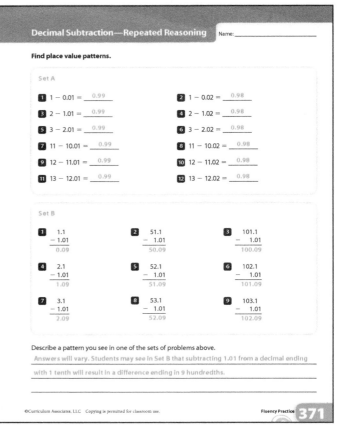

### Decimal Subtraction—Repeated Reasoning
Name: _____

**Find place value patterns.**

Set A

**1** 1 − 0.01 = ___0.99___   **2** 1 − 0.02 = ___0.98___

**3** 2 − 1.01 = ___0.99___   **4** 2 − 1.02 = ___0.98___

**5** 3 − 2.01 = ___0.99___   **6** 3 − 2.02 = ___0.98___

**7** 11 − 10.01 = ___0.99___   **8** 11 − 10.02 = ___0.98___

**9** 12 − 11.01 = ___0.99___   **10** 12 − 11.02 = ___0.98___

**11** 13 − 12.01 = ___0.99___   **12** 13 − 12.02 = ___0.98___

Set B

**1**  1.1
   − 1.01
   ‾‾‾‾‾
   0.09

**2**  51.1
   − 1.01
   ‾‾‾‾‾
   50.09

**3**  101.1
   − 1.01
   ‾‾‾‾‾
   100.09

**4**  2.1
   − 1.01
   ‾‾‾‾‾
   1.09

**5**  52.1
   − 1.01
   ‾‾‾‾‾
   51.09

**6**  102.1
   − 1.01
   ‾‾‾‾‾
   101.09

**7**  3.1
   − 1.01
   ‾‾‾‾‾
   2.09

**8**  53.1
   − 1.01
   ‾‾‾‾‾
   52.09

**9**  103.1
   − 1.01
   ‾‾‾‾‾
   102.09

Describe a pattern you see in one of the sets of problems above.

Answers will vary. Students may see in Set B that subtracting 1.01 from a decimal ending
with 1 tenth will result in a difference ending in 9 hundredths.

©Curriculum Associates, LLC   Copying is permitted for classroom use.

---

©Curriculum Associates, LLC   Copying is not permitted.

## Decimal Multiplication—Skills Practice  Form A

Name: _____

Multiply.

**1** $3 \times 0.6 =$ ___1.8___   **2** $1.2 \times 1.2 =$ ___1.44___   **3** $0.5 \times 4 =$ ___2___

**4** $0.7 \times 0.2 =$ ___0.14___   **5** $7 \times 0.02 =$ ___0.14___   **6** $5.5 \times 0.1 =$ ___0.55___

**7** $25 \times 0.01 =$ ___0.25___   **8** $0.4 \times 0.08 =$ ___0.032___   **9** $0.09 \times 10 =$ ___0.9___

**10**  3.7
  $\times\ 0.4$
  ‾‾‾‾‾
  1.48

**11**  1.8
  $\times\ \ 4$
  ‾‾‾‾‾
  7.2

**12**  6.12
  $\times\ 0.5$
  ‾‾‾‾‾
  3.06

**13**  3.06
  $\times\ \ 2$
  ‾‾‾‾‾
  6.12

**14**  0.31
  $\times\ 0.6$
  ‾‾‾‾‾
  0.186

**15**  1.75
  $\times\ 2.5$
  ‾‾‾‾‾
  4.375

**16**  0.11
  $\times\ 14$
  ‾‾‾‾‾
  1.54

**17**  4.1
  $\times\ 5.2$
  ‾‾‾‾‾
  21.32

**18**  3.33
  $\times\ 2.2$
  ‾‾‾‾‾
  7.326

**19**  33.3
  $\times\ 0.22$
  ‾‾‾‾‾
  7.326

**20**  0.5
  $\times\ 15$
  ‾‾‾‾‾
  7.5

**21**  11.1
  $\times\ 0.09$
  ‾‾‾‾‾
  0.999

   ©Curriculum Associates, LLC   Copying is permitted for classroom use.

---

## Decimal Multiplication—Skills Practice  Form B

Name: _____

Multiply.

**1** $4 \times 0.4 =$ ___1.6___   **2** $1.1 \times 1.1 =$ ___1.21___   **3** $0.5 \times 6 =$ ___3___

**4** $0.6 \times 0.2 =$ ___0.12___   **5** $6 \times 0.02 =$ ___0.12___   **6** $8.8 \times 0.1 =$ ___0.88___

**7** $15 \times 0.01 =$ ___0.15___   **8** $0.9 \times 0.04 =$ ___0.036___   **9** $0.03 \times 10 =$ ___0.3___

**10**  5.4
  $\times\ 0.3$
  ‾‾‾‾‾
  1.62

**11**  1.3
  $\times\ \ 5$
  ‾‾‾‾‾
  6.5

**12**  8.24
  $\times\ 0.5$
  ‾‾‾‾‾
  4.12

**13**  4.12
  $\times\ \ 2$
  ‾‾‾‾‾
  8.24

**14**  0.72
  $\times\ 0.3$
  ‾‾‾‾‾
  0.216

**15**  1.25
  $\times\ 7.5$
  ‾‾‾‾‾
  9.375

**16**  0.11
  $\times\ 16$
  ‾‾‾‾‾
  1.76

**17**  6.2
  $\times\ 5.1$
  ‾‾‾‾‾
  31.62

**18**  2.22
  $\times\ 4.4$
  ‾‾‾‾‾
  9.768

**19**  22.2
  $\times\ 0.44$
  ‾‾‾‾‾
  9.768

**20**  0.5
  $\times\ 25$
  ‾‾‾‾‾
  12.5

**21**  11.1
  $\times\ 0.08$
  ‾‾‾‾‾
  0.888

©Curriculum Associates, LLC   Copying is permitted for classroom use.

---

## Decimal Multiplication—Repeated Reasoning

Name: _____

Find place value patterns.

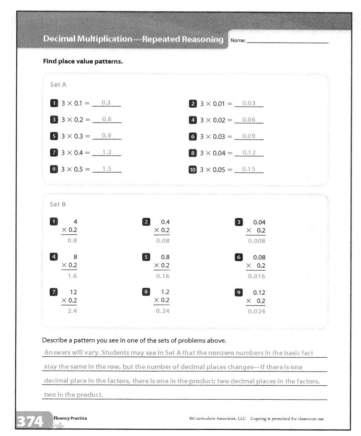

### Set A

**1** $3 \times 0.1 =$ ___0.3___   **2** $3 \times 0.01 =$ ___0.03___

**3** $3 \times 0.2 =$ ___0.6___   **4** $3 \times 0.02 =$ ___0.06___

**5** $3 \times 0.3 =$ ___0.9___   **6** $3 \times 0.03 =$ ___0.09___

**7** $3 \times 0.4 =$ ___1.2___   **8** $3 \times 0.04 =$ ___0.12___

**9** $3 \times 0.5 =$ ___1.5___   **10** $3 \times 0.05 =$ ___0.15___

### Set B

**1**  4
  $\times\ 0.2$
  ‾‾‾‾‾
  0.8

**2**  0.4
  $\times\ 0.2$
  ‾‾‾‾‾
  0.08

**3**  0.04
  $\times\ 0.2$
  ‾‾‾‾‾
  0.008

**4**  8
  $\times\ 0.2$
  ‾‾‾‾‾
  1.6

**5**  0.8
  $\times\ 0.2$
  ‾‾‾‾‾
  0.16

**6**  0.08
  $\times\ 0.2$
  ‾‾‾‾‾
  0.016

**7**  12
  $\times\ 0.2$
  ‾‾‾‾‾
  2.4

**8**  1.2
  $\times\ 0.2$
  ‾‾‾‾‾
  0.24

**9**  0.12
  $\times\ 0.2$
  ‾‾‾‾‾
  0.024

Describe a pattern you see in one of the sets of problems above.

Answers will vary. Students may see in Set A that the nonzero numbers in the basic fact
stay the same in the row, but the number of decimal places changes—if there is one
decimal place in the factors, there is one in the product; two decimal places in the factors,
two in the product.

   ©Curriculum Associates, LLC   Copying is permitted for classroom use.

---

## Decimal Division—Skills Practice

Name: _____

Divide decimals through hundredths.  Form A

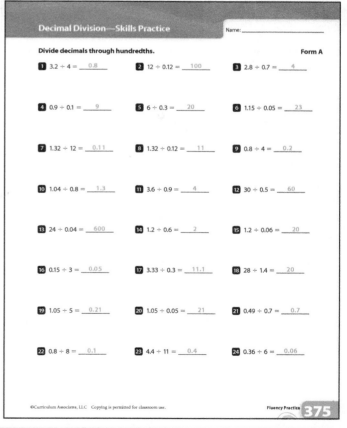

**1** $3.2 \div 4 =$ ___0.8___   **2** $12 \div 0.12 =$ ___100___   **3** $2.8 \div 0.7 =$ ___4___

**4** $0.9 \div 0.1 =$ ___9___   **5** $6 \div 0.3 =$ ___20___   **6** $1.15 \div 0.05 =$ ___23___

**7** $1.32 \div 12 =$ ___0.11___   **8** $1.32 \div 0.12 =$ ___11___   **9** $0.8 \div 4 =$ ___0.2___

**10** $1.04 \div 0.8 =$ ___1.3___   **11** $3.6 \div 0.9 =$ ___4___   **12** $30 \div 0.5 =$ ___60___

**13** $24 \div 0.04 =$ ___600___   **14** $1.2 \div 0.6 =$ ___2___   **15** $1.2 \div 0.06 =$ ___20___

**16** $0.15 \div 3 =$ ___0.05___   **17** $3.33 \div 0.3 =$ ___11.1___   **18** $28 \div 1.4 =$ ___20___

**19** $1.05 \div 5 =$ ___0.21___   **20** $1.05 \div 0.05 =$ ___21___   **21** $0.49 \div 0.7 =$ ___0.7___

**22** $0.8 \div 8 =$ ___0.1___   **23** $4.4 \div 11 =$ ___0.4___   **24** $0.36 \div 6 =$ ___0.06___

©Curriculum Associates, LLC   Copying is permitted for classroom use.

---

©Curriculum Associates, LLC   Copying is not permitted.

## Decimal Division—Skills Practice   Name: _____

**Divide decimals through hundredths.**                         Form B

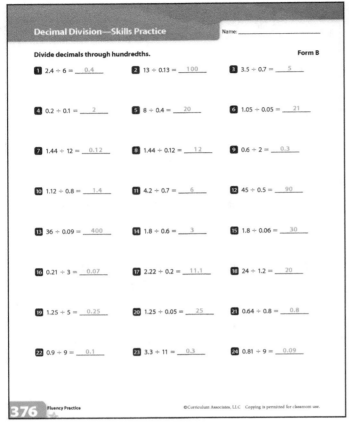

1  $2.4 \div 6 = \underline{0.4}$   2  $13 \div 0.13 = \underline{100}$   3  $3.5 \div 0.7 = \underline{5}$

4  $0.2 \div 0.1 = \underline{2}$   5  $8 \div 0.4 = \underline{20}$   6  $1.05 \div 0.05 = \underline{21}$

7  $1.44 \div 12 = \underline{0.12}$   8  $1.44 \div 0.12 = \underline{12}$   9  $0.6 \div 2 = \underline{0.3}$

10  $1.12 \div 0.8 = \underline{1.4}$   11  $4.2 \div 0.7 = \underline{6}$   12  $45 \div 0.5 = \underline{90}$

13  $36 \div 0.09 = \underline{400}$   14  $1.8 \div 0.6 = \underline{3}$   15  $1.8 \div 0.06 = \underline{30}$

16  $0.21 \div 3 = \underline{0.07}$   17  $2.22 \div 0.2 = \underline{11.1}$   18  $24 \div 1.2 = \underline{20}$

19  $1.25 \div 5 = \underline{0.25}$   20  $1.25 \div 0.05 = \underline{25}$   21  $0.64 \div 0.8 = \underline{0.8}$

22  $0.9 \div 9 = \underline{0.1}$   23  $3.3 \div 11 = \underline{0.3}$   24  $0.81 \div 9 = \underline{0.09}$

©Curriculum Associates, LLC   Copying is permitted for classroom use.

---

## Decimal Division—Repeated Reasoning   Name: _____

**Find place value patterns.**

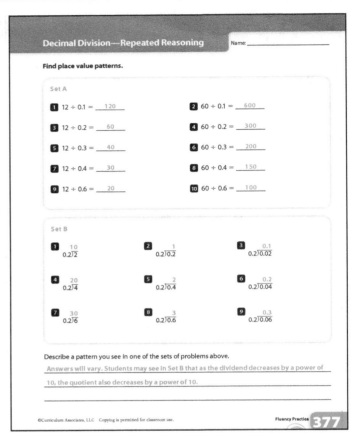

**Set A**

1  $12 \div 0.1 = \underline{120}$   2  $60 \div 0.1 = \underline{600}$

3  $12 \div 0.2 = \underline{60}$   4  $60 \div 0.2 = \underline{300}$

5  $12 \div 0.3 = \underline{40}$   6  $60 \div 0.3 = \underline{200}$

7  $12 \div 0.4 = \underline{30}$   8  $60 \div 0.4 = \underline{150}$

9  $12 \div 0.6 = \underline{20}$   10  $60 \div 0.6 = \underline{100}$

**Set B**

1  $0.2\overline{)2}$ = $10$   2  $0.2\overline{)0.2}$ = $1$   3  $0.2\overline{)0.02}$ = $0.1$

4  $0.2\overline{)4}$ = $20$   5  $0.2\overline{)0.4}$ = $2$   6  $0.2\overline{)0.04}$ = $0.2$

7  $0.2\overline{)6}$ = $30$   8  $0.2\overline{)0.6}$ = $3$   9  $0.2\overline{)0.06}$ = $0.3$

Describe a pattern you see in one of the sets of problems above.

Answers will vary. Students may see in Set B that as the dividend decreases by a power of 10, the quotient also decreases by a power of 10.

©Curriculum Associates, LLC   Copying is permitted for classroom use.

---

## Fraction Addition—Skills Practice   Name: _____

**Add fractions or mixed numbers.**                         Form A

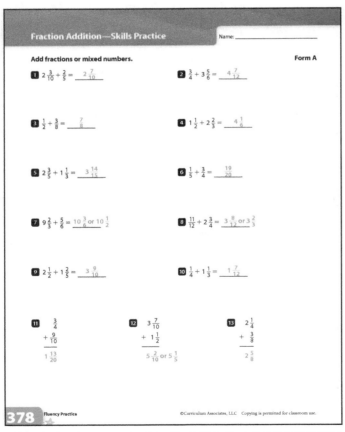

1  $2\frac{3}{10} + \frac{2}{5} = \underline{2\frac{7}{10}}$   2  $\frac{3}{4} + 3\frac{5}{6} = \underline{4\frac{7}{12}}$

3  $\frac{1}{2} + \frac{3}{8} = \underline{\frac{7}{8}}$   4  $1\frac{1}{2} + 2\frac{2}{3} = \underline{4\frac{1}{6}}$

5  $2\frac{3}{5} + 1\frac{1}{3} = \underline{3\frac{14}{15}}$   6  $\frac{1}{5} + \frac{3}{4} = \underline{\frac{19}{20}}$

7  $9\frac{2}{3} + \frac{5}{6} = \underline{10\frac{3}{6} \text{ or } 10\frac{1}{2}}$   8  $\frac{11}{12} + 2\frac{3}{4} = \underline{3\frac{8}{12} \text{ or } 3\frac{2}{3}}$

9  $2\frac{1}{2} + 1\frac{2}{5} = \underline{3\frac{9}{10}}$   10  $\frac{1}{4} + 1\frac{1}{3} = \underline{1\frac{7}{12}}$

11  $\begin{array}{r} \frac{3}{4} \\ + \frac{9}{10} \\ \hline 1\frac{13}{20} \end{array}$   12  $\begin{array}{r} 3\frac{7}{10} \\ + 1\frac{1}{2} \\ \hline 5\frac{2}{10} \text{ or } 5\frac{1}{5} \end{array}$   13  $\begin{array}{r} 2\frac{1}{4} \\ + \frac{3}{8} \\ \hline 2\frac{5}{8} \end{array}$

©Curriculum Associates, LLC   Copying is permitted for classroom use.

---

## Fraction Addition—Skills Practice   Name: _____

**Add fractions or mixed numbers.**                         Form B

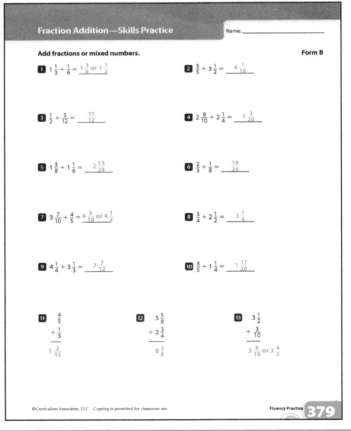

1  $1\frac{1}{3} + \frac{1}{6} = \underline{1\frac{3}{6} \text{ or } 1\frac{1}{2}}$   2  $\frac{3}{5} + 3\frac{1}{2} = \underline{4\frac{1}{10}}$

3  $\frac{1}{2} + \frac{5}{12} = \underline{\frac{11}{12}}$   4  $2\frac{9}{10} + 2\frac{1}{4} = \underline{5\frac{3}{20}}$

5  $1\frac{3}{8} + 1\frac{1}{6} = \underline{2\frac{13}{24}}$   6  $\frac{2}{3} + \frac{1}{8} = \underline{\frac{19}{24}}$

7  $3\frac{7}{10} + \frac{4}{5} = \underline{4\frac{5}{10} \text{ or } 4\frac{1}{2}}$   8  $\frac{3}{4} + 2\frac{1}{2} = \underline{3\frac{1}{4}}$

9  $4\frac{1}{4} + 3\frac{1}{3} = \underline{7\frac{7}{12}}$   10  $\frac{3}{5} + 1\frac{1}{4} = \underline{1\frac{17}{20}}$

11  $\begin{array}{r} \frac{4}{5} \\ + \frac{1}{3} \\ \hline 1\frac{2}{15} \end{array}$   12  $\begin{array}{r} 5\frac{5}{8} \\ + 2\frac{3}{4} \\ \hline 8\frac{3}{8} \end{array}$   13  $\begin{array}{r} 3\frac{1}{2} \\ + \frac{3}{10} \\ \hline 3\frac{8}{10} \text{ or } 3\frac{4}{5} \end{array}$

©Curriculum Associates, LLC   Copying is permitted for classroom use.

©Curriculum Associates, LLC   Copying is not permitted.

## Page 380

### Fraction Addition—Repeated Reasoning

Name: _____

**Find regrouping patterns.**

**Set A**

1. $1\frac{3}{4} + \frac{1}{4} = \underline{\quad 2 \quad}$

2. $1\frac{3}{4} + \frac{1}{2} = \underline{\quad 2\frac{1}{4} \quad}$

3. $2\frac{3}{4} + \frac{1}{4} = \underline{\quad 3 \quad}$

4. $2\frac{3}{4} + \frac{1}{2} = \underline{\quad 3\frac{1}{4} \quad}$

5. $3\frac{3}{4} + \frac{1}{4} = \underline{\quad 4 \quad}$

6. $3\frac{3}{4} + \frac{1}{2} = \underline{\quad 4\frac{1}{4} \quad}$

7. $4\frac{3}{4} + \frac{1}{4} = \underline{\quad 5 \quad}$

8. $4\frac{3}{4} + \frac{1}{2} = \underline{\quad 5\frac{1}{4} \quad}$

**Set B**

1. $2\frac{7}{8}$ $+ \frac{1}{8}$ ___ $3$

2. $2\frac{7}{8}$ $+ \frac{1}{4}$ ___ $3\frac{1}{8}$

3. $2\frac{7}{8}$ $+ \frac{1}{2}$ ___ $3\frac{3}{8}$

4. $3\frac{7}{8}$ $+ \frac{1}{8}$ ___ $4$

5. $3\frac{7}{8}$ $+ \frac{1}{4}$ ___ $4\frac{1}{8}$

6. $3\frac{7}{8}$ $+ \frac{1}{2}$ ___ $4\frac{3}{8}$

7. $4\frac{7}{8}$ $+ \frac{1}{8}$ ___ $5$

8. $4\frac{7}{8}$ $+ \frac{1}{4}$ ___ $5\frac{1}{8}$

9. $4\frac{7}{8}$ $+ \frac{1}{2}$ ___ $5\frac{3}{8}$

Describe a pattern you see in one of the sets of problems above.
Answers will vary. Students may see in Set A that adding $\frac{1}{2}$ to a mixed number that has $\frac{3}{4}$ as
its fraction part is the same as adding $1\frac{1}{4}$ to the whole-number part.

©Curriculum Associates, LLC Copying is permitted for classroom use.

## Page 381

### Fraction Subtraction—Skills Practice

Name: _____

**Subtract fractions or mixed numbers.**     Form A

1. $3\frac{3}{4} - \frac{3}{8} = \underline{\quad 3\frac{3}{8} \quad}$

2. $\frac{4}{5} - \frac{2}{3} = \underline{\quad \frac{2}{15} \quad}$

3. $4\frac{1}{10} - 1 = \underline{\quad 3\frac{1}{10} \quad}$

4. $4\frac{1}{4} - 2\frac{5}{12} = \underline{\quad 1\frac{10}{12} \text{ or } 1\frac{5}{6} \quad}$

5. $2\frac{1}{2} - \frac{3}{5} = \underline{\quad 1\frac{9}{10} \quad}$

6. $5\frac{1}{3} - 1\frac{1}{6} = \underline{\quad 4\frac{1}{6} \quad}$

7. $3 - \frac{3}{8} = \underline{\quad 2\frac{5}{8} \quad}$

8. $\frac{5}{6} - \frac{5}{8} = \underline{\quad \frac{5}{24} \quad}$

9. $5\frac{3}{10} - 4\frac{1}{2} = \underline{\quad \frac{8}{10} \text{ or } \frac{4}{5} \quad}$

10. $3\frac{3}{5} - 1\frac{3}{4} = \underline{\quad 1\frac{17}{20} \quad}$

11. $5$ $- 2\frac{1}{6}$ ___ $2\frac{5}{6}$

12. $1\frac{1}{3}$ $- \frac{3}{12}$ ___ $1\frac{1}{12}$

13. $3\frac{7}{8}$ $- 2\frac{2}{3}$ ___ $1\frac{5}{24}$

©Curriculum Associates, LLC Copying is permitted for classroom use.

## Page 382

### Fraction Subtraction—Skills Practice

Name: _____

**Subtract fractions or mixed numbers.**     Form B

1. $4\frac{11}{12} - \frac{5}{6} = \underline{\quad 4\frac{1}{12} \quad}$

2. $\frac{5}{6} - \frac{3}{4} = \underline{\quad \frac{2}{24} \text{ or } \frac{1}{12} \quad}$

3. $5\frac{1}{8} - 4 = \underline{\quad 1\frac{1}{8} \quad}$

4. $5\frac{1}{5} - 2\frac{7}{10} = \underline{\quad 2\frac{5}{10} \text{ or } 2\frac{1}{2} \quad}$

5. $3\frac{2}{3} - \frac{1}{2} = \underline{\quad 3\frac{1}{6} \quad}$

6. $2\frac{5}{12} - 2\frac{1}{4} = \underline{\quad \frac{2}{12} \text{ or } \frac{1}{6} \quad}$

7. $2 - \frac{3}{5} = \underline{\quad 1\frac{2}{5} \quad}$

8. $\frac{3}{4} - \frac{2}{3} = \underline{\quad \frac{1}{12} \quad}$

9. $4 - 2\frac{5}{12} = \underline{\quad 1\frac{7}{12} \quad}$

10. $4\frac{1}{6} - 2\frac{5}{8} = \underline{\quad 1\frac{13}{24} \quad}$

11. $4$ $- 2\frac{5}{12}$ ___ $1\frac{7}{12}$

12. $2\frac{3}{4}$ $- \frac{1}{12}$ ___ $2\frac{8}{12} \text{ or } 2\frac{2}{3}$

13. $8\frac{3}{10}$ $- 3\frac{1}{4}$ ___ $5\frac{1}{20}$

©Curriculum Associates, LLC Copying is permitted for classroom use.

## Page 383

### Fraction Subtraction—Repeated Reasoning

Name: _____

**Find regrouping patterns.**

**Set A**

1. $1\frac{3}{4} - \frac{1}{2} = \underline{\quad 1\frac{1}{4} \quad}$

2. $1\frac{1}{2} - \frac{3}{4} = \underline{\quad \frac{3}{4} \quad}$

3. $2\frac{3}{4} - \frac{1}{2} = \underline{\quad 2\frac{1}{4} \quad}$

4. $2\frac{1}{2} - \frac{3}{4} = \underline{\quad 1\frac{3}{4} \quad}$

5. $3\frac{3}{4} - \frac{1}{2} = \underline{\quad 3\frac{1}{4} \quad}$

6. $3\frac{1}{2} - \frac{3}{4} = \underline{\quad 2\frac{3}{4} \quad}$

7. $4\frac{3}{4} - \frac{1}{2} = \underline{\quad 4\frac{1}{4} \quad}$

8. $4\frac{1}{2} - \frac{3}{4} = \underline{\quad 3\frac{3}{4} \quad}$

**Set B**

1. $6\frac{1}{4}$ $- \frac{1}{4}$ ___ $6$

2. $6\frac{1}{4}$ $- \frac{1}{2}$ ___ $5\frac{3}{4}$

3. $6\frac{1}{4}$ $- \frac{3}{4}$ ___ $5\frac{1}{2}$

4. $7\frac{1}{4}$ $- \frac{1}{4}$ ___ $7$

5. $7\frac{1}{4}$ $- \frac{1}{2}$ ___ $6\frac{3}{4}$

6. $7\frac{1}{4}$ $- \frac{3}{4}$ ___ $6\frac{1}{2}$

7. $8\frac{1}{4}$ $- \frac{1}{4}$ ___ $8$

8. $8\frac{1}{4}$ $- \frac{1}{2}$ ___ $7\frac{3}{4}$

9. $8\frac{1}{4}$ $- \frac{3}{4}$ ___ $7\frac{1}{2}$

Describe a pattern you see in one of the sets of problems above.
Answers will vary. Students may see in Set A that subtracting $\frac{3}{4}$ from a mixed number that
has $\frac{1}{2}$ for its fraction part results in a difference that is 1 less for the whole-number part and
has $\frac{3}{4}$ for the fraction part.

©Curriculum Associates, LLC Copying is permitted for classroom use.

©Curriculum Associates, LLC   Copying is not permitted.

## Fraction Multiplication—Skills Practice

Name: _____

**Multiply fractions and whole numbers.** Form A

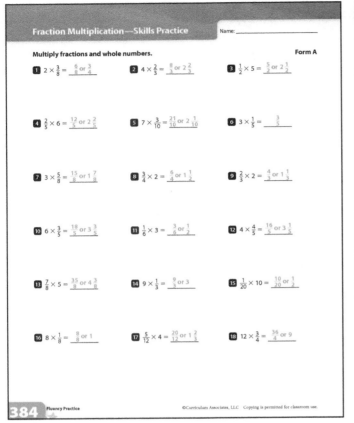

1. $2 \times \frac{3}{8} = \frac{6}{8}$ or $\frac{3}{4}$
2. $4 \times \frac{2}{3} = \frac{8}{3}$ or $2\frac{2}{3}$
3. $\frac{1}{2} \times 5 = \frac{5}{2}$ or $2\frac{1}{2}$
4. $\frac{2}{5} \times 6 = \frac{12}{5}$ or $2\frac{2}{5}$
5. $7 \times \frac{3}{10} = \frac{21}{10}$ or $2\frac{1}{10}$
6. $3 \times \frac{1}{5} = \frac{3}{5}$
7. $3 \times \frac{5}{8} = \frac{15}{8}$ or $1\frac{7}{8}$
8. $\frac{3}{4} \times 2 = \frac{6}{4}$ or $1\frac{1}{2}$
9. $\frac{2}{3} \times 2 = \frac{4}{3}$ or $1\frac{1}{3}$
10. $6 \times \frac{3}{5} = \frac{18}{5}$ or $3\frac{3}{5}$
11. $\frac{1}{6} \times 3 = \frac{3}{6}$ or $\frac{1}{2}$
12. $4 \times \frac{4}{5} = \frac{16}{5}$ or $3\frac{1}{5}$
13. $\frac{7}{8} \times 5 = \frac{35}{8}$ or $4\frac{3}{8}$
14. $9 \times \frac{1}{3} = \frac{9}{3}$ or $3$
15. $\frac{1}{20} \times 10 = \frac{10}{20}$ or $\frac{1}{2}$
16. $8 \times \frac{1}{8} = \frac{8}{8}$ or $1$
17. $\frac{5}{12} \times 4 = \frac{20}{12}$ or $1\frac{2}{3}$
18. $12 \times \frac{3}{4} = \frac{36}{4}$ or $9$

©Curriculum Associates, LLC Copying is permitted for classroom use.

## Fraction Multiplication—Skills Practice

Name: _____

**Multiply fractions and whole numbers.** Form B

1. $\frac{3}{8} \times 3 = \frac{9}{8}$ or $1\frac{1}{8}$
2. $\frac{2}{3} \times 6 = \frac{12}{3}$ or $4$
3. $9 \times \frac{1}{2} = \frac{9}{2}$ or $4\frac{1}{2}$
4. $\frac{2}{5} \times 5 = \frac{10}{5}$ or $2$
5. $\frac{3}{10} \times 3 = \frac{9}{10}$
6. $2 \times \frac{1}{5} = \frac{2}{5}$
7. $2 \times \frac{5}{8} = \frac{10}{8}$ or $1\frac{1}{4}$
8. $\frac{3}{4} \times 3 = \frac{9}{4}$ or $2\frac{1}{4}$
9. $4 \times \frac{2}{3} = \frac{8}{3}$ or $2\frac{2}{3}$
10. $\frac{3}{5} \times 8 = \frac{24}{5}$ or $4\frac{4}{5}$
11. $4 \times \frac{1}{6} = \frac{4}{6}$ or $\frac{2}{3}$
12. $\frac{4}{5} \times 5 = \frac{20}{5}$ or $4$
13. $\frac{7}{8} \times 2 = \frac{14}{8}$ or $1\frac{3}{4}$
14. $6 \times \frac{1}{3} = \frac{6}{3}$ or $2$
15. $\frac{1}{20} \times 5 = \frac{5}{20}$ or $\frac{1}{4}$
16. $6 \times \frac{1}{6} = \frac{6}{6}$ or $1$
17. $\frac{5}{12} \times 3 = \frac{15}{12}$ or $1\frac{1}{4}$
18. $8 \times \frac{3}{4} = \frac{24}{4}$ or $6$

©Curriculum Associates, LLC Copying is permitted for classroom use.

## Fraction Multiplication—Skills Practice

Name: _____

**Multiply fractions by fractions.** Form A

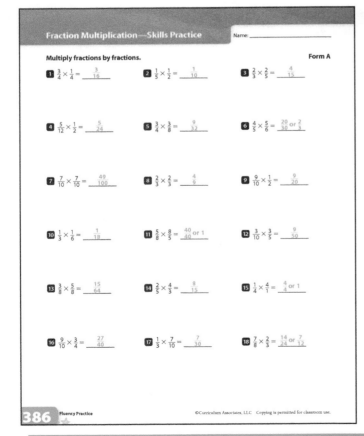

1. $\frac{3}{4} \times \frac{1}{4} = \frac{3}{16}$
2. $\frac{1}{5} \times \frac{1}{2} = \frac{1}{10}$
3. $\frac{2}{3} \times \frac{2}{5} = \frac{4}{15}$
4. $\frac{5}{12} \times \frac{1}{2} = \frac{5}{24}$
5. $\frac{3}{4} \times \frac{3}{8} = \frac{9}{32}$
6. $\frac{4}{5} \times \frac{5}{6} = \frac{20}{30}$ or $\frac{2}{3}$
7. $\frac{7}{10} \times \frac{7}{10} = \frac{49}{100}$
8. $\frac{2}{3} \times \frac{2}{3} = \frac{4}{9}$
9. $\frac{9}{10} \times \frac{1}{2} = \frac{9}{20}$
10. $\frac{1}{3} \times \frac{1}{6} = \frac{1}{18}$
11. $\frac{5}{8} \times \frac{8}{5} = \frac{40}{40}$ or $1$
12. $\frac{3}{10} \times \frac{3}{5} = \frac{9}{50}$
13. $\frac{3}{8} \times \frac{5}{8} = \frac{15}{64}$
14. $\frac{2}{5} \times \frac{4}{3} = \frac{8}{15}$
15. $\frac{1}{4} \times \frac{4}{1} = \frac{4}{4}$ or $1$
16. $\frac{9}{10} \times \frac{3}{4} = \frac{27}{40}$
17. $\frac{1}{3} \times \frac{7}{10} = \frac{7}{30}$
18. $\frac{7}{8} \times \frac{2}{3} = \frac{14}{24}$ or $\frac{7}{12}$

©Curriculum Associates, LLC Copying is permitted for classroom use.

## Fraction Multiplication—Skills Practice

Name: _____

**Multiply fractions by fractions.** Form B

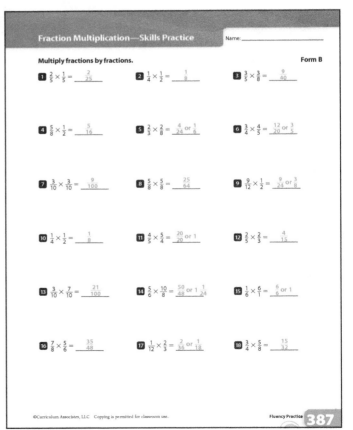

1. $\frac{2}{5} \times \frac{1}{5} = \frac{2}{25}$
2. $\frac{1}{4} \times \frac{1}{2} = \frac{1}{8}$
3. $\frac{3}{5} \times \frac{3}{8} = \frac{9}{40}$
4. $\frac{5}{8} \times \frac{1}{2} = \frac{5}{16}$
5. $\frac{2}{3} \times \frac{2}{8} = \frac{4}{24}$ or $\frac{1}{6}$
6. $\frac{3}{4} \times \frac{4}{5} = \frac{12}{20}$ or $\frac{3}{5}$
7. $\frac{3}{10} \times \frac{3}{10} = \frac{9}{100}$
8. $\frac{5}{8} \times \frac{5}{8} = \frac{25}{64}$
9. $\frac{9}{12} \times \frac{1}{2} = \frac{9}{24}$ or $\frac{3}{8}$
10. $\frac{1}{4} \times \frac{1}{2} = \frac{1}{8}$
11. $\frac{4}{5} \times \frac{5}{4} = \frac{20}{20}$ or $1$
12. $\frac{2}{5} \times \frac{2}{3} = \frac{4}{15}$
13. $\frac{3}{10} \times \frac{7}{10} = \frac{21}{100}$
14. $\frac{5}{6} \times \frac{10}{8} = \frac{50}{48}$ or $1\frac{1}{24}$
15. $\frac{1}{6} \times \frac{6}{1} = \frac{6}{6}$ or $1$
16. $\frac{7}{8} \times \frac{5}{6} = \frac{35}{48}$
17. $\frac{1}{12} \times \frac{2}{3} = \frac{2}{36}$ or $\frac{1}{18}$
18. $\frac{3}{4} \times \frac{5}{8} = \frac{15}{32}$

©Curriculum Associates, LLC Copying is permitted for classroom use.

©Curriculum Associates, LLC Copying is not permitted.

## Fraction Multiplication—Repeated Reasoning    Name: _____

**Multiply by a unit fraction to find patterns.**

### Set A

**1** $12 \div 2 = \underline{\quad 6 \quad}$

**2** $12 \times \frac{1}{2} = \dfrac{12}{2} = \underline{\quad 6 \quad}$

**3** $12 \div 3 = \underline{\quad 4 \quad}$

**4** $12 \times \frac{1}{3} = \dfrac{12}{3} = \underline{\quad 4 \quad}$

**5** $12 \div 4 = \underline{\quad 3 \quad}$

**6** $12 \times \frac{1}{4} = \dfrac{12}{4} = \underline{\quad 3 \quad}$

**7** $12 \div 6 = \underline{\quad 2 \quad}$

**8** $12 \times \frac{1}{6} = \dfrac{12}{6} = \underline{\quad 2 \quad}$

**9** $12 \div 12 = \underline{\quad 1 \quad}$

**10** $12 \times \frac{1}{12} = \dfrac{12}{12} = \underline{\quad 1 \quad}$

### Set B

**1** $6 \div 6 = \underline{\quad 1 \quad}$

**2** $6 \times \frac{1}{6} = \dfrac{6}{6} = \underline{\quad 1 \quad}$

**3** $60 \div 60 = \underline{\quad 1 \quad}$

**4** $60 \times \frac{1}{60} = \dfrac{60}{60} = \underline{\quad 1 \quad}$

**5** $600 \div 600 = \underline{\quad 1 \quad}$

**6** $600 \times \frac{1}{600} = \dfrac{600}{600} = \underline{\quad 1 \quad}$

Describe a pattern you see in one of the sets of problems above.

Answers will vary. Students may see that if you divide a number by one of its factors the
answer is the same as when you multiply the number by a unit fraction with the factor as
its denominator.

## Fraction Division—Skills Practice    Name: _____

**Divide a fraction by a whole number and divide a whole number by a fraction.**    **Form A**

**1** $2 \div \frac{1}{3} = \underline{\quad 6 \quad}$
**2** $3 \div \frac{1}{2} = \underline{\quad 6 \quad}$
**3** $5 \div \frac{1}{5} = \underline{\quad 25 \quad}$

**4** $\frac{1}{3} \div 3 = \underline{\quad \frac{1}{9} \quad}$
**5** $\frac{1}{4} \div 5 = \underline{\quad \frac{1}{20} \quad}$
**6** $\frac{1}{5} \div 4 = \underline{\quad \frac{1}{20} \quad}$

**7** $3 \div \frac{1}{4} = \underline{\quad 12 \quad}$
**8** $4 \div \frac{1}{3} = \underline{\quad 12 \quad}$
**9** $6 \div \frac{1}{5} = \underline{\quad 30 \quad}$

**10** $\frac{1}{5} \div 2 = \underline{\quad \frac{1}{10} \quad}$
**11** $\frac{1}{3} \div 6 = \underline{\quad \frac{1}{18} \quad}$
**12** $\frac{1}{6} \div 3 = \underline{\quad \frac{1}{18} \quad}$

**13** $2 \div \frac{1}{6} = \underline{\quad 12 \quad}$
**14** $5 \div \frac{1}{4} = \underline{\quad 20 \quad}$
**15** $4 \div \frac{1}{5} = \underline{\quad 20 \quad}$

**16** $\frac{1}{5} \div 2 = \underline{\quad \frac{1}{10} \quad}$
**17** $\frac{1}{2} \div 5 = \underline{\quad \frac{1}{10} \quad}$
**18** $\frac{1}{3} \div 2 = \underline{\quad \frac{1}{6} \quad}$

## Fraction Division—Skills Practice    Name: _____

**Divide a fraction by a whole number and divide a whole number by a fraction.**    **Form B**

**1** $5 \div \frac{1}{3} = \underline{\quad 15 \quad}$
**2** $3 \div \frac{1}{5} = \underline{\quad 15 \quad}$
**3** $2 \div \frac{1}{2} = \underline{\quad 4 \quad}$

**4** $\frac{1}{2} \div 2 = \underline{\quad \frac{1}{4} \quad}$
**5** $\frac{1}{4} \div 2 = \underline{\quad \frac{1}{8} \quad}$
**6** $\frac{1}{2} \div 4 = \underline{\quad \frac{1}{8} \quad}$

**7** $2 \div \frac{1}{5} = \underline{\quad 10 \quad}$
**8** $5 \div \frac{1}{2} = \underline{\quad 10 \quad}$
**9** $4 \div \frac{1}{6} = \underline{\quad 24 \quad}$

**10** $\frac{1}{5} \div 5 = \underline{\quad \frac{1}{25} \quad}$
**11** $\frac{1}{6} \div 4 = \underline{\quad \frac{1}{24} \quad}$
**12** $\frac{1}{4} \div 6 = \underline{\quad \frac{1}{24} \quad}$

**13** $6 \div \frac{1}{3} = \underline{\quad 18 \quad}$
**14** $10 \div \frac{1}{2} = \underline{\quad 20 \quad}$
**15** $2 \div \frac{1}{10} = \underline{\quad 20 \quad}$

**16** $\frac{1}{2} \div 6 = \underline{\quad \frac{1}{12} \quad}$
**17** $\frac{1}{6} \div 2 = \underline{\quad \frac{1}{12} \quad}$
**18** $\frac{1}{8} \div 5 = \underline{\quad \frac{1}{40} \quad}$

## Fraction Division—Repeated Reasoning    Name: _____

**Divide by a unit fraction to find patterns.**

### Set A

**1** $6 \times 2 = \underline{\quad 12 \quad}$

**2** $6 \div \frac{1}{2} = \underline{\quad 12 \quad}$

**3** $6 \times 3 = \underline{\quad 18 \quad}$

**4** $6 \div \frac{1}{3} = \underline{\quad 18 \quad}$

**5** $6 \times \underline{\quad 4 \quad} = 24$

**6** $6 \div \dfrac{1}{4} = 24$

**7** $6 \times \underline{\quad 5 \quad} = 30$

**8** $6 \div \dfrac{1}{5} = 30$

**9** $6 \times \underline{\quad 6 \quad} = 36$

**10** $6 \div \dfrac{1}{6} = 36$

### Set B

**1** $7 \times 10 = \underline{\quad 70 \quad}$
**2** $7 \div \frac{1}{10} = \underline{\quad 70 \quad}$

**3** $8 \times 10 = \underline{\quad 80 \quad}$
**4** $8 \div \frac{1}{10} = \underline{\quad 80 \quad}$

**5** $9 \times 10 = \underline{\quad 90 \quad}$
**6** $9 \div \frac{1}{10} = \underline{\quad 90 \quad}$

**7** $10 \times 10 = \underline{\quad 100 \quad}$
**8** $10 \div \frac{1}{10} = \underline{\quad 100 \quad}$

Describe a pattern you see in one of the sets of problems above.

Answers will vary. Students may see in Set B that both multiplying a number by 10 and
dividing it by $\frac{1}{10}$ increases the value of the number 10 times.

©Curriculum Associates, LLC   Copying is not permitted.

# Unit Game Teacher Resource
# Table of Contents

Name: _____

## Decimal Race to 100 Recording Sheet

| | |
|---|---|
| _____ **Player A Name** | _____ **Player B Name** |

**Player A**

1.  _____

2.  + _____

    _____

3.  + _____

    _____

4.  + _____

    _____

5.  + _____

    _____

        100.00

    – _____

    _____

**Final Score Player A** [ ]

**Player B**

1.  _____

2.  + _____

    _____

3.  + _____

    _____

4.  + _____

    _____

5.  + _____

    _____

        100.00

    – _____

    _____

**Final Score Player B** [ ]

©Curriculum Associates, LLC   Copying is permitted for classroom use.

**Digit Cards**

✂

| 0 | 1 | 2 | 3 | 4 |
| 5 | 6 | 7 | 8 | 9 |
| 0 | 1 | 2 | 3 | 4 |
| 5 | 6 | 7 | 8 | 9 |

©Curriculum Associates, LLC   Copying is permitted for classroom use.

Name: _____

## Fraction Sums and Differences Recording Sheet

---

**Player A Name**

Digits: ☐ ☐ ☐ ☐

**Greatest Sum**

1. $\frac{\square}{\square} + \frac{\square}{\square} = \square$

**Greatest Difference**

2. $\frac{\square}{\square} - \frac{\square}{\square} = \square$

**Least Sum**

3. $\frac{\square}{\square} + \frac{\square}{\square} = \square$

**Least Difference**

4. $\frac{\square}{\square} - \frac{\square}{\square} = \square$

**Players' Choice**

5. $\frac{\square}{\square} \ \square \ \frac{\square}{\square} = \square$

---

**Player B Name**

Digits: ☐ ☐ ☐ ☐

**Greatest Sum**

1. $\frac{\square}{\square} + \frac{\square}{\square} = \square$

**Greatest Difference**

2. $\frac{\square}{\square} - \frac{\square}{\square} = \square$

**Least Sum**

3. $\frac{\square}{\square} + \frac{\square}{\square} = \square$

**Least Difference**

4. $\frac{\square}{\square} - \frac{\square}{\square} = \square$

**Players' Choice**

5. $\frac{\square}{\square} \ \square \ \frac{\square}{\square} = \square$

©Curriculum Associates, LLC   Copying is permitted for classroom use.

## Most Valuable Expressions Recording Sheet

---

_____
**Player A Name**

1. _____ = _____

2. _____ = _____

3. _____ = _____

4. _____ = _____

5. _____ = _____

6. _____ = _____

7. _____ = _____

8. _____ = _____

**Player A Score Tally:** [ _____ ]

---

_____
**Player B Name**

1. _____ = _____

2. _____ = _____

3. _____ = _____

4. _____ = _____

5. _____ = _____

6. _____ = _____

7. _____ = _____

8. _____ = _____

**Player B Score Tally:** [ _____ ]

## Digit, Decimal, and Fraction Cards

| | | | |
|---|---|---|---|
| 0 | 1 | 2 | 3 |
| 4 | 5 | 6 | 7 |
| 8 | 9 | $\frac{1}{2}$ | $\frac{1}{4}$ |
| $\frac{1}{5}$ | $\frac{1}{10}$ | 0.1 | 0.25 |

©Curriculum Associates, LLC   Copying is permitted for classroom use.

Name: _____

## Measurement Match Recording Sheet

1. _____ = _____

2. _____ = _____

3. _____ = _____

4. _____ = _____

5. _____ = _____

6. _____ = _____

7. _____ = _____

8. _____ = _____

9. _____ = _____

10. _____ = _____

11. _____ = _____

12. _____ = _____

©Curriculum Associates, LLC   Copying is permitted for classroom use.

**Measurement Cards**

| | | |
|---|---|---|
| 3 centimeters | 3 meters | 300 millimeters |
| 5 kilometers | 50 meters | 0.5 meter |
| 300 centimeters | 0.03 meter | 30 centimeters |
| 0.05 kilometer | 5,000 meters | 50 centimeters |

   ©Curriculum Associates, LLC   Copying is permitted for classroom use.

## Measurement Cards (continued)

✂

| | | |
|---|---|---|
| 800 centimeters | 80 meters | 0.8 meter |
| 0.6 kilometer | 60 meters | 600,000 centimeters |
| 8,000 centimeters | 8 meters | 800 millimeters |
| 6 kilometers | 600 meters | 6,000 centimeters |

©Curriculum Associates, LLC   Copying is permitted for classroom use.

Name: _____

## Triangle Bingo Recording Sheet

**1.** equilateral triangle

_____

_____

**2.** isosceles triangle

_____

_____

**3.** scalene triangle

_____

_____

**4.** acute triangle

_____

_____

**5.** obtuse triangle

_____

_____

**6.** right triangle

_____

_____

©Curriculum Associates, LLC   Copying is permitted for classroom use.

Name: _____

## Triangle Bingo Game Board

**Triangle Bingo Game Cards**

✂

| | | |
|---|---|---|
| scalene triangle | isosceles triangle | equilateral triangle |
| obtuse triangle | right triangle | acute triangle |
| scalene triangle | isosceles triangle | equilateral triangle |
| obtuse triangle | right triangle | acute triangle |

©Curriculum Associates, LLC   Copying is permitted for classroom use.